RISE of the RANGES of LIGHT

DAVID SCOTT GILLIGAN

RISE of the RANGES of LIGHT

LANDSCAPES AND CHANGE IN THE MOUNTAINS OF CALIFORNIA

Heyday, Berkeley, California

Library of Congress Cataloging-in-Publication Data
Gilligan, David, 1972-
  Rise of the ranges of light : landscapes and change in the mountains of California / David Scott Gilligan.
    p. cm.
  Includes bibliographical references and index.
  ISBN 978-1-59714-151-2 (pbk. : alk. paper)
  1. Mountains--California. 2. Natural history--California. 3. Mountains--Sierra Nevada (Calif. and Nev.) 4. Natural history--Sierra Nevada (Calif. and Nev.) 5. Philosophy of nature--California. 6. Philosophy of nature--Sierra Nevada (Calif. and Nev.) I. Title.
  GB525.5.C34G55 2011
  508.794--dc22
                              2010045283

Book Design: Lorraine Rath
Printing and Binding: Thomson-Shore, Dexter, MI

Orders, inquiries, and correspondence should be addressed to:
Heyday
P. O. Box 9145, Berkeley, CA 94709
(510) 549-3564, Fax (510) 549-1889
www.heydaybooks.com

10   9   8   7   6   5   4   3   2   1

CONTENTS

A HUNDRED AND FORTY YEARS AGO, while looking east to the sunlit, granite, snow-covered peaks of the Sierra Nevada from Pacheco Pass, John Muir dubbed the Sierra the "Range of Light" and famously extolled the unparalleled aesthetic virtues of this singular mountain range. Muir's name stuck, and eventually found wider usage to include all of the Sierra-Cascade axis from Tehachapi clear to Shasta. Although the Sierra-Cascade axis undoubtedly forms the crown of the mountains of California, the entire state is characterized by mountains. There are more different kinds of mountains in California, in fact, than in any similar-sized chunk of land in all of North America. *Rise of the Ranges of Light* is the story of all of these ranges, and it expands on Muir's name for the Sierra Nevada to include all the ranges that together bathe in the golden light of California. It is a continuation, or modern rendition of, and certainly a tribute to Muir's classic work *The Mountains of California.*

California

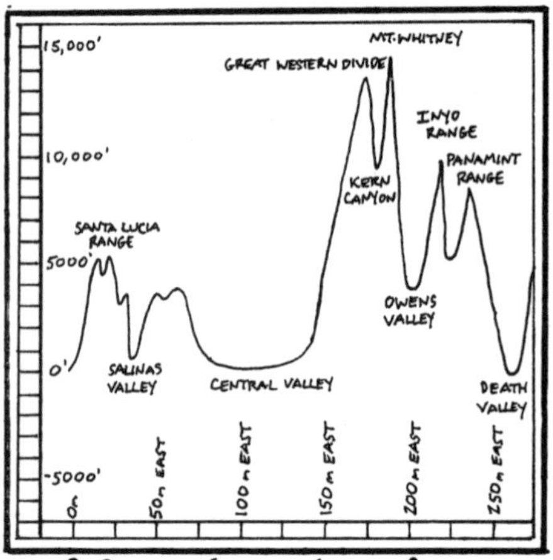
15,000'
10,000'
5000'
0'
-5000'
MT. WHITNEY
GREAT WESTERN DIVIDE
INYO RANGE
PANAMINT RANGE
KERN CANYON
SANTA LUCIA RANGE
OWENS VALLEY
SALINAS VALLEY
CENTRAL VALLEY
DEATH VALLEY
0 m
50 m EAST
100 m EAST
150 m EAST
200 m EAST
250 m EAST

★ West-East Cross Section

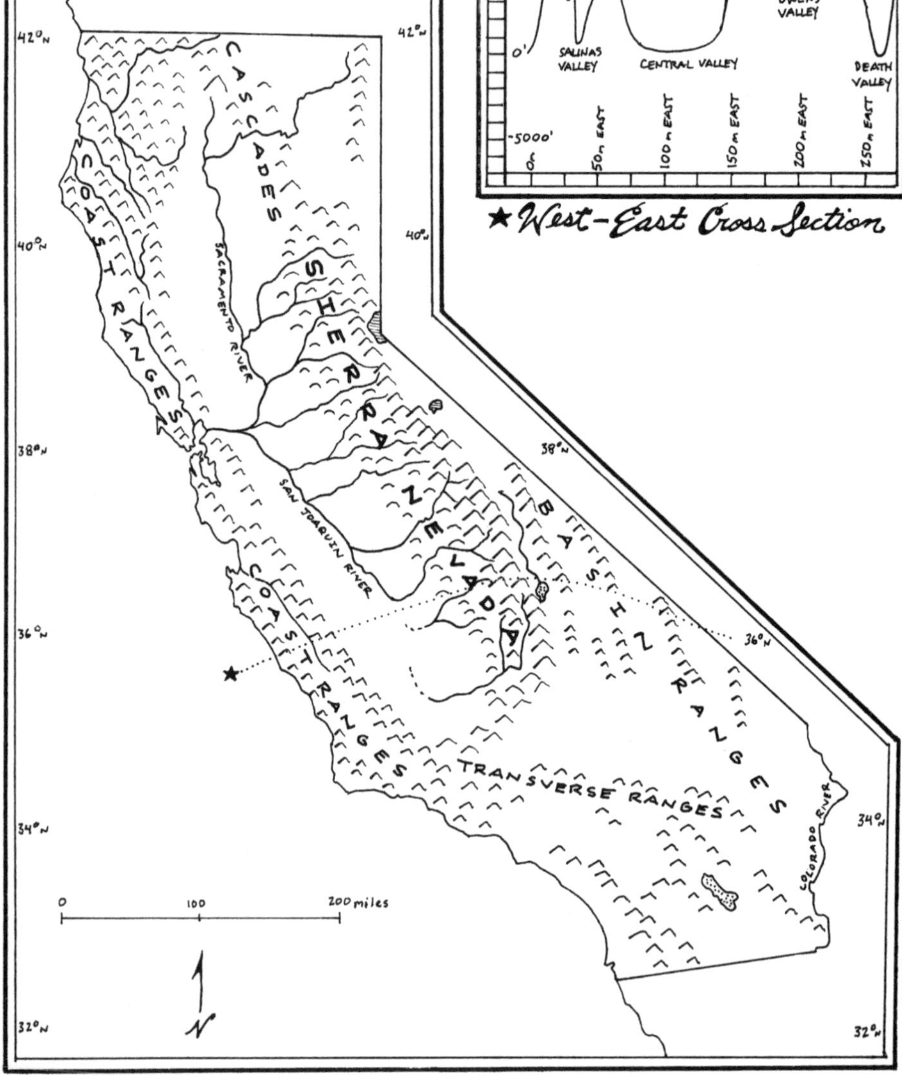
42° N
40° N
38° N
36° N
34° N
32° N
CASCADES
COAST RANGES
SIERRA NEVADA
SACRAMENTO RIVER
SAN JOAQUIN RIVER
BASIN RANGES
TRANSVERSE RANGES
COLORADO RIVER
0
100
200 miles
N

PREFACE

High on a windswept alpine flat in the Sierra Nevada, unseen pocket gophers grope in the dark beneath an overlying quilt of dry meadow grasses, sedges, perennial herbs, and wildflowers. The rodents, in their quest for food and fatness, sever the root systems of the plants. In time the plants dry up, wither, decompose, and blow away, lifeless in the chapping wind. The climate is changing, drying. What was once a fragrant, green meadow turns into a parched gravel flat. The pocket gophers go elsewhere to slake their hunger. The gravel flat, seemingly desolate compared to its luxuriant predecessor, hosts new life of its own. Prostrate *Eriogonums* and *Calyptridiums* soon garnish the bright granitic sand and pebbles. They bloom and emit perfumes new and different. The death of one thing brings the life of another. The landscape evolves and none can foresee the ends to come.

The Hindu religious tradition recognizes a trinity of gods that together represent the nature of the phenomenal world. The first member of the trinity is Brahma, the creator, who brings things into being and breathes life into the world. The second member of the trinity is Vishnu, the preserver, who sustains life and being through time. The third and most widely worshiped member of the trinity is Siva, the destroyer, who makes wreckage of being and life and reduces the efforts of Brahma and Vishnu to utter ruin. Thus the slate is cleared for Brahma to come and make the world anew and Vishnu to hold its course. But without the change that Siva brings, the evolution of the world as we know it would stop, and there would be no continued renewal, no reinvention, no evolution.

This book is about Brahma, Vishnu, and Siva. It is about ongoing change in the world of phenomenal nature. It is about why change is occurring; what, if any, its patterns are; and how we perceive change in the world around us. It is also about the unfolding story of the evolution of place—the mountains of California—and one man's relationship with place. These two threads, of change and of personal experience of place, meet and intertwine when landscapes and life evolve and we are there to interpret the evidence, to tell the story. That means being out with the living land, roaming its curves and recesses, observing, questioning, speculating, and interacting with it. It can even mean being affectionate towards it.

This book is not an exhaustive analysis of any one topic, but rather a synthesis of disparate topics, unified by the worldview that recognizes change as the rule, not the exception, in the manifest nature of the world. In the stories and anecdotes to come, I hope to braid aspects of natural history, geography, geology, biology, ecology, cosmology, and even a bit of philosophy and present a holistic way of perceiving the physical world. There are libraries full of books on any one of the above-mentioned subjects. There are few in the stacks that look at them synthetically. Each book in the stack is but a page in the great book of all time, which is the combination of efforts of many over millennia. This work is an attempt to summarize of a part of that great book. Ultimately I hope to integrate my sources and take an evolutionary step. I've borrowed significantly from my predecessors. It is an unavoidable practice, and I do it with utmost humility and respect. I look over at my bookshelf. Goethe, Emerson, Thoreau, Muir, Leopold, Eiseley, McPhee, Snyder, Darwin, Mayr, Gould, Hawking, Wilber, Aurobindo, Ramacharaka, Lao Tzu, Shakespeare, Homer, Campbell, and Kazantzakis share space with holy books so old no one knows who wrote them and files stuffed thick with scientific articles. All of these have been sources not just of information but of inspiration.

In the pages to come I will follow a simple course. In the opening chapter I will introduce the two overarching themes that twine their way

Era	Period	Epoch	Years (mya)	Diversity of Life
Cenozoic	Quaternary	Holocene		
		Pleistocene	1.65	
	Tertiary	Pliocene		
		Miocene		
		Oligocene		
		Eocene		
		Paleocene	65	
Mesozoic	Cretaceous			
			135-145	
	Jurassic			
			205-210	
	Triassic			
			240-245	
Paleozoic	Permian			
			285-290	
	Pennsylvanian			
			320	
	Mississippian			
			360	
	Devonian			
			408-410	
	Silurian			
			435-440	
	Ordovician			
			505	
	Cambrian			
			530-570	
Proterozoic			2500	
Archean			~4600	ORIGIN OF THE EARTH

xi

throughout the book and provide context for the action that follows. Chapters two and three will further investigate these themes, first through mountain building and plate tectonics, then the geography of natural communities and the evolution of species. Subsequent chapters will integrate these two themes as they have manifested themselves for over five hundred million years in the evolution of the earth.

The story is set in the mountains of California because here there are more different kinds of mountains, habitats, and species of plants and animals than in any other similar-sized piece of land in temperate North America, if not the temperate world. The diversity, geological and biological, of California is unprecedented largely due to the state's position at the edge of the continent of North America. Here is a place of intense and immediate tectonic activity, which begets topographic diversity, which begets climatic diversity, which begets habitat diversity, which begets biological diversity. California's geographic position at the latitudinal junction between the subtropics and temperate regions also makes it a natural biological meeting place for a stunning array of life, where species with Arctic, desert, and neotropical origins meet and intermingle. The place is also, quite literally, one of the newest on earth, freshly hewn, young and full of vitality, a place where you can literally watch the earth in the making. It is at the leading edge of the world in both a physical and biological sense. It is *happening*.

In short, California has a good story because it is a particularly rich one. But the idea of change and its application to landscapes extends far beyond California to just about anywhere on planet Earth, from the poles to the tropics, from the mountains to the sea. Everywhere you go the story is much the same. But the details are different, and understanding the details is part of what makes life rich and beautiful.

Change can be tough to metabolize, but it makes the world a dynamic and mysterious place to live. Not so long ago the great German poet-scientist Johann Wolfgang von Goethe wrote, "When something has acquired a form it metamorphoses immediately into a new one. If we wish to arrive at some living perception of nature we ourselves must remain as quick and flexible as nature and follow the example she gives." Change keeps us on our toes. It keeps us awestruck with the world.

ONE

A Flash in the Pan

The universe is expanding, the earth is contracting, and somehow amidst it all life makes a bloom. The universe is expanding due to an unfathomable explosion that happened billions of years ago, while the earth is contracting as gravity pulls the exploded pieces of the universe back together. With these seemingly opposing forces of expansion and contraction at work, the whole phenomenal world is in a constant state of change. I am seeking evidence of this change in the mountain landscapes of California. I have questions and I am looking for answers.

I sit soaking the morning away in the slippery waters of Whitmore Hot Springs, staring up at the Eiger-like east face of Mount Morrison as the first light of day illuminates its bold countenance. I have looked at this mountain for years. It is undoubtedly one of the most aesthetically prominent and intriguing mountains on the eastern crest of the Sierra Nevada. Geologically, it is enticing. Most people are attracted to the aesthetic qualities of swirls and folds in rocks, and Morrison is loaded with them. Up there amid the late-lying snows of winter, underlying the thin, transient veneer of seasons, is some of the oldest rock in the Sierra Nevada of California. Rock that has been the floor of a sea. Rock that has been twisted and bent, rock that has buckled under the pressure of rising volcanoes. Rock that has been relentlessly ground down by the combined forces of water and gravity. Rock that has been injected from beneath by one of the biggest reservoirs of magma on the planet. Rock that has been boldly uplifted to nearly thirteen thousand feet while the rest of the West was stretched to become some of the thinnest crust on earth. Rock that is swirled and richly folded, contorted, and beautiful. Rock that is making perhaps its last precarious stand on the surface of this wildly spinning globe. Stone with a story. Today I will climb its flanks and try to read the story.

Last night I sat up late and examined the stars. I tried to discern if they were really moving away from each other. I didn't see any movement and figured that as short-lived humans in a universe some fifteen billion years old, perhaps we are a little too new on the scene to see much action. But the stars really *are* moving away from each other and I know this. I have studied it. I have discussed its implications among friends and colleagues to the point of mental exhaustion. Everything I could see from my vantage point at Whitmore Hot Springs, times a million and a million times that, was once condensed into a incomprehensibly small space—smaller than an orange, smaller even than a pinhead—with an incomprehensibly high density. It's not that there was ever any less stuff in the universe, it was just all packed together. Now, billions of years later, it is scattered from me to the cosmic horizon. Scientists tell us that the pressure got so intense that the super-condensed universe just exploded. They call it the Big Bang. The Yogic tradition, which predates that of science by over five millennia, calls this the dawn of the Day of Brahm. It happened somewhere around fifteen billion years ago, and the initial blast is still affecting us to this very day. In fact, the background radiation resulting from such an explosion is still humming away as the infinite first sound of the universe. While long, long ago the power of contraction brought the stuff of the universe together and held it there for who knows how long, now it's the power of expansion that is blowing it all apart. Contraction, as Goethe suggested long ago, is a prerequisite for the "next step" in nature, whatever that step may be. Thus contraction necessarily precedes the expansion of the universe, and though one theme or the other may dominate the universal dynamic, both themes are always at play. Contraction equals convergence and unification. Expansion equals divergence, diversification, and individuation. Our universe is expanding, but galaxies, solar systems, even the very earth beneath our feet, are contracting.

If there are two opposing forces that keep the whole show of change going on in the world, these are those forces. Why did life start simple and get complex? Why are there more species on the earth than there ever have been? Why do *we* start simple and get complex? Why life at all? Why does everything out there seem to be moving farther and farther away from everything else? Why does energy always experience entropy? Why do things like species, languages, cultures, families, market products, occupations, and just about everything else experience constant divergence of character? Why do the old days seem golden and easy, while the new seem uncertain and complex? As long as the stuff of the universe keeps expanding and contracting, we have something to work with. Under the current expansion regime of the last fifteen billion years or so, our laws of thermodynamics, evolution, and perhaps even our philosophies hold up. When and if it stops, we'll probably find that things change quite a bit. That's if we're around to find out.

While the whole universe spills itself out like a jar of marbles dropped onto the pavement, expansion isn't all we see going on. True, most matter moves away from all other matter, and perhaps even the primordial epicenter of the Big Bang, but somehow, amidst all this separation, matter is also drawn to itself. Science calls this gravity; spiritual traditions have referred to it as individuation. It means that we get things like planets, solar systems, and galaxies, not to mention other expressions of contraction such as interpersonal mutual attraction, symbiosis in cellular evolution, and fusion of gamete nuclei. It's like some universal recollection of the initial attraction that drew the stuff of the universe together for the big explosion in the first place. It also hints that the same thing could possibly happen again. Contraction as expressed in gravity, magnetic forces, and nuclear forces not only gives us a place to live but also makes that place interesting. The earth was somewhat hastily thrown together during its formation, and it has been sorting out its component parts ever since. As the earth pulls on itself, the heaviest stuff, like iron and nickel, moves towards the center. The lighter stuff gets displaced outward. All the while the innards of the earth decay, giving off the radioactive heat that gives the push to the pump. This gravitational differentiation burps out atmosphere through volcanoes, spits out oceans, and throws up mountains all around the earth's surface. We get to watch all this happen.

A culture and the stories it tells about itself are reflective of one another. Ancient cultures called these stories myths and today we call them science, but the myths of ancient cultures were as real to them as science is to us today. Not only do cultures and their mythologies reflect each other, but they also inform one another. When one changes significantly, the other does too. The Norse myth of Ragnarok was indicative of the impending doom that a shift to Christianity would bring to the culture of the northmen. As ancient Greece shifted from the age of heroes to the age of reason, the old pantheon was abandoned in favor of more practical divinity. In our own times, the old mechanistic worldview given to us by Newton and the physicists of the sixteenth, seventeenth, and eighteenth centuries is being replaced by a worldview that suggests the kind of dynamic change and evolution that no machine can deliver.

Two ideas seem to be shifting the way we view the manifest world, both of which are dictated by the larger theme of an expanding universe. The first to come on the scene was the evolution of species through the processes of natural selection, publicized by Charles Darwin in his *On the Origin of Species* in 1859. This was the Big Bang of the biological world. Darwin's ideas did not develop in isolation, however, and it is important that we recognize the revolutionary contributions of other scientists, such as Goethe, Buffon, Erasmus Darwin, Lyell, Lamarck, and Wallace, not to mention ideas outside of the sphere of science that had been circulating around planet Earth for thousands of years. The idea of the evolution of species was huge because not only did it serve to begin shifting our consciousness of the natural world from a Newtonian mechanistic view to an evolutionary view, but it also shed light on the fact that species underwent constant diversification and divergence of character through things like geographic isolation, environmental changes, and specialization under stable conditions. In other words, life on earth at any moment was a snapshot in time. Life was constantly changing and diverging, and perhaps even more importantly, it was expanding.

The second idea was soon to follow. Around a hundred years after Darwin's biological revolution, geologists had a revolution all their own. The crust of the earth was moving, as evidenced by the matching outlines of the continents, the spreading of seafloors, and the consequent devouring of the seafloors at their edges beneath the crust of the continents. The earth's surface was moving, and it was doing so because the planet was slowly cooling and settling down as gravity continually pulled everything together. Contraction. Our experiences of volcanic eruptions, earthquakes, and even hot springs were all evidence of this dynamic. With the theory of plate tectonics, we could suddenly explain just about all of the earth's surface processes—island arcs like Japan, continental mountains like the Himalaya and the Alps, oceanic trenches and ridges, island archipelagos, and so much more. The Big Bang of geology.

The notion of an expanding universe gave context to the evolution of species and landscapes, amplifying their significance by showing them to be tangible illustrations of what had been at work for billions of years. Scientists had postulated the possibility of a great explosion being the origin of our universe for some time, but it was not until 1965 that empirical proof emerged to back the theory. Two physicists working for Bell Labs in New Jersey were testing an ultrasensitive microwave detector. Inadvertently, they picked up a microwave background that seemed to be coming from everywhere at once. This was the breakthrough discovery that for decades physicists had been looking for and been unable to find. These waves were the cosmic microwave background radiation given off by the initial Big Bang. It was out there like a song singing clearly of the events that had birthed it. We finally found it.

NIGHT IS THE TIME FOR PONDERING IDEAS. Day is the time for seeing them at work, for testing these heady themes against the hard stone

of the earth. Up there on Mount Morrison there might be some
answer to at least the smallest of my questions. Maybe in a rare fossilized organism, so infrequently preserved in the tormented metamorphic rock. Maybe in the place of contact where two different rock
types met. Maybe in a rare stand of limber pines, isolated from their
Rocky Mountain counterparts by hundreds of miles. Maybe in the
splash of color given by an endemic alpine wildflower, unique
to the ecological conditions of this area of the Sierra Nevada.
Maybe in the sheer physical effort of ascending over five thousand
vertical feet in a day. Maybe in the lucid trance of the summit
experience.

Hours later, after negotiating the tangle of vegetation and churning
waters of the Convict Lake inlet, I work my way upstream along the
northern bank of the creek. Here I know I will find signs of a trail,
a dashed line obscured by patches of hard snow. Morning has long
since turned in its golden beginnings for the brighter, whiter light
of midday, and my decision to take the scenic route around the lake
has cost me precious hours. I make haste along the segments of trail,
easily linking them together as I crunch across the old snow. Some
miles up I cross a rotting snow bridge, probing seriously with a long
fir pole before committing my full weight to the snow. I keep my
sights on the rusty brown of the north slope of Morrison, watching
for a good line upward.

I am unsure which route, if any, leads to the summit ridge, and
after a time of indecision I conclude that any way up is better than
not trying. After crossing a broad, steepening belt of loose scree and
talus, I follow one of the many thin, streaming cascades of snowmelt
water that plummet down over the bedrock of the mountain. Careful
to avoid the wet rocks, I scramble on, growing increasingly discour-
aged by the steep, loose material that defines Morrison. I aim for a
long, fingerlike snowfield, hoping that by this time of day it will be
soft enough to kick steps into. Sure enough, it is, and once on the
snow I move more swiftly. As I get higher, now over a thousand feet
above the creek, I cannot help but notice a fine chute just east of me
that seems to provide a more certain route to the summit ridge. It
is inaccessible from where I am; to reroute myself I would have to

descend all the way to the apron of scree below. I stubbornly continue on my route for several hundred more feet before realizing it goes nowhere. I have to go back down.

It is afternoon by the time I descend, traverse, and climb up and into the chute. But although it is late, the route looks good and the thought of making the summit overshadows any thought of retreat. Ascending the chute soon requires moving up scree at an impossibly steep angle of repose, then negotiating equally steep snow and ice. Progress is slow, as the chute is well shaded from the rays of the sun, and the snow is as hard as it was at midnight. I put my adze to good use hacking steps. I am not sure what to expect up ahead, if the chute will go, if I will get cliffed out, or if the snow will get icier. Although I am not cold, I start to feel cold. Beads of sweat seem to be freezing on the back of my neck. The walls of the chute grow narrow, the way ahead choked. My breath grows labored, and my legs turn to bags of sand. I stop and crane my neck for a look up. Fifty feet above me, a slightly rounded boulder the size of a cement mixer sits wedged into the chute. It blocks the way ahead completely. Only the narrowing walls of the chute keep it from continuing its way downslope, totally crushing anything and everything in its path. I stand there on my cut steps, chips of ice flecked across the lenses of my sunglasses, my eyes glazed over, frustrated and befuddled.

There is a boom like a thousand thunders and I can hear the mountain suddenly give way and start to fall apart. Small pieces of rock fly by as larger ones sound decidedly from above. I drive my axe into the snow as hard as I can and lean over it, covering my head with my arms. The world groans as some great tectonic hand grabs it tightly and squeezes. The mountain shakes and I hold on tight, too gripped to pray, too scared to move. The chockstone that was my nemesis just moments before is now my salvation. Somehow it holds the breaking rock from above and dams up the chute. All I suffer is a light sprinkling of pebbles and dust.

Almost as soon as it began, the shaking stops, and I listen as bits of rock and dirt fall onto the snow like fine rain. If it was thunder then it came from nowhere and went back there just as fast. If it was a slide then it must have been massive to make the earth tremble and shake like it did. I imagine the earth in a state of eternal convulsion, pulling in on itself in order to make right its hasty design, roiling all the while. Yet even while it contracts, life on earth diversifies, evolves, and expands. The earth, with everything in it and on it, including me, is an expression, a manifestation of the universe. In this supreme moment, I am in awe of this curious ball of metal and dust, rock, water, and life hurtling through the singing cosmos, and I am keenly aware of myself, a speck in the midst of it all, a flash in the pan in a universe forever in the making.

TWO

Mountains in the Making

There are more mountains, there is more land, and there are more species on Earth today than ever before in the history of the planet. There is more land because once the earth's crust is sorted to the outside of the planet, it stays there. There are more mountains because there is more land, and a handful of geologic events are all happening coincidentally that have never done so before. The Atlantic Ocean grows and pushes the Americas and Europe and Africa apart. Around the bend, the Pacific gets swallowed up as the western Americas and Asia close in on one another. Africa and India drift northward. Ice that once covered a third of the Northern Hemisphere is suddenly removed. All this leads to more mountains. There are more species because there is more land and there are more mountains, and life has had more time to diverge and diversify today than it did yesterday.

I lie sleepless beneath the night sky of Nine Lakes Basin, deep in the heart of the Southern Sierra Nevada, thinking to myself that the stars in the sky seem particularly innumerable on this night. Some sets of stars are brighter than others, casting a pale silvery glow across the broken granite floor of the basin. The sky is black velvet, stark

9

in contrast to silver. I lie there for some time, a thin veneer of life over the hard stone. I wait for the mood of night to make way for the first faint smudges of dawn. I wait for five a.m. When it comes, I will crawl out into the cold alpine air, pull my shoes on, strap on my daypack, and walk on down Big Arroyo Canyon.

I am still only halfway into waking reality when River comes to get me up. I can't believe she is awake. River Gates, friend and teaching assistant from Monterey, California, field ecologist, naturalist, Buddhist who eats with chopsticks except when she eats cheeseburgers (which she eats with her hands), lover of poetry and master of statistics, who *always* likes to sleep in, looks me square in the face with the most awake of eyes and says, "Get up, slacker, we're going." I was sure she would sleep through dawn, and I even secretly hoped she would so I could too. No use. In less than fifteen minutes we are both ready to go. We set out to climb the Black Kaweah: the biggest, baddest, and most sinister mountain on the Great Western Divide of the Sierra Nevada. From its lofty heights we hope to look out across the vast mountain landscape of California and consider what it means to be a mountain.

We move quickly from the eastern shore of Heart Lake to meet the Big Arroyo trail as it winds downstream. We breathe in cold air as we move across the wet meadows. Soon the lodgepole pines of treeline flank us on either side, decorated by anxious white-crowned sparrows flitting about. A group of five reddish-colored mule deer drift noiselessly across the herbage, browsing their way through the dim, quiet hours of morning. We walk by swiftly.

At the sound of the first tributary stream to our left, we abandon the trail and begin the long slog up steep talus slopes and out of Big Arroyo Canyon. The cold air seems to expand as the inside of my lungs warms it up, and I feel like my rib cage might crack wide open. Without stopping and without a word to one another, we ascend purposefully and arrive at an obvious band of foxtail pines that lines the upper lip of the canyon. From there we stop and look up, only to find that the talus continues as a huge pile of morainal material, stretching all the way up to the very foot of the Black Kaweah. We breathe deeply and begin again, ascending the rocks through brilliant patches of wet meadow alongside elaborately braided streamlets. Many false rises await us before we arrive at the outlet of the lowest lake. Here we are awarded our first view of our route. We realize that our southwest chute, still shaded from the rising sun, might be too cold a spot for an early start. We decide to continue up to the bottom of the chute and wait awhile.

Despite the physical exertion of ascending rugged terrain with relentless elevation gain, we reach the base of the chute cold. An apron of hard, icy snow spreads out from the bases of two prominent chutes on the southwest side of the mountain. The chute to the right appears to have an easier start, but it soon gets walled out by the dark rock above. The chute to the left looks to have some long, hard moves at the start, but then it appears to provide a decent route upward to the west of the summit blocks. We resolve to try the left-hand chute.

We wait, shivering, collecting water from the slightest meltwater trickles and chewing on handfuls of peanuts and chocolate chips. By nine o'clock the late-morning sun warms our shoulders. The chute, however, still has several hours to go before it will afford such comfort. After ten minutes of sunbathing, we step up the hard snow to the bottom of the chute and duck back into the cold.

We enter the chute via a slick granite crack to the right, leaving our cold-handled ice axes at the snow-choked base of the rock. Getting off the ground involves a series of solid yet committing jams that leave our bodies dangling momentarily over potentially treacherous landings some ten feet below. The exposure is soon over, however, and easier moves on less solid rock follow. The subsequent few hundred feet of the chute require some negotiating and some long moves, and we quickly become familiar with the fragmented style of the Black Kaweah as countless potential handholds become dislodged. As we leave the comfort of the wide granite below us, things get worse. Even the big stuff is loose, some chunks as big as a person. Slowly and delicately, we creep up to where the chute begins to open up and become less vertical. We don't talk about the downclimb.

As the chute opens, the rock changes from granite to metavolcanic material, rhyodacite with plagioclase feldspar crystals forming somewhere along the way. This is the rock that the Black Kaweah is known for. It lacks the hint of structural integrity of the granite below, thus it is more open and lies at a lower angle. It proves only a slightly better substrate for climbing on because it doesn't necessitate the long moves of the granitic material below. The abundance of loose material, however, is hardly worth the trade-off.

We continue upward, keeping to the main chute as it weaves its way among precipitous cliffs to the base of the summit block. When we can no longer see up the chute, we pull ourselves up and onto the serrated west ridge. Straddling the spine of the Black Kaweah, we peer over to the north side of the mountain. From the sharp arete we are seated on, the mountain falls out from under us in a cracked but singular wall, wholly black until giving way to a snowy bib far below. The snowfield spreads out splendidly, merging with the ice-blue frozen slush of Lake 11,700'+, the longest lake in the Kaweahs. The summit of Queen Kaweah looms above the lake. It seemed so lofty when we climbed its summit two days ago, but now the Queen seems but a small heap of talus, not a defined, intimidating elemental mass of stone like the legendary and ominous Black Kaweah upon which we stand. An updraft brings cold air to the ridge and my balance tinkers. We keep moving

The summit is now in sight. The way is obvious: the path of least resistance. Yet resistance seems to emanate from this mountain as a low hum from a cold, dark place. We make our way across the west ridge like Tai Chi masters at 13,700 feet, slowly shifting around the loose, blocky stone with hands, butts, and knees until we can safely get back on our feet. The exposure is extraordinary and the route exhilarating as we nimbly prance the last ten yards of broken rock to the hard hunched back of the Black Kaweah.

The landscape of the entire Sierra Nevada lays spread out like some fantasy of endless mountains. Over one hundred and fifty miles to the north I can clearly make out the distinct forms of Mount Ritter and Banner Peak, the Cathedral Range, and the strangely disjunct summits of the Clark Range. Closer at hand, I fancy I can make out the tilted block of the summit of Mount Humphreys, and the evolution region extending southward to the unmistakable crest of the Palisades. The Kings–Kern Divide country, just thirty miles north, is much more sharply defined, the south slopes of the mountains free of snow and standing tall and bold. The summits are nearly uncountable: Junction, Stanford, Caltech, Geneva, Jordan, on over to the northern summits of the Great Western Divide: Table, Thunder, South Guard, Brewer, North Guard, to name but a few. South of there the crest is split, the western ridge sweeping south to meet with the Kaweahs, then continuing still further south to Sawtooth, Milestone, Rainbow, and Florence before falling into the trees. The eastern crest just gets bigger and bigger, as if the hulking Palisade Crest and innumerable 13,000-foot summits were not enough. The crest culminates with Mount Whitney, the high jewel of the crown, surrounded by Mount Russell, Keeler Needle, Day Needle, spire-like Mount Muir, convoluted LeConte and Corcoran, the tips of Mallory, Irvine, and McAdie, and the broad back of Mount Langley. Southward, the mountains fall into the trees except for the lonely, isolated alpine summit of Olancha Peak. Even further south the mountains sweep around to the west in a faint blue line, the ghostly form of the Tehachapis peering out from the summer smog that covers up the otherworld of the lowlands. To the west I can barely discern the purple wave that suggests the Coast Ranges of Central California—the Santa Lucias out there like a distant dream. This is the clearest day the summer has yet known, and the mountains of California seem to be gathered together to recognize it.

As the midsummer sun beats down on my bare brow and warms the dark rocks of the summit block, it occurs to me that I can think of no other place in the lower forty-eight where I could sit and be so utterly surrounded by so many high mountains so close at hand. All of my experiences in other ranges in the contiguous United States seem to shrink next to the scene before me. Here are more mountains of more different types than I will ever climb in this little life, with more different stories than I could ever tell. And of all the dozens of ranges that make up California, none seem so profound and aesthetically perfect as the Sierra Nevada. So many superlatives describe this place that one wonders by what divine grace were so many fantastic things gifted to one mountain range. Here is the longest singular mountain range in North America, and the highest in the lower forty-eight. The Sierra Nevada is home to the highest alpine lake in the

variations in climate and associated biological phenomena from its base to its summit." Specifics aside, land becomes a mountain when it is uplifted. No one seems to dispute this.

A look at a physical map of the world will quickly reveal where the bulk of the world's mountains occur. It is no small coincidence that these are also the places where the bulk of the world's volcanic and earthquake activity occurs. The Pacific Ocean is literally surrounded by mountains along its fringe. From the Patagonian to the Peruvian Andes the span of mountains is continuous, reaching up through Central America and into the multiple mountain systems of North America. From the Sierra San Pedro Martir and the Sierra Madre, on through the scattered Rockies, the Sierra Nevada, Cascades, and Coast Ranges, on up to the convoluted ranges of Alaska, the trend of mountains continues. The Aleutian Islands, mountaintops rising out of the sea, span the rim of the Pacific to Asia, where the arc of mountains sweeps south, forming Japan, Indonesia, the island arcs of the South Pacific, and New Zealand. All of these ranges together form the vast system now known as the Pacific Rim Cordillera. A second system occurs along the underbelly of Eurasia. Here are the Alps, the Caucasus, the Zagros, the Pamirs, the Karakoram, the Himalaya, among dozens of smaller ranges, collectively referred to as the Alpine-Himalayan Belt.

Long aware of the global distribution of mountains, as well as their coincidence with catastrophic geologic phenomena, geologists and geographers were stumped for centuries by the question of mountain origins. It was in the early 1900s that scientists began to put the puzzle pieces together and see the big picture. It had been obvious for some time that the continental margins surrounding the Atlantic Ocean seemed to fit together almost perfectly. This gave rise to further speculations and theories. The American geologist F. B. Taylor asserted that drifting continents squeezed and depressed the ocean floors between them. Sediments filled in the oceanic troughs as they deepened until continued movement of the continents squeezed the material up and out. This process explained the Pacific Rim Cordillera. The Alpine-Himalayan Belt could be similarly explained by applying the same concepts to continental collisions. Another

American geologist, H. Baker, suggested the idea of a supercontinent that had split into the present disjunct landmasses around twenty million years ago. Alfred Wegener, a German meteorologist, gave further credence to the theory of continental drift by matching up the continental margins along the continental shelves, rather than their present-day coastlines. His ideas were first asserted in 1912 and were translated in 1924 as *The Origin of Continents and Oceans*. Wegener backed up the theory with both geologic and paleontological evidence. Africa and South America had once shared the same rocks, the same climatic conditions, *and* the same assemblages of plant species. These continents also showed evidence of previous coincidental glaciation. The geologic community scoffed at Wegener and assumed him to be a radical (he was, after all, not a "trained" geologist). Other dissident geologists and paleontologists caught the bug, however, and the evidence began stacking up. The debate came to head in 1937 when the South African geologist (and ardent supporter of Wegener) A. L. Du Toit published his paper entitled "Our Wandering Continents," which openly attacked and effectively derailed the conservative contingency. Continental drift was on the map.

Although the efforts of Wegener and Du Toit brought continental drift to the attention of the world, it was not until the 1950s and 1960s that physicists' studies in paleomagnetism tested and confirmed the theory. These studies indicated that as the mineral constituents of rocks solidified (especially iron-rich volcanic rocks), they would align themselves with the magnetic poles. This meant that rocks acted as compasses and indicated the relative movement of the crust in relation to the poles. Despite the complications of wandering continents pointing towards magnetic poles that are themselves migrating, physicists were able to construct models indicating the past positions of continents, as well as the timing of drift. These results matched up with the models put forth by Wegener and Du Toit. All but the most stubborn of the conservative American geologists were convinced.

As the theory of continental drift became increasingly accepted, the geologic community turned their attention to the mechanism that caused such movement. Yes, the crust of the earth has moved, but *why* does it move and *how* does it happen? Taylor had suggested it was a result of tidal action within the earth created by capture of the moon. Baker also made a case for tidal activity, speculating that varying planetary orbits brought Earth and Venus so close together that tidal distortion ripped off a hunk of Earth's crust and formed the moon. Subsequently, the surrounding continents broke and moved in to fill the empty space. Wegener's speculations were less fantastic. He pondered the spin of the earth, tidal effects, and the wobble of the earth's axis but made no significant breakthroughs. It was the Scottish geologist Arthur Holmes who intuited the mechanism for continental drift. Holmes asserted that due to inconsistent radioactive decay of the earth's interior, hotter material was constantly differentiating outward. This plastic flow of material contacted the rigid underside of the crust, pushing and breaking it in places, and flowing beneath in others. As the material cooled, it differentiated back towards the core, sinking, dragging the crust down into the mantle along with it. The result of all this action was a series of huge convection cells within the earth—which, according to Holmes, was the cause of continental drift and consequent mountain building. Wegener, for one, accepted Holmes's ideas with little hesitation.

Equipped with the theories of continental drift and thermal convection, geologists combed the globe to prove or disprove these unorthodox ideas. A search began for the oldest rocks. From there it was thought that the story of the earth might be unraveled. It had long been assumed that the oldest rocks lay beneath the waters of the sea, thus it was to the seafloors that geologists turned their attention. Surveys had recently revealed that the earth was embroidered with an elaborate system of oceanic mountain ranges which were centers of volcanic and earthquake activity. The largest and best known of these was the Mid-Atlantic Ridge, which runs roughly north-south through the middle of the Atlantic Ocean in a curve that parallels the coasts of the Americas and Europe and Africa. In search of the oldest rocks, geologists pulled samples from the depths of the brine in vain. Here, they found not the oldest rocks of the earth but the youngest. Probing into other recesses of the Atlantic, they found that the rocks grew progressively older as they moved away from the Mid-Atlantic Ridge. The oldest rocks they pulled read 180 million years ago, a geologic blink of an eye when compared to the three-billion-year-old samples from the continents. It appeared that new crust was continually being created along the Mid-Atlantic Ridge, displacing the slightly older crust outward towards the continents. If new material was being created, what was happening to the crust it displaced at the other end? There was no convincing evidence that the earth was expanding. The only explanation was that somewhere, somehow, material was being destroyed.

Answers came with further exploration of the deep sea trenches that rim the Pacific. Here, offshore of the surrounding continents, the abyssal plains that stretched out from the oceanic ridges suddenly took a submissive dive down into unfathomable depths. Here too were found the oldest rocks of the ocean floors, disappearing into the deep ocean trenches as the crust of the ocean floor was devoured. Adjacent to these trenches rose the mountain ranges and island arcs of the Pacific Rim. Earthquakes and volcanoes abounded along these boundaries. Further seismic research revealed that the deepest quakes occurred along the plane where the subducting oceanic crust rubbed up against the underside of the crust that was overriding it. These quakes were the simple result of a whole lot of friction between two pieces of crust with different agendas. Monitoring these quakes allowed geologists to measure the actual angle at which crust was subducting, which varied, indicating differences in speed and momentum among pieces of crust. The quakes ceased altogether at around seven hundred kilometers depth. Here the crust began to melt.

Shortly after its formation 4.6 billion years ago, the earth began sorting out its constituent parts. Gravity's pull is greatest on those parts with the greatest density, pulling them ever closer to the center of the planet, while the less dense material is differentiated outward. The result is a series of concentric spheres within the earth, like those of a jawbreaker candy or an onion, organized according to density. A cross section of the earth illustrates that the core is composed of solid nickel and iron. Outward from the core, the percentage of such dark, heavy materials decreases, revealing minerals with higher silica contents towards the crust, and even less dense material, such as water and atmosphere (and life), around the crust. Wrapped around the innards of the earth like an eggshell, the earth's crust is composed of solidified material floating atop a semi-molten interior layer. If something causes the eggshell to crack, the egg whites ooze out. The oceanic crust is primarily hardened egg whites—basaltic volcanic rock extruded from the interior, of high density relative to other common rocks of the crust but necessarily of lower density than the material deeper than it. The continental crust is primarily granitic, even lower in density than the stuff of the ocean floors. Because the continents are less dense, they are more buoyant than the heavier ocean floors and ride higher on the semi-molten interior.

The earth is far from being finished sorting itself out. The thermal convection cells theorized by Holmes way back in 1928 provide the vehicles on which all this continually differentiating material rides. As long as radioactive decay of the earth's parts continues, thermal convection will keep pumping out the heat, and the earth will keep differentiating and redifferentiating. Holmes couldn't have been more right in his assertions. Where upwelling of heat occurs, the lithosphere of the earth diverges, is torn, and a spreading center occurs. Where cooling and sinking occur, the lithosphere converges and subduction happens.

The result of all these processes is that the outer sphere of the earth is broken up into a series of plates which are constantly changing and evolving as thermal convection and gravitational differentiation work together to provide movement. A single plate may host both oceanic and continental crust, the proportions constantly shifting as spreading takes place on one and subduction on the other. Spreading centers start small and get bigger. First they may stretch continental crust so thin it cracks and breaks into blocks, such as is presently occurring in the Great Basin of the American West, or the Rift Valley of Ethiopia. A few more tens of millions of years and the ripping and stretching gets so intense that seawater rushes in, such as is occurring in the Red Sea of Africa. Further action opens up such seas into oceans. Presently, all the major ocean basins of the world have ridges indicating that spreading action has taken place. These ridges mark the trailing edge of the world's plates, which all move steadily away from the spreading centers. The Mid-Atlantic Ridge, for example, is the trailing edge of the North American Plate, which is westward-bound and includes most of the North American continent (there are smaller plates pasted onto the western margin) and the western North Atlantic. The ridge is also the trailing edge of the Eurasian Plate, which is eastward-bound and includes most of Eurasia (there are numerous new additions here as well) and the eastern North Atlantic. As the Atlantic opens up and plates diverge from one another, the Pacific gets devoured by the leading edges of those same growing plates as they converge on the opposite side of the globe.

When continental and oceanic crust collide, such as is occurring along the western margins of the Americas, the more dense oceanic crust subducts beneath the encroaching continent and re-enters the semi-molten interior. As it subducts, it often scrapes the less dense material off of the underside of the continent and mixes with it. This new mix of semi-molten oceanic and continental crust is too light to stay deep, so it differentiates outward, melting more and more of the continental crust into it as it intrudes back into the solid crust. The more continental material it integrates into its semi-molten body, the more it rises. Enough of this will cause the magma to extrude out of the earth's surface, resulting in extensive volcanic arcs, such as the Cascades and the Andes, just inland from subduction zones. Beneath these volcanic arcs, below the earth's surface, huge reservoirs of magma collect and solidify, forming vast bodies of granite and adding to the bulk of the continent.

On the other side of the Pacific, there are smaller oceanic plates that buffer the encroaching continents from full-on collision with the oceanic crust of the Pacific. Here, oceanic crust meets oceanic crust, and the less dense of the two (typically the older) subducts, often causing both leading edges to bend downward as the subducting plate tugs on its overriding neighbor. The consequent buildup of magma beneath the overriding plate intrudes into the crust, melting the dominant crust much as in a continental-oceanic collision. Volcanic island arcs form just in from the leading edge of the overriding plate. Japan, the Aleutians, and countless other islands find their origins here.

All of the cordilleran-type mountains of the Pacific Rim are the result of the subduction of oceanic crust that occurs when plates collide. The lofty mountains of the Alpine-Himalayan Belt, however, have different origins. While oceanic crust is continually being created and destroyed, continental crust is here to stay. When it converges with oceanic crust, it overrides the latter. Eventually, two continental landmasses approaching from different directions will subduct all of the oceanic crust between them, and the continents themselves will collide. When continental crust collides with other continental crust, it buckles, folds, faults, contorts, and builds up in the most massive mountain-building events the world has known. The heat and pressure associated with such events result in widespread metamorphism of rock material. When India finally met Asia, the bottom of the ocean that once stood between them was thrust up to the top of Mount Everest. Africa and Italy into the rest of Europe made the Alps. Eventually, North America and Asia will meet.

Every few hundred million years the landmasses of the earth converge to form a supercontinent. The earliest evidence of this is from around 750 million years ago, when all of the protocontinents were gathered together into a single landmass we now call Rodinia. Most of our knowledge of Rodinia is sketchy at best, but it is generally believed that western North America was connected to Siberia, and possibly Antarctica. Eventually the massive supercontinent presumably overinsulated the thermal convection cells within the earth, and by 550 million years ago Rodinia had broken apart. The continents moved away from their new spreading centers and the ocean basin which was to become the Pacific was born. For over three hundred million years the continental landmasses migrated, closing up the ancestral Atlantic and reorganizing the shape of the earth's surface. By 270 million years ago they had reunited into the supercontinent known as Pangea. Eastern North America crashed into Europe and Africa, while South America collided with southern North America, creating the beginnings of the Appalachians, the Scottish Highlands, the mountains of Scandinavia, the Urals, the Pyrenees, the Atlas Mountains, and the ancestral Rockies. Pangea's demise was due to the same overinsulation of thermal convection cells that presumably broke up Rodinia. Again the continents rifted, each taking some chunks of others as they separated. North America rifted from Eurasia and Africa and began its trip west. The Atlantic opened up at one end, while the Pacific Rim Cordillera and its associated mountains were born on the other. Australia and India divorced South America, and Antarctica began cruising north towards Asia at record-breaking speeds, squeezing out island arcs and the Himalaya along the way. Africa switched directions a few times, eventually settling on the collision with Europe that is throwing up the Alps. When North America and Asia meet, the cycle will begin anew.

I LOOK WEST AND IMAGINE the great island arc of Japan closing in, and all the basalt and seafloor sediments of the Pacific subducting and stacking up to Himalayan proportions in between. As the gentle west wind plays with my hair, it is not too difficult to feel as if things are moving in that direction. River sits quietly and looks south, watching the southern tail of the range slowly bend towards the west. The mountains all around us are testimony to the fact that yes, we are close to the edge of the continent, the meeting place of two evolving pieces of the earth's crust. After a prolonged period of silence, I look over at River and say, "This is totally incredible. I can't believe I almost forgot, took it for granted, got comfortable, believed the books, believed my own memory. I'm never staying home again."

River has a small rusted box in her hands—the summit register of the Black Kaweah. I am drawn to the box by its apparent antiquity. A brief survey of the relatively few names reveals the scrawl of the legendary Norman Clyde from 1932. From an age yet older is the name of Walter Starr Jr. (Pete), year 1929. Starr wrote his name in blood. Presumably he had neither pen nor pencil. It seems an eerie foreshadowing of his death to come, years later, in the shadow of the Minarets. The seventy-year interval since these pioneering mountain explorers were here seems a long time. Then, for perspective, I think of the seventy thousand years since this mountain was shaped by glacial ice, over seventy million years since the rock was formed, and over seven hundred million years of contributing events before that. Suddenly it seems as if Clyde and Starr were here earlier this morning.

The sun reminds us we have to go down. The summit block seems to drop off to vertical walls on all sides. There is the brief temptation to step off and let gravity do the rest, accompanied by the imagined sensation of flying. I let both pass and begin looking for the line across the ridge that will lead us to the chute.

Statistics in the widely read journal *Accidents in North American Mountaineering* indicate that 85 percent of mountaineering accidents happen on the descent. Every time I start to climb down, a haunting mantra echoes through my head. The only way to squeeze it out is through concentration. The Black Kaweah demands it. The mountain's fee of utmost respect is non-negotiable. Loose rock and lots of air have a way of wringing focus out of even the most distractible people. But downclimbing has its advantages. You've been on the route before and can anticipate difficult sections. You're warmed up and familiar with the character of the rock. Gravity is compliant with your direction of travel.

We step off the summit rocks and begin the long, slow, deliberate series of movements that will bring us off the mountain. As we descend, the scraps of attention not fixed on my kinesthetic relationship with the Black Kaweah wander to imaginings of crawling back into the mantle of the earth. As I finger the volcanic rock, I think of its origin. Here is the crust of an old seafloor, once subducted beneath the continent and redistilled as semi-molten material through the thick, solid crust of North America. It reached the surface of the continent over a hundred million years ago and found escape as a frustrated volcano. Broken, angular pieces of this ancient volcano clink beneath my feet, against the mountainside.

Ever careful not to get above or below each other, we downclimb slowly, side by side where space allows, and one at a time where the chute becomes constricted. Dust and pebbles land on my helmet more than a few times. It is painstaking work. We are thankful when we reach the more solid granite of the lower mountain, where the moves become longer but the danger of rockfall less. When we hit the snow at the base of the climb, it is soft, and we both stand there touching its surface for a minute, transfixed by its malleable, forgiving texture after a full day on hard stone. Retrieving our ice axes, we enjoy a swift glissade down to waiting hunks of sun-warmed talus. Below us, shimmering lakes glisten in the afternoon glow, their surfaces teased by the updrafts of valley breezes.

Eventually the lure of the high mountains gives way to the need to return to camp. We descend the lower flank of the Kaweah massif, quickly re-entering the open groves of foxtail pines and scattered whitebarks. Continuing down, we trade the stark aesthetic of the alpine country for the fragrant comforts of the montane forest. Red mountain heather garnishes the granitic boulders we hop across. Hummingbirds whir amongst the magenta corollas of mountain pride penstemons. Water gurgles from beneath the rocks. We have returned to the land of plenty.

We sift our way through the trees and back up the wide valley of Big Arroyo. As the afternoon waxes into early evening, we tread across the open granite slabs of Nine Lakes Basin to our snug camp along the eastern shore of Heart Lake. We are both beaming, still basking in the ambiance of so many mountains, in the knowing that we have seen things rarely seen and imagined things that can only be prompted by rare experience, in the realization that today a mountain is a mountain because of the climb.

THREE

Life on the Rise

Roam where you will across the wrinkled mountain landscape of California and you will find more species of plants and animals than occur in any similar-sized chunk of land in temperate North America, if not the entire temperate world. Over five thousand species of native plants occur here, over half of which occur nowhere else in the world. There are lush forests of redwoods, dry oak savannas, parched grasslands, sun-drenched deserts, fertile ribbons of streamside woodland, stately conifer forests, and windswept expanses of alpine tundra. The synopsis of all this is that diverse topography means diverse habitats, and diverse habitats means more species. The upshot: where there are more mountains there is greater diversity of life. But first we need the mountains.

Early explorers and geographers, and perhaps even their far-reaching Stone Age predecessors, found that they could predict, with a reasonable degree of success, the types of landscapes they would encounter on their travels. It was no mystery that the equatorial regions were warm, even hot, while the polar regions were bitter cold, often to the point of being encased in ice. Everything in between,

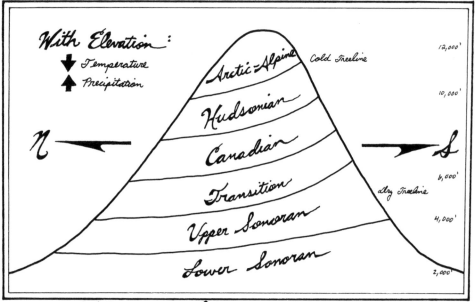

C.H. Merriam's Lifezone Concept (simplified & adapted)

whether north or south of the equator, became increasingly cool the farther one traveled. Explorers discovered many things (often the hard way) that today we take for granted as common knowledge. In the tropics they encountered dense, often impenetrable jungles of rainforest crawling with insects, ornate birds, and vocal monkeys. Diversity among species here was extraordinary. In search of fabled cities of gold, they tore deep into the hot, humid, green realms of the indigenous Americans of Central and South America. In analogous equatorial regions of sub-Saharan Africa, Southeast Asia, and Oceana they found the same types of landscapes. The particular species may have differed considerably, but the climatic conditions, the soils, and the structure and functions of the flora and fauna were the same. Traveling north, the trend continued. Deserts dominated the subtropical arid regions in latitudes of twenty to forty degrees north and south of the equator, including the Sahara, the Australian, the Arabian, the Sonoran, the Chihuahuan, the Atacama. The species of plants and animals varied from place to place, but the climatic conditions and soils as well as the adaptations plants made to cope with these physical factors were the same. In temperate latitudes, where storms were more common and moisture was adequate, forests grew, cloaking most of Europe, Asia, and much of North America. These temperate forests were deciduous in areas with consistent year-round moisture, and coniferous in areas that experienced dry times. Where pronounced dry seasons occurred, expansive grasslands replaced the trees: the steppes of Eurasia, the Great Plains of North America, California's Central Valley. Further north, in latitudes that came to be known as the Roaring Forties and Furious Fifties, where the growing season was shortened and snow covered the ground for much of the year, the forests changed dramatically. Here, conifers ruled, conical and flexible to shed snow, evergreen to take advantage of short warm spells and get a head start on summer. A few notable exceptions to the evergreen rule made a living in these boreal forests of the north: fluttering aspens, bright paper birches, chaste alders and willows. Overall, however, diversity of species was low, though the numbers of individuals of the same species were overwhelming. Still further north, above sixty degrees, the storm systems settled down considerably, but the growing-season temperatures were so cold that the trees stopped growing altogether. Permafrost crept into the ground. Beneath the mysterious green warping skies of the aurora borealis and the amber light of the midnight sun, the trees gave way to vast tundra: prostrate plants in an elaborate system of bogs, meadows, and fell fields extending into the high Arctic. Eventually even these plants couldn't make it, and only a few tenacious lichens survived in the extreme polar regions.

Although new land is what they sought, the explorers and geographers of the golden age were first and foremost sailors. Their realm to roam was the sea, and it was here that some of their most important contributions to science were made. From the earliest times, those who focused their attention on the sea took note of massive ocean currents, for their success at sea depended on intimate knowledge of these. After enough shipwreck stories passed down through the years, sailors could hit the waters with a certain degree of confidence of where the ocean wanted to take them. In short, the ocean basins were like giant washtubs, with their waters moving in a predictable fashion. As we now know, the waters of the North Pacific and North Atlantic both circulate in a clockwise fashion. In the Atlantic, warm equatorial waters are drawn west from the coast of Africa. These waters move north along the Antilles and the Bahamas, continuing up along the coastline of the southern United States before diverging from the continent and heading northeast directly towards Ireland, Great Britain, and Scandinavia. The warm waters delivered by the North Atlantic Current moderate the climate of whatever lands they contact, thus simulating the climatic conditions of lower latitudes. Bermuda, at a latitude comparable to the Carolinas, has a tropical climate. Great Britain, at the same latitude as Labrador, rarely sees snow, has a lengthy growing season, and once supported one of the most extensive empires the world has ever known. Palm trees planted along the west coast of Scotland grow and thrive. Northern Norway, at the same latitude as the ice caps of central Greenland and Baffin Island, supports vast forests of birch and alder, though far above the Arctic Circle.

Eventually the ocean waters do cool, circulating back down the west coast of Europe towards Africa, where again the water is warmed and the cycle begins anew. In the Pacific, the story is much the same, with warm waters moderating southeastern China and Japan, veering off towards southeastern Alaska, and cool waters circulating down the west coast of North America. South of the equator the situation is reversed, and the oceans circulate in a counterclockwise fashion. A quick look at a map will show that in the Southern Hemisphere things are much as they are in the north. Warm waters moderate the east coasts at lower latitudes and eventually diverge and head west. The west coasts at higher latitudes are moderated by these warm ocean currents. Eventually the waters cool down, and these cold waters circulate along the west coasts back towards the equatorial regions. That's the general idea. In reality, things get much more complicated.

Later, research in the fields of climatology, soil science, ecology, and geography confirmed what explorers had speculated for so long. Maps generated from all of these disparate branches of science illustrated striking similarities. The climate maps matched the vegetation maps, and the soil maps matched both. The matching of these maps illustrated clearly that the world could be divided up into distinct climatic regions, or distinct soil regions, or distinct biogeographical regions, and that the boundaries of all of these different classifications were essentially the same. In short, climate maps vegetation, which maps soil, which maps climate, which maps vegetation, which maps soil, which maps…Seem like an impenetrable feedback cycle? Or perhaps a holy trinity of geography. Actually, even during the early stages of this geographic research it was recognized that although climate, vegetation, and soils all influence each other, climate is the ultimate arbiter of the geography of life and soils. Climate, of course, as demonstrated by the findings of the early explorers, is strongly dictated by latitude.

Equipped with accounts of early discoveries, new maps, and bits and pieces of quantitative data becoming more and more available, scientists set out to define vegetation formations and delineate their geography. "Biome" is the modern scientific term used to describe these formations, and it is the broadest category we have to describe vegetation formations. Several different systems have come forward for identifying the major biomes of the earth, all of which focus on the climatic conditions that give rise to each biome. The ecologist Paul Colinvaux identifies eight terrestrial biomes (note that these are terrestrial and do not include marine or other aquatic systems). There are, of course, innumerable more specific systems that nest within these eight major biomes, such as temperate rainforests, hot versus cold deserts, and so forth:

Tundra: Characterized by prostrate vegetation adapted to cold and short growing season. Occurs in polar and subpolar latitudes and altitudes with growing season temperatures that average less than fifty degrees Fahrenheit. Permafrost is often present.

Boreal forest: Characterized by monotypic conifers with few associates, adapted to cold, snow, and short growing seasons. Usually at least 30 to 100 percent canopy coverage by trees. Occurs in subpolar latitudes and altitudes with growing season temperatures that average greater than fifty degrees Fahrenheit. Winters are bitter cold and vegetation is super cold hardy. Permafrost is patchy or not present.

Temperate forest: Characterized by mixed stands of conifers and/ or deciduous trees, dependent on ample moisture, longer growing seasons, and cold but not bitter cold winters. Usually at least 30 to 100 percent canopy coverage by trees. Occurs in temperate latitudes.

Temperate grassland: Characterized by treeless vegetation dominated by graminoids (grasses and grasslike plants, such as sedges and rushes), dependent on ample precipitation punctuated by a pronounced dry season. Often maintained by fire and/or grazing mammals. Occurs in temperate latitudes.

Chaparral: Characterized by a continuous canopy of arid-adapted and fire-dependent shrubs. Most common on acidic (often granitic) soils. Maintained by fire. Occurs in temperate to subtropical latitudes.

Desert: Characterized by sparse arid-adapted vegetation. Evaporation rates exceed precipitation rates. Occurs in subtropical latitudes, mountain rain shadows, and extreme polar regions.

Tropical savanna: Characterized by grassland interspersed with widely spaced trees. Canopy coverage by trees is less than 30 percent. Growing season is year-round. Occurs in tropical regions with pronounced dry seasons.

Tropical rainforest: Characterized by a continuous multilayered canopy of trees (typically broad-leaved evergreens). Growing season is year-round. Occurs in tropical regions with abundant precipitation.

If you were to walk a straight line from the central coast of California to the Nevada border, you could boast of having seen six, and arguably seven, of the eight terrestrial biomes of the world. There is no place else in North America where you could make such a boast, and few places in the world. Pick just about any spot on the globe and you will find one, maybe two, rarely three of these eight biomes represented there. Alaska has Arctic tundra, boreal forest, and arguably some temperate forest in the southeast. Equatorial Africa has tropical savanna and tropical rainforest. Siberia has only boreal forest. Australia, an entire continent, is predominantly desert, with smaller areas of temperate forest and grassland on the eastern seaboard, and tropical rainforest along the north coast. To find the place where the most of the world's biomes are represented in the smallest area, you need to either pick a long, skinny piece of land with a vast latitudinal span, such as Chile, or find somewhere where a wide latitudinal range is simulated by a wide range of elevation. To do that you need mountains.

It had long been known that going up a mountain was like traveling north, but it was not until the late nineteenth century that the naturalist C. Hart Merriam consolidated and published his lifezone concept to explain it. Merriam had traveled widely in the far north of Canada and spent time amongst the spire-like spruces of the great boreal forests and the wide tundra to the north. While surveying on the Colorado Plateau of Northern Arizona, Merriam was struck by the readily apparent bands of vegetation along the flanks of San Francisco Mountain. Only fifty miles away, at the bottom of the Grand Canyon, Merriam had stood amongst the cacti and dusty shrubs indicative of the warm lower Sonoran Desert. Climbing out of the canyon, he passed through the blackbrush and scattered junipers of the colder upper Sonoran Desert. Approaching the San Francisco Peaks, the open woodland of juniper and pinyon thickened to a forest of ponderosa pine and oak. Up on the slopes, the pines and oaks gave way to glowing stands of aspen and thick, dark firs. Further up, past 9,000 feet these trees, reminiscent of what might be seen in Canada, gave way to Engelmann spruces and bristlecone pines, analogous to the boreal forests of the Hudson Bay region. Above 11,500 feet, even the stalwart trees of the north bent down to the prostrate mats and shrubs of the tundra, reaching past 12,600 feet, the summit of Humphreys Peak. He named his lifezones accordingly: Lower Sonoran, Upper Sonoran, Transition, Canadian, Hudsonian, Arctic-Alpine.

What Merriam encountered in that small cross section of Northern Arizona was nothing new. It is because he wrote it down that he is so remembered, and thus Merriam's lifezone theory has become a cornerstone in our modern understanding of the natural world. The short version is that temperature decreases with elevation, now quantified at a rate of three to five and a half degrees Fahrenheit for every thousand feet, depending on the relative humidity of the air mass. Not by mere coincidence, precipitation rates increase with elevation. The upshot: mountains are colder and wetter than the surrounding lowlands, thus simulating more northerly climes. Going up the mountain a thousand feet is like going north two hundred miles.

Merriam's idea was a simple one, yet profound. Modern scientists have been quick to criticize his lack of attention to details and apt not to recognize that the only reason there are details is because Merriam got the basics down for all who follow to footnote. Further observations have shown that slope aspect greatly affects lifezones. In the Northern Hemisphere the sun is in the southern sky, and slopes with southerly exposure are warmer and drier than those facing north. Accordingly, north-facing slopes host lifezone communities at a far lower elevation than their southerly counterparts. Engelmann spruce, the quintessential Hudsonian species on San Francisco Mountain, may occur just above eight thousand feet on north-facing slopes, while on the south-facing slopes it is rare below ten thousand feet. West-facing slopes are also warmer and drier, as the afternoon sun is more intense than that of the morning, and more heating of the earth's surface has occurred by that time of day. Southwest-facing slopes, then, tend to be the warmest, and northeast-facing slopes the coolest. Another detail of great importance is the drainage effect. Just as hot air rises during the day as the earth's surface is heated, cold air sinks at night as things cool down. This sinking air takes the path of least resistance downslope, moving much like water, and follows natural drainages, creating a temperature inversion relative to the area around it. Thus drainages are cool and moist relative to the land surrounding them, and they may host vegetation typically found thousands of feet higher. Subsequent analysis of Merriam's lifezone theory found that distinct plant associations were not quantifiable, and that each species responded to its own set of ecological conditions independent of other species. What Merriam saw as distinct bands of vegetation was actually a spectrum of species, each with its own unique ecological niche, a seamless continuum. Yet somehow we still see what we see. Merriam's terms are still in use, and the basic idea that elevation simulates latitude is still at the forefront of our consciousness as we journey up the mountain.

Perhaps nowhere else on the continent is this idea more drastic, more stunning, more overstated than in the canyon of the Kings River, the deepest canyon in North America. Here, the waters of the south-central Sierra Nevada gather from the highest snow-encrusted peaks and ridges and cut down through the landscape in an incessant quest for the sea. Nine thousand feet of elevation are spanned by the walls of the canyon, from the chilling alpine heights at fourteen thousand feet to the warm pine woodlands and chaparral of the canyon bottom, at five thousand feet. The Kings is deeper than the Grand Canyon, and in contrast to its southwestern counterpart, to look in you must climb up to its rims, to the skyscraping granite tops of innumerable mountains.

From an ecological perspective, walking the nine thousand vertical feet from the canyon floor to the surrounding summits is like walking eighteen hundred miles north. On such a lengthy northerly sojourn, you would pass through semi-arid conifer woodlands laced with lush riparian gallery forests, interspersed with open grassland and temperate savanna, shrubby chaparral, cold sagebrush desert, sweet-smelling pine forests, well-ordered boreal forests, and finally, the windswept expanse of the Arctic tundra. You would end your journey after months, if not years, of traveling to tell the tale that going north it gets colder, the weather changes, and the plants and the soils they grow upon change correspondingly. You would be standing on the permanently frozen soils of the Yukon Plateau, perhaps looking up at a shimmering display of aurora borealis and settling in for a night of subpolar slumber as the mercury dropped to fifty degrees below zero. You could spend just a few days walking in Kings Canyon and see things much the same.

I LEAVE ROAD'S END with six students to simulate the journey to the Arctic. My students have long since heard of the idea that going up the mountain is like going north. Now is their chance to prove it. We have been out in the backcountry together for over two weeks already, as part of a ten-week field quarter studying natural history and ecology in the mountains of California. Thus, our bodies are becoming accustomed to the rigors of life in the field and the strain of carrying on our backs everything we need for eleven days in the mountains. Our noses are burnt and peeled, calves taut, we know what each other likes to eat, who stays up late and who sleeps in, what each other smells like, and who is the turtle and who the hare on the trail. Laden with necessities and strengthened by some experience, we set out across the hot, dusty, pine-scented flats of the canyon. Thoughts of cool alpine meadows and crunchy snowfields give meaning to the sweat that soaks our packs as they press into our backs; we knew well the toll that nine thousand vertical feet would exact on our legs before we would ever reach such high places.

We ascend steeply up the Bubbs Creek drainage, trudging up

switchbacks on a slope that cruelly faces southwest. It is a textbook ecological situation. Here, along the hot and dry southwest slope, are woodland and chaparral species, species that Merriam would have called Upper Sonoran, growing higher than the lower montane Transition zone species of the valley floor, where cold air pools regularly every night. We pass canyon live oaks, bush chinquapin, manzanita, whitethorn, and even a stray pinyon, leaving drops of sweat on their parched leaf surfaces as we walk by. When we reach the top of the slope, we tuck into the valley of Bubbs Creek, thankfully noticing gigantic sugar pine cones littering the ground as the forest trees of the Transition zone close in around us.

Continuing upward, we find ourselves once again pounded by the midday sun as we plod up the rocky switchbacks along Sphinx Creek. The terrain is typical of the Sierra Nevada: flat treads of valley walking characterized by meandering or rushing streams and placid lakes, interspersed with huge, steep risers of bare granite and plummeting waterfalls. This is the glacial staircase, an undulating stair-step topography fit for the most giant of giants, which we will follow up to its uttermost summit. The switchbacks seem endless, each hopefully the last but leading inevitably to yet more. The valley of the Kings gapes large and far away, now three thousand feet below us, with its forest dark green and thick. Eventually the riser bends into another tread, and we follow a less hurried Sphinx Creek into its sheltered drainage. Tucked away from the sun, huge trees grow here, and the massive trunks of red firs and western white pines grow up to thick branches and green scented boughs. Beneath the canopy, numerous small streams intersect flowering red mountain heather and pinemat manzanita, cascading down the slope towards Sphinx Creek. Paralleling Sphinx Creek, we cross these tributaries, one after the other, each decorated with vibrant seep-spring monkeyflowers, largeleaf lupines, big red paintbrushes, cinquefoils, and secretive bog orchids. This forest is decidedly more northern than the one below. At the Sphinx Creek crossing, we rest. We lean comfortably against rocks and logs, and spontaneously and simultaneously fall asleep.

We awaken an hour later to the high wail of thousands of mosquitoes. Surely we must be in Canada now.

With another thousand feet up to go that day, we hoist our ten days' worth of food, clothing, shelter, notebooks, textbooks, ice axes, and helmets and set out off-trail. We follow Sphinx Creek more closely this time, ascending yet another riser towards where we hope to find some slabs to camp on. Passing through forest-line wet meadows abloom with goldenrod, rose-smelling Kelly's tiger lilies, and Jeffrey's shooting stars, we emerge into an extensive stand of quaking aspen, leaves aflutter in the up-valley afternoon breeze. Here we pause and listen to the sound of the wind in the trees, green leaves all shaking against each other. As in all places where they grow, the aspens here are pioneering a recently disturbed area, in this case an area where a combination of rockslides and avalanches falling from the steep valley walls above has scraped off any pre-existing vegetation and scoured the underlying soil. If there was any doubt we were in a mid-montane Canadian-type forest, this sight dispels it. Not only is this forest similar to those of the north in terms of its climatic conditions, structure, and organism functions, but actual species are the same. This is the very same *Populus tremuloides* found in the Canadian-type forests of Alaska, all the way across Canada to the North Woods of Maine. Biogeographers appropriately call this northern forest the boreal forest, after Borealis, the Greek god of the north wind. This is the largest and most contiguous terrestrial biome in the world, covering much of Alaska and Canada and patches of the lower forty-eight, as well as most of northern Europe and all of Siberia. Here in the Sierra Nevada we are in a southern extension of the boreal forest, a finger of northern forest that extends conspicuously far south, following the cold, wet spines of the mountains. Here, because it is elevation rather than northerly latitude that creates the ecological conditions conducive to this type of forest, biogeographers refer to the forest as montane boreal.

The last stretch is a grunt up the steep riser and through the trees. Soaked with sweat and covered in dirt and debris from bushwhacking, we let our packs drop and roll across blessed flat slabs of granite. We have made it to camp.

For three days we study the ecology of pollination while watching rufous hummingbirds draw nectar from *Penstemon newberryi*. We discuss and debate the ecological causes and potential value of the diversity of life on earth while keying out innumerable species of wildflowers, turning our heads upside-down to peek into the corollas of crimson columbines. We study the evolutionary characteristics of mammals while fending off *Ursus americana,* the ubiquitous black bear of the Sierra Nevada. Eventually it is time to ascend another three thousand feet, through the uppermost montane forest and into the land above the trees. With our packs three days lighter and the wide expanse of the alpine Sierra Nevada on our minds, we rise to the task at hand.

As we ascend the glacial staircase from our camp at 9,000 feet, we strain our legs once again and wind our way up the steep granite slabs and through the trees. As the riser we camped against rounds out to the next tread, we come to the marshy shore of a shallow lake, nestled like a babe in cradling arms of granite. Here, the undulating glacial ice of the Pleistocene had carved out a small basin, the way a waterfall does when it falls with force down a steep slope and abruptly meets a flat bed. Since the ice pulled back, the lake has slowly but surely been filling in with sediments washed down from the heights above. The banks of the lake are lined with willows, tolerant of the fluctuating lake levels and prolonged periods of inundation. Further in from the shore, rooted aquatic plants grow, their foliage floating on the water's surface. Over time, as sediments have washed into it, this lake has grown increasingly shallow, and its waters have spilled outward into the surrounding forest. We peer down into the lake at dozens of submerged logs, trees that once lined the shore and then collapsed into the lake as its waters widened. Mosquitoes whir around us by the thousands, urging us to keep going, up, up, above the trees and into the wind. Judging by the scene before us, we might be in Alaska, or deep in the lake country of Ontario, Manitoba, or Quebec. We could be in Scotland, on the shore of some haunted loch, or chasing reindeer herds across northern Scandinavia. But this is the Sierra Nevada, and one look above the lodgepole pines that line the lake reveals walls of glinting granite mountains. The glacier that carved this basin was no sprawling gargantuan continental ice sheet, but a steep and undulating alpine glacier. We are not in the boreal forests of the north, but rather the montane boreal forest of the Sierra Nevada of California!

Two more risers and another lake later, we emerge from the trees and into the wide-open sunlit space of the High Sierra. At just below 11,000 feet, this is an unusually low elevation for treeline, and sure enough, as we traverse the shores of Sphinx Lakes, sporadic trees continue to make appearances all the way up to 12,000 feet, hugging warm south- and west-facing slopes. We cross granite slabs glistening in the sun, worn and polished by the undersides of long-past glaciers, striations etched into their shining surfaces by the rocks and sand that were once pressed between the bedrock and the overbearing ice. We crunch our way across extensive gravel flats, where drought-resistant pussy-paws and wild buckwheats eke out a living. Bright green ribbons of dense vegetation burst forth from the ground just a few feet away, where snowmelt water gurgles in countless threaded streams and delivers moisture to wet meadows all summer long. Flowers grow here in lavish abundance and uncountable numbers, and the buzz of flying insects fills the air. In between are dry and moist meadows, rich with sedges and early flowering dwarf bilberries and kalmias. Snowfields persist in nooks and crannies and cover the north- and east-facing slopes, melting in the heat of summer and watering the ground. Here is the tundra, where small is beautiful and a closer look reveals entire miniature worlds.

Tucked into a rock crevice at 11,000 feet, just up from the lower Sphinx Lakes, a cluster of columbines catches our attention. Unlike the crimson columbine, whose bright red nodding flowers are so common along streamsides in the montane forest, this plant bears larger, paler flowers, creamy whitish-yellow with rosy streaks. The flowers face sideways, with a horizontal orientation, rather than down, and have only half the nod of their montane counterparts. The place where they are growing is different as well. This is no streamside, but a rock cranny. Leaving the matter for speculation, we continue to ascend.

We keep climbing, from treads filled with sparkling lakes to steep risers of big granite. At 11,500 feet, we begin our final climb across old glacial moraine and huge chunks of angular talus, picking our way carefully, slowly but surely, to an obscure pass at over 12,000 feet. Our journey north is complete, and if not for the serrated peaks surrounding us on all sides, we might be in the Arctic, the midnight sun just coming down from its midsummer apex, spiraling around the polar skies. Merriam's lifezones, just a concept before, become as solid in our experience of the world as eating and breathing. Elevation really does simulate latitude, and the truth is written across every feature of the snow-crusted, tundra-graced alpine zone of the Sierra Nevada.

As we rest over food and drink, we gaze southeast across yet another basin to a long ridge extending from the high summit of Mount Brewer. Along that ridge there is an obvious col, a low saddle carved by glaciers long ago. Through that col is our next camp.

The last phase of a long day in the mountains is always unpredictable. Sometimes tiredness sets in and undoes the group. Other times knowing that the packs will soon come off and camp will be made affords a second wind, and faces become aglow with grins. We are somewhere in between those extremes, making our way across the ambient granite and up to our resting place. On our way up to the col, a few of us gather around a familiar sight. It is a columbine, yet different than either of the ones we have seen before. This one has large, purely pale, cream-colored flowers that grow erect, with no detectable nod. It is growing at the edge of a gravel flat, tucked and shaded against a large granite boulder. We compare it to the columbines below. The crimson columbine had a bright red, nodding, tight, relatively small flower, half the size of this one, and grew along stream banks. This one has a looser, pale cream, erect, relatively large flower, twice the size of its crimson relative, and grows in rocky places. The columbine at Sphinx Creek was somewhere in the middle. Have we been looking at two different species? Speculations arise which quickly turn to hypotheses. We discuss them as we continue ascending, and engaging in a dialogue about evolution helps keep us going. Clearly this new columbine, at nearly 12,000 feet, is no crimson columbine but something different, perhaps unique to the alpine zone. But what about the Sphinx Lakes columbine? Is it an unusual crimson or more akin to the new flower? Is it a third species, unique in its own right? Are we witnessing evolution in action? Questions fly like pollen on the wind. What is a species anyway? How does speciation occur?

For much of our time on earth, humans have perceived the world around them as a set creation, made by a creator and set in motion complete. Judeo-Christian mythologies, though often criticized for perpetuating this belief system, are but one mythos of an innumerable many that have reflected the worldview of humans for thousands of years. What on earth would make people believe anything different? Even today, only a select handful of scientists have actually seen organic evolution happening, and this has been among organisms so small they are invisible to the naked eye. Yet we are witnessing such evolution in action every day, all the time. Every time an organism is born, dies, or engages in reproductive activity, evolution is at work, ever changing the face of life as it moves into tomorrow.

Charles Darwin published his monumental work, *On the Origin of Species,* in 1859, revolutionizing biology and forever changing the way we view the world. In this work, Darwin articulated the process of natural selection as the mechanism by which species evolve over time. Not only did Darwin provide the mechanism by which species evolve, but he also gave overwhelming evidence to support such evolution of species. In light of the Newtonian mechanistic worldview that dominated Western culture at the time, as well as the creationist view of the Church, Darwin's assertion was bold because it suggested that the universe, rather than being predictable and mechanistic, or static and pre-created, was dynamic and changing. This potentially reinfused Western thought with a teleological sense of purpose that it had lacked since the Greco-Roman era. Like Merriam, Darwin was a spokesperson for ideas that had been on the table for some time. Because he was the first to put them in popular print, and no less due to his painstaking efforts in figuring out the mechanism of natural selection, his name will be forever known. But there were others who preceded him, a few who were his contemporaries, and still more who are filling out the details of evolution in his wake.

During the fifteenth century, Europe was hemmed into a tight corner. To the north were frozen wastes. To the east and south the iron curtain of Islam kept all but a few Westerners from penetrating this ever-growing cultural boundary. To the west was the mighty Atlantic, stretching further than the eye could see to the edge of the world. When finally these confines were breached, and explorers and geographers began pulling into their home harbors laden with otherworldly specimens and descriptions of exotic lands, the very foundations of Western thought began to shake and tremble. Where were these species during the great flood of Noah? Were they on board the ark? How could they possibly have all fit? How could God have done all this in just six days? Although they may seem like trite questions to us today, these and many other like questions posed serious challenges to the church-state that shaped the Western mind. As science gained credence, further biological and geological discoveries came filing in. Naturalists were perplexed by the similarities between analogous body parts of different organisms. The human hand, the flippers of marine mammals, and the wings of bats shared structural similarities that seemed beyond mere coincidence. Humans' bony protrusions in the rear of the pelvis corresponded suspiciously to the bony parts of tails. During the early stages of development, human embryos looked just like hundreds of other organisms, including fish. Early geologists discovered fossilized marine organisms deep below the surface of the earth. The organisms were more simple the deeper they dug, becoming increasingly complex towards the surface. The deeper rocks were older, and this suggested that marine organisms were becoming more and more complex as time progressed. If creation was complete, and all species had remained the same since creation was set in motion, how could this be?

By the eighteenth century, the amount of evidence suggesting the evolution of species was overwhelming. Georges-Louis Leclerc, Comte de Buffon, was among the first to articulate evolutionary ideas to the scientific community. He was the first to define the concept of species, describing them as distinct entities which do not interbreed with each other. This fundamental definition is still in use today. Buffon also recognized that traits were passed on from parents to their offspring, and that an increasing number of combinations of traits arose with each successive generation. Buffon didn't stop there. He was also the first to recognize that species adapt to the environments in which they live, and over time the environment determines the way species evolve. Inheritance, in combination with changing environments, determined the evolution of species. Buffon was halfway there. But he lacked the mechanism by which evolution actually took place.

In England, Erasmus Darwin, the grandfather of Charles, followed closely in the wake of Buffon. Perhaps the coincidence of two evolutionary theorists of the name Darwin is proof enough for the idea of heredity! Erasmus was a keen observer of animals, questioning the development of such obscurities as elephants' trunks, specialized beaks, cumbersome antlers, porcupine quills, and brightly colored insects. He emphasized the relationship between environment and heredity, demonstrating that the vast majority of morphological characteristics revolved around either gathering food, protection from predators, or reproduction. Characteristics that allowed for a higher degree of success in foraging, evading predators, or breeding were passed on to offspring as successful adaptations. But how did such adaptations arise?

Meanwhile, in France, the famous botanist and renowned naturalist Jean-Baptiste de Monet, Chevalier de Lamarck, was coming up with his own recipe. Lamarck recognized two fundamental ideas essential to our modern understanding of evolution. First, that all living things were an integrated whole, the life of each affecting the lives of others. Second, that all of nature, organic and inorganic, was in a constant state of change. In the Newtonian world of mechanical predictability, these ideas were revolutionary. Lamarck emphasized that the idea of species was a human construct, and what we observed as species were actually snapshots of change in action. The most complicated organisms were those that had been changing the longest, while the most simple organisms were the youngest. Further, once life reached a certain degree of complication, such as multicellular life evolving from unicellular life, or placental mammals evolving from marsupials, there was no going back. Even if a group of organisms died in one area, they would be replaced by the innumerable forms of life evolving "below" them.

Many of Lamarck's best ideas are central not only to our modern understanding of the evolution of species but also to our understanding of the evolution of landscapes, and even the universe. An understanding of the interrelatedness of all living things was an essential step in the development of our emerging ecological worldview, in which all living (organic) *and* nonliving (inorganic) things are connected. Lamarck's notion that change is *the* fundamental aspect of nature, and that species are snapshots of change in action, is central to our understanding of the universe, from galaxies to solar systems, from landscapes to organisms, as a dynamic system. His idea that evolution moves towards ever-increasing complexity echoes loudly in our understanding of species divergence, most commonly illustrated in the "family trees" of organisms, in which successive groups of organisms diverge and branch off from a common ancestor. Lamarck was also the first to begin to articulate the idea of "niche," though he did not name it as such. His idea of evolving organisms "moving up" to fill in the spaces left by those that died off suggested that nature abhors a vacuum, and that organisms have interconnected roles that need to be filled for the whole system to function.

Unfortunately, Lamarck's best ideas were shrouded by his most famous one, for which he became the subject of ridicule. Lamarck suggested that all characteristics gained throughout the life of one organism were passed on to its offspring. This Lamarckian idea is classically illustrated by African giraffes. Originally a grazing animal, giraffes began stretching their necks to reach leaves in trees. As the height at which leaves were available increased, the giraffes had to stretch still more. The parents who had stretched gave birth to offspring with stretched necks, and now we have long-necked giraffes. According to this theory, if you pruned the tree out in your front yard for a long enough period, the offspring of that tree would have pruned characteristics. Similarly, if a parent spent enough time in the sun and always had tanned skin, their children would be born with tanned skin. If this were the case, evolution would work much more rapidly than it does, and entirely new "species" could evolve in just a few generations. Modern biology assures us that, while changes in the genotype affect the phenotype of an organism, changes in the phenotype do not affect the genotype. This means changes must occur in the *genetic* makeup of an organism in order to be passed on to the next generation. Thus we remember Charles Darwin, and the name of Lamarck remains covered with dust.

The very same year that Lamarck published his ideas, Charles Darwin was born. Shortly after Lamarck's death, in 1829, this strapping young man stepped onto the creaking wooden deck of the HMS *Beagle,* bound for the tropics and the Southern Hemisphere. Darwin had studied medicine at Edinburgh, but his time there was brief and he is said to have fainted at the sight of blood. Nevertheless, he learned much in the fields of geology and natural history along the way. Perhaps disenchanted by the lack of answers these disciplines provided, or simply due to lack of motivation (he was known to prioritize hunting above studying), he took the advice of his father and went on to study divinity at Cambridge. Embarking on the five-year journey that would change both his life and, eventually, the lives of billions, Darwin was far from the cutting-edge thinker he would be upon his return. He was invited along to keep the captain company and provide the conversations and intellectual stimulation the wine-soaked crew could not. As the story goes, at the time of his departure Darwin was dead set against the growing idea of evolution. No mechanism for such an idea had been realized. When he sailed from Europe, Darwin was a creationist.

On a spattering of volcanic islands five hundred miles off the coast of Ecuador, Darwin found the unlooked-for answer to hundreds of years of evolutionary thinking. While exploring the Galapagos, he identified thirteen different species of finch, the only group of terrestrial birds on the islands. Each species that Darwin found was confined to its own island, geographically isolated from other species. While Darwin's finches were distantly related to a seed-eating ground finch found in Ecuador (presumably blown in from the South American mainland in ages past), each of the thirteen species had evolved distinct adaptations specific to the environmental conditions of the island it inhabited. The most notable of these adaptations involved foraging for food. On tree-covered islands, the finches foraged for insects among the trees. Some of these birds gleaned insects from the surfaces of branches, and from shallow grooves and cracks in the bark. These finches had needlelike bills similar to those of warblers. Other birds foraged for insects beneath the bark, and in the wood of trees. These finches were more robust and had more substantial, longer bills, similar to those of woodpeckers. On other islands, where trees were absent or not abundant, different birds were found. These fed on seeds, foraging on the ground or on the low, spiny cactus plants that grew there. Their bills were thick and conical, ideal for the seed cracking behavior common to most finches. Even among these birds, however, no two species were alike, and each was particular to its own island. With no other terrestrial birds to compete with, the Galapagos finches had adapted rapidly to the specific conditions of each island, radiating into a multiplicity of niches that were usually occupied by many different birds. Where there were no warblers, the finches became warbler-like. Where there were no woodpeckers, the finches became woodpecker-like. There was no job a Galapagos finch couldn't do.

Darwin recognized that organisms reproduced exponentially but food did not. Because of this simple inequity, there would only ever be enough food for a fixed number of individuals, unless some change occurred that allowed more efficient use of resources. This led to Darwin's idea of competition. According to Darwin, those individuals that best fit their environmental conditions got the most food, evaded predators most easily, and bred the most successfully. Less fit individuals struggled for food, fell more easily to predators, and were less likely to survive to reproduce. While the characteristics of fit individuals were passed on to successive generations, those of less fit organisms were gradually weaned out. On a tree-covered island where insects abounded, those birds with needlelike bills were the most efficient foragers, thus they survived to breed, and the characteristic was passed on to their young. Those birds lacking the characteristic of needle-shaped bills did not survive to breed, thus their thick-billed characteristics were not passed down. After several generations, only birds with needlelike bills were left on the island. Darwin called this mechanism for evolution "natural selection." This was his key contribution to our understanding of evolution. He further asserted that as an environment changes, nature will select for those individuals best suited to the changes. Thus environment governs the evolution of species. Here was Darwin's genius.

Contemporary with Darwin's work was that of a young upstart named Alfred Russell Wallace. While Darwin cruised the Galapagos, Wallace hopped the islands of Southeast Asia in search of answers to the same questions, and he found them. Never a favorite among the academic bigwigs of Europe at the time (among whom was the famous geologist Charles Lyell), Wallace lacked the support for his ideas that was essential for them to be taken seriously. Although he sent papers to Lyell and to Darwin himself, Wallace remained obscure. His work, however, was highly influential (and controversial) within the scientific community of the time. While Darwin sat on his *Beagle* journals, afraid of being labeled a heretic, Wallace cleared the way and provided Darwin with the competition he needed to come out of his shell. *On the Origin of Species* was published soon after Wallace mailed a paper directly to Darwin, a paper which Darwin may have later denied reading.

Darwin's theory of evolution depended on variation among organisms in order for different traits to come up. Unable to unravel this mystery, he let the matter rest. Though it was a hot topic when it emerged, Darwin's theory of evolution took a break in the late nineteenth century. It was not revisited for several decades, until the discovery of genetics by the famous Austrian monk Gregor Mendel, which confirmed Darwin's theory by providing a mechanism for Darwin's mechanism. Genetic variation, inherent among all organisms, allowed for variable traits. Evolution was on the books.

BY NIGHTFALL, OVER CUPS OF TEA with the flush of alpenglow on the west face of South Guard, my students unravel the mystery of the columbines. The crimson is the elder of the genus *Aquilegia*. As the mountains rose, a new species began to diverge from the crimson columbine in response to the changing environmental conditions. This new species, the Coville's columbine, is more successful in the rocky conditions that dominate the alpine Sierra. Because it grows higher, where the growing season is shorter and pollination activity less, its flowers are larger, erect, and less strictly colored, so it can attract a wider variety of pollinators than its crimson cousin. The Sphinx Creek columbine is a hybrid, with characteristics of both species, and is living evidence that the divergence of the columbines is both recent and incomplete. I smile, immeasurably proud of my students for tackling such a sophisticated riddle, and knowing that this will lead to more and bigger questions.

We sleep soundly, knowing our slumber was well deserved after such an ascent. Through my mind the ideas of Buffon, Lamarck, and Darwin circulate like wind in a thunderhead. All life evolved from other life. New species do not spontaneously appear on earth, but arise as modified versions of previous species. Each species transcends and includes its predecessors. Without primates there could be no humans. Without mammals there could be no primates. Without vertebrates there could be no mammals. And so we reach back deep into the vaults of time, to the dawn of life, and beyond.

FOUR

Under Ancient Seas

In the sound of the sea the song of the universe echoes more clearly than in any other sound on earth. Far from the places where briny ocean waters lap up against the land leaving salty foam and sand, that song is still heard. It is in the fossils embedded in the limestone of the summit of Mount Everest. It is in the bent and folded, garnet-encrusted, ancient seafloor walls of the Pennine Alps. It is in the oranges, reds, and tans of the sandstones, limestones, and shales of the Grand Canyon. It is in the marble canyons, Basin ranges, and shifting dunes of Death Valley. In all of these places the sea has left its story, though its waters no longer remain.

Dust swirls around sandy flats as I drive northwest from Stovepipe Wells Village, Death Valley, along the road to Marble Canyon. The twisted shapes of the Cottonwood Mountains grow up to my left, pale and cold in the dusk of December. But even in the waning light of midwinter, I can see lines in the mountain escarpment, brown, rust, gray, and tan. They are bent and folded, almost like waves in some places, in others more like the flutes and lines of a chocolate soft-serve ice cream cone. Sometimes water cuts down through those lines, finding weaknesses in the rock and working them over millions of years into deep canyons. That's what I am looking for. That's where I am going. There is a story to be unraveled. These mountains, the rocks of this place, were laid down at the bottom of an ancient sea. I want to get inside the rocks, deep inside some lonely canyon, to the heart of that old seafloor.

I keep my momentum going as I ride through the sand, wary of slowing down and getting stuck in the loose, bottomless grains. I think of being on the East Coast, driving on the beach, and imagine the sound of surf pounding against the shore, sifting billions of grains of sand around in its backwash. I remember getting stuck while driving across Atlantic sand and running miles for help as the tide rose. I think of quiet walks for miles along the wide swath of Assateague, in Virginia, Cape Hatteras, in North Carolina, Edisto, in South Carolina, Anastasia, in Florida. I think to myself, "This is like being at the beach, except there's no beach."

Soon the sand gives way to cobbles, fist-sized to head-sized. These are rounded and have spent time in fast-moving water, rolling down out of the mountains along rocky beds. The tumbling bashed off any angularities and polished them up with waterborne sand. The cobbles have come a long way. The mountain front is still miles off. The flood must have been big. Big enough to squeeze through some unnamed canyon in a flashing fury and rush out miles along a wide alluvial fan of sand, to rest here. The cobbles are everywhere. Soon I realize the road became at some time past the path of least resistance for the floodwaters, and I am driving in an ephemeral stream bed. The front end of my '83 Subaru doesn't take it so well. She bucks like a wild horse. My head hits the ceiling as we bounce.

As dusk falls, the cobbles become incessant. I slow down to a steady crawl, ever vigilant for rocks the size of bowling balls, scanning the inadequate field of view offered by my headlights. Eventually I make the eight miles to the mouth of Cottonwood Canyon, where again floodwaters long squeezed in by canyon walls finally spread out luxuriously across the open valley floor. What is left of the road continues up the canyon along the wash. As I approach the wash, I realize the road ahead drops out from under me. As I come to an abrupt and dusty halt, I am reminded of nightmarish dreams I have had of driving cars over the edges of bridges to nowhere. As the dust settles in the yellow glow of the headlights, I get out of the car to have a look at the drop-off in the road. It is a steep, eroded escarpment of about thirty degrees. The drop is eight feet. Looking at the front end of the Subaru, carefully considering its shape and upward curve from the wheels, I figure I can make it. I get back in, put the car in four-wheel low, and drop in.

I roll into the wash with a surge of adrenaline, and in one tumbling second I discover success. I have gambled and won.

Ahead, the canyon works its way into the dark shapes of the mountains. I shift up to four-wheel high and set out across the last stretch of cobbles. They are worse than before. The Subaru seems to plead with me to stop. She creaks and groans, flexing with each bounce and thunk. I try to reason with her. In two miles we will make the confluence with Marble Canyon, the point of rest I have fixed in my mind. It is too much for her. She lasts through the first, but I know the second mile will be her undoing. I spot a raised silty flat, a fine bed for the night, and come to a stop.

I emerge from the shell of my car and enter into the desert night. It is still. The sky is deep indigo-black and spattered with countless stars. The stars seem to be vibrating. They look like quivering beads of silver light strewn across the dark cloak of night. There is no moon. She seems to have left the stars alone for a time, as if not wanting to distract the world from their spectacle. It is cold, and the cold seems to make the air cleaner, the silhouettes of the canyon walls more sharp, the night sky more crisp. As I crawl into my sleeping bag, I am sure I can see five thousand stars.

I lie there thinking about stars, and space, and time, transfixed for a while beneath the stark clarity of the desert sky. Modern physicists tell us that space *is* time, and that before there was space there was no time at all, not even light. Before the Big Bang, the stuff of the universe was so dense that light couldn't even escape. When it exploded, fifteen billion years ago, light was one of the first things to issue forth into the void. Time began, perhaps with light as its envoy. The world as we know it was set in motion.

Meteors periodically brighten the sky. Wild things are on the loose up there. Wild things we can't touch or change. Orange, crimson, and blue tails gush from behind them, spraying out across the star-strewn heavens.

Morning comes cold and slow, as is its wont in canyons in winter. I arise and step out into the cold still air, my brain empty of thoughts, as it is on the best mornings. Brushing the dust from my pot, I fill it with cereal and milk and sit there eating, looking up-canyon as the first ideas of the day begin to formulate. It is dead quiet. It is so quiet I grow self-conscious about the noise my spoon makes as it clinks against my pot, reverberating off of the canyon walls. Chewing becomes deafening. I wonder if the silent creatures around are looking at me and wondering. Occasionally I stop chewing to listen, but then even my breathing seems to drown out any other subtle sounds that are out there. Feeling like a clumsy buffoon, I finish breakfast and rummage through my belongings, looking for the food, water, and clothes I need for the day.

I set out up the lonely wash of Cottonwood Canyon, crunching my way across loose sand and gravel, over half-buried cobbles of brown, burgundy, orange, and elephant gray, over hard-packed silt that feels smooth when crushed in the hand. Soon I reach the Marble confluence, evidenced by a substantial tributary channel coming in from the right. Here, I leave the Cottonwood wash and follow Marble. The canyon is wide for several miles, giving the floodwaters a chance to spread out before the next constriction downstream, near the mouth of Cottonwood Canyon. Here, on this wide channel, the waters slow down, dropping not only cobbles and small stones but even sand and silt. Patches of vegetation grow on temporary islands that rise above flood level. But no trees grow here, nor any shrubs of substantial age. During big flood years, all of these island refugia were swarmed with brown, surging waters, and the canyon was full from wall to wall.

These canyons cut deep into the desert mountains, incisions into the otherwise often obscured stone bones of the Basin ranges. The landscape is vast, wide, sweeping, quiet. Sometimes it feels as if the space is aching to be filled, or at least we ache to fill it. It will cram your psyche with the striped confines of marbleized limestone slot canyons and spill you out to impossible panoramas of bent, broken earth, wide, dropping, salt-encrusted, sinking valleys, cleanly uplifted mountain ranges, lowest, highest, thinnest, driest. The expanse of Basin and Range that spans the deserts of western North America transcends morality, duality, causality. This place exists independent of our belief, trust, faith, or love for it and does not revolve around the whims of the human psyche. This is no wilderness playground for seekers of nectar and decadent backcountry promises. There is little sweetness on which to be drunk when the winds blast sand and grit and it's you and the earth and not a whole lot of forgiveness. The desert helps only as much as it harms, gives only as much as it takes away, and any troubles, darkness, or drama that we find here are projections of what we bring with us when we come. In the desert mirage is a mirror that shows only ourselves. It cuts away the fat, then the flesh, and gets down to the bones. This place is all bones.

The narrows begin like a gateway into another world. The canyon closes up and reduces the bed of the wash from a hundred meters wide to a mere few. It is cold in here. Cold and shady. The atmosphere of the canyon hints at its deep, dark past. When these rocks were laid down, there was no light, no sun, but trace suggestions of it filtered through the waters of a shallow sea. The name "Marble" betrays the canyon's history. Marble is marine limestone that is exposed to tremendous pressure, hardened and often bent and folded during the process. Such limestone only forms in shallow seas, such as occur when ocean waters rise and flood the land, or where continental shelves extend out to sea, as is the case in eastern North America today. In most seas, the ocean floor is so deep that all of the nutrients required for living, growing things are hundreds, thousands, even tens of thousands of feet below the surface of the water, beyond even the blue of the ocean, deep in the black endless night. But living things need not only nutrients, they need sunlight as well. Without both of these things, the ocean is a vast, wet desert. Only in shallow seas do both nutrients and sunlight occur together. Here, life is abundant. Over millions of years, billions of marine organisms die and leave their shells and skeletons to disintegrate on the seafloor. They pile up, mixing with sand and other sediments, packing together beneath the immense pressure of the sea above. In time, they lithify—they become rock. Rich in the calcium and carbonate minerals of shells and skeletons, the rock is limey. Marine limestone.

I enter the narrows, running my fingers along the smooth, polished walls as I step into the quiet space. The floor is sand. Here in this tight space, floodwaters moved so fast and with such force that even human-sized boulders were transported through the canyon and ejected at the mouth of the narrows. They were out there, strewn across the sand, testimony to the power of water stopping at nothing to get back to the sea. It was not water that had sculpted the feminine curves of this canyon, but rocks and sand suspended in the water, acting like coarse-grit sandpaper every time a flood came through.

The canyon walls are high enough that the sky above appears as a thin ribbon of blue. Along their contours, the walls are gracefully striped, in places as marked as a zebra, accentuating every convexity and concavity. A closer look reveals small pockets in the surface of the rock, some the size of fingertips, others fist-sized, large enough for floodwaters to deposit sediments in them. From these pockets, the lush green leaves of the rock lady *Maurandya* pour forth, little hanging gardens in stark contrast to the clean, striped stone. The pockets are left where the marble dissolved. The calcium and carbonate minerals that make up limestone both dissolve in solution, making limestone water soluble. Marble shares this characteristic with its parent limestone. Here in Marble Canyon, hundreds of millions of years of dissolving and re-precipitating have given the canyon its distinct striped appearance. It is an endless cycle, water dissolving the rock and forming grooves along natural points of weakness, minerals re-precipitating out of the water and filling in the grooves. I could follow those lines with my eyes for hours.

When Marble Canyon was at the bottom of the sea, California was but a figment of the earth's imagination. Its shoulders would not rise above the surface of the ocean for hundreds of millions of years, and even then its assembly would be incomplete. The story of the rocks of Marble Canyon begins far back in a past as dim as the seafloor where it was made. Just as we remember more about what happened yesterday than what happened a thousand days ago, so our knowledge of the earth's past is greater the closer we get to the present. We know precious little about the early days, and considering that the origin of the earth was 4.6 billion years ago, it's amazing we know anything at all.

The sea that was eventually to lay down the limestone of Marble Canyon, as well as seafloor sediments all over the American West, first lapped upon the west coast of the continent around 550 million years ago, just before the dawn of the Paleozoic geologic era. It was then that the supercontinent known as Rodinia broke apart, setting the embryonic North America free. Rodinia, brought together by thermal convection cells deep within the earth, had sat on top of those convection cells too long, like a lid on a pot of boiling water. Eventually the pressure was too great, and the lid gave way. The building thermal convection ripped the overlying continent wide open. At first, rifts appeared in the surface of Rodinia, like the surface of a sidewalk when tree roots push up from underneath. Magma from deep within the earth welled up to fill in the gaps and paste things back together. This worked for a while, but eventually the tearing was too great, and the continental crust couldn't hold together. The sea came rushing in, and the ocean that was to become the mighty Pacific was born.

As the proto–North America drifted across the globe, the west coast, which then ran through what is now central Utah, was the trailing edge. The continental crust to the west of this had subsided, sinking below sea level following the rifting of Rodinia. Much like the eastern seaboard of North America today, rivers drained the land, washing sediments from the uplands to the sea, depositing them in broad river deltas reaching out onto the sunken continental shelf. But unlike the present-day east of North America, in the west, five hundred million years ago, there was not a hint of vegetation in all the land. Without the roots of plants to hold the ground together, it quickly washed away, and erosion rates during this time must have been something like the erosion rates of deserts during flash floods. Over millions of years, these sediments piled up. When sea levels lowered relative to the land, the seas became increasingly shallow, and their waters began to settle. These sunlit waters allowed for the abundant life that gave their shells and skeletons back to the seafloor, forming limestone. Elsewhere, and at other times, sand, silt, and mud was deposited. Over time, these sedimentary sequences settled and compacted, eventually forming the bulk of the limestones, sandstones, and shales of the American West.

Throughout the Paleozoic Era, while North America was experiencing its first wave of westward expansion, life on land was making its debut. Out at sea, red, brown, green, and yellow-green algae fed a world of fishes. Slowly, hesitantly, some of these algae developed a tolerance for freshwater and eked out a living along stream corridors and ponds on land. Over still more time, these plants became the forebears of the mosses and liverworts we know today. These primitive plants were the latest expression of multicellular life. They had rigid cell walls for structure, specially developed cuticles to keep them from drying out in the air, and highly developed chloroplasts capable of storing food. Closely related to their algae parents, they did not produce seeds, let alone flowers or fruits, but rather depended on water to transport their millions of tiny spores from plant to plant. They had no moisture transportation system, no roots, stems, or leaves, but got their water by laying low and soaking it up like a sponge. Like the mosses of today, they lived in a horizontal world.

With time, the newly evolved mosses and liverworts developed elongated cells, enabling them to transport moisture around a greater area. They hesitantly reached upward, off the ground like tiny fingers exploring a vertical world of possibility. Eventually, as generation after generation of these primitive plants was successful on land, they developed vascular tissues—the means of transporting moisture to and from innumerable cells. These new plants grew erect, taking advantage of the vertical niches their forebears were unable to use. These were the first ferns. More specially adapted to living on land, not only did they grow erect but they kicked their dependence on water, by developing airborne spores. The ferns and their allies were so successful that they covered the ground, changing the face of the earth forever. For the first time, looking at the earth from space, the land was green.

As ferns, horsetails, and other spore-producing plants grew to tree size, animals discovered the new land-based food source and crept out of the briny waters of the sea. These early land animals were arthropods, the predecessors of today's insects, arachnids, scorpions, millipedes, and centipedes. Arthropods were pre-adapted for success on land because they already had exoskeletons, necessary for support in an environment where the added buoyancy of water did not exist. Following the insects were fishes, drawn onto land by this abundant new food resource, as well as the possibility of escaping the intense competition of sea life. Slowly they wriggled their way onto land. Lobe-finned bony fishes with well-developed fin bones were among the first to develop the limbs to aid them in land-based travel. Over successive generations, these bold pioneers adapted to increasingly longer periods out of the water and became the first amphibians. Like their aquatic relatives, amphibians were still dependent on water for reproduction and the early stages of life. Their skins were semi-permeable, thus they remained dependent on water to prevent loss of body fluids. Amphibians retain these qualities even to this day.

The continents drew closer together and Pangea was imminent. The southern supercontinent, known to geologists as Gondwanaland, composed of South America, Africa, Antarctica, India, and Australia, migrated across the poles several times as it lined up for the big collision. As it crossed the pole a substantial ice cap developed over the land, evidenced today by glacial deposits in Brazil and Africa. As the ice thickened and the climate cooled, ocean currents fluctuated, bringing cold waters to lower latitudes. Over a period of five million years, thousands of species of warm-water marine organisms went extinct. Invertebrates, plankton, and fish alike were wiped off the face of the planet forever, leaving only fossils as traces of their time on earth. Mass extinction had occurred.

Mass extinctions were not new to the earth. At least one major extinction had occurred less than a hundred million years before, during the Ordovician Period of the Paleozoic Era, around 505 to 435 million years ago. The Ordovician extinction had killed off marine species by the thousands. As a result, the slate was clean for fishes to evolve into forms more diverse than ever before. Similarly, this second mass extinction cleaned the slate of many invertebrates and fishes, thereby reducing interspecific competition and allowing insects, amphibians, and reptiles to diversify. Death brings forth new life. With the earth in a state of constant stability, evolution would move along at a snail's pace. All niches would be filled, and only competition at the level of the finest details would occur. But the earth is ever in a state of flux. Catastrophic events rock the ark, and the most specialized organisms fall prey to chance and change. With niches wide open, surviving groups of organisms are released from the competition that for so long kept their evolution suppressed. Nature is given the chance at novelty, and the new and different replace the same-old same-old.

As insects, amphibians, and reptiles diversified and cruised the continents, plants were undergoing an evolutionary revolution of their own. During this time, from 370 to 240 million years ago, the first seed plants evolved. Early spore-producing plants, closer to their aquatic ancestors, were still partially dependent on water for successful reproduction. Without water, spores quickly dried up and died, and even though a single plant could produce millions of spores, only one in a million would ever grow into a mature plant. Early seeds were tiny, but many times the size of spores. They had the advantage of not only a waterproof coating to prevent desiccation, but also a nutrient package to get them started once germination occurred. Although each seed cost the plant more energy to make, the survival rate of seeds was much greater than that of spores. It was a success. The seed producers thrived, diversified, and covered the land.

The early seed producers of the late Paleozoic were the predecessors of today's conifers, cypresses, yews, and ephedras. Their seeds were exceedingly rich in fats and proteins, both coveted by land-dwelling animals. Before seeds, plant foods were primarily limited to herbage, which supplies substantially less energy to its consumers than seeds. The condensed calorie package made available to animals through the evolution of seed plants may have been essential to the development of higher metabolisms among animals, which eventually led to the diversification of reptiles and warm-blooded mammals.

As the first feet of larger land animals padded across the surface of the planet, the earth beneath them was also shifting, changing, and evolving. While North America kept growing westward, its eastern seaboard was devouring the ancient Iapetus Ocean, the predecessor of the Atlantic, throwing up volcanoes and creating deep ocean trenches. On the opposite side of the Iapetus, the continental landmasses of Eurasia and Africa were doing the same thing. The ocean floor was being consumed from both sides, and North America and Europe and Africa were on a crash course. As the two landmasses closed in on each other, they squeezed out the intervening ocean, along with any islands that once existed between them. Mountains grew along these collision zones—the mountains of New England, the Highlands of Scotland, the Caledonians of Norway. While much of the ancient seafloor material was subducted beneath the overriding continents, some of it was pushed up and onto the continents, and twisted, bent, and metamorphosed during the process. Shale became slates, phyllites, and schists. Sandstones became quartzite. The volcanic basement complex of the seafloor became greenstone, or mixed with overlying sediments and seawater to become serpentine. When finally the continents themselves met, they pushed together like two carpets sliding across the floor. Where the ends of each carpet met, they both buckled up and wrinkled, forming huge nappes. Mountains grew all along this collision zone, and the Appalachians were born. They grew like the Himalaya, reaching heights in excess of 20,000 feet above sea level. South, the story was much the same. South America joined with Africa and what was to become Antarctica, Australia, and India, and rammed into the underbelly of North America. All the land of the earth converged. Pangea was born. Time: 280 to 240 million years ago.

As Pangea converged into a single united landmass, the climatic conditions on earth became so unstable and hostile that nearly all life perished. The supercontinent, spanning both poles, developed extensive ice caps at both ends. Never before in the history of the planet had continental-scale glaciation occurred on both poles. Global temperatures plummeted. The massive supercontinent blocked the circulation of ocean waters, severely limiting the moderating effects resulting from normal circulation of equatorial waters. With so much atmospheric moisture locked up in polar ice sheets, dry air swept across the midlands of Pangea, and the temperate regions became deserts. The convergence of the continents, along with the buildup of ice, lowered sea levels substantially, and newly exposed land absorbed considerable amounts of oxygen from the atmosphere, lowering global atmospheric oxygen by up to 15 percent. Volcanic eruptions abounded, pumping sulfates into the atmosphere and blotting out the sun with vast clouds of ash. From 90 to 95 percent of all marine life died out. On land, tree ferns and horsetails yielded to the dominance of more adaptable species of seed plants. Amphibians withered and died in the cold, dry world, along with the earliest reptiles. All told, 75 percent of the vertebrates vanished. This was the greatest crisis life had ever known, and everything since has paled in comparison to the Permian extinction. This time, night fell long, dark, and cold.

MESMERIZED BY THE SWIRLING folds of the walls of Marble Canyon, I enter a second narrows. Warmer air circulates through the slot, and outside the sun blares bright and unchallenged. I can't stop touching the cold stone. As my fingers feel its grooves and flutes, I follow with my eyes. Thinking of ancient seas, I look for the fossils of countless marine organisms from ages past, so common in the limestones of Arizona and Utah. Speculating that I will find none where water has polished the marble smooth, I find a low-angle place and begin working my way up the canyon wall. Using smooth, sloped holds, progress is slow, but eventually I get high enough that the scouring is notably less. Then it occurs to me. I could look for fossils for hours here and it might be in vain. Looking for fossils in metamorphic rock is like trying to find a grain of sugar in a cooked cookie. Metamorphism tends to either cook fossils or squish them out, wiping away even the ghostly echo of beings long since passed away from the spheres of the earth. But there are nodules of charcoal-gray chert the size of golf balls, eggs, even tennis balls, embedded in the otherwise smooth canyon walls, often forming a rounded, wartlike protrusion in the surface. Chocolate chips in the cookie. Perhaps some lonesome sponge cruised the seafloor, eventually to be buried by accumulating sediments, its silica-rich body mixing with silica-rich fluids that flooded its rounded space, minerals eventually precipitating out of solution and hardening into one of these strange spheres.

Such nodules of silica-rich stuff made excellent stone points for the hunter-gatherer bands that once roamed here, once *lived* here, in this place that we now call Death Valley. I imagine the singing, laughing voices of those people, sitting in the shade, making conversation to pass the heat of the day, pecking petroglyphs of ravens and spirals into the face of the stone. Fossils. Imprints. One day I will be just the same.

A cool wind blows up Marble Canyon, through its sensuous walls laid down long before the dinosaurs or furry or feathered things, when North America was but a whisper and Rodinia a memory and Pangea yet to come. In places the folds and recumbent folds are so complex it looks like some ancient wanderer put primitive pencils between each finger like claws and spent days caressing the canyon walls. And there are cracks like chaotic webs imposed on the rock, and every one of them is filled, pasted, glued back together by white-hot mineral-laden fluids injected from below, above, the sides. Directions become meaningless as I crane my head around and upside-down seeking a pattern. None emerges.

I search up-canyon for evidence of what happened next. I pass the confluence of Marble and Dead Horse Canyons, bend right, and head up Marble. Within a few hundred feet the canyon closes in again. Before me, in the exact alcove where I sat waiting out a rainstorm one year before, a pile of broken rock that would fill the bed of a dump truck sits conspicuously on the sand, smashed to bits, recently broken off from the roof of the alcove above. The pile is big enough to have leveled a small building, crushed a car into a steel pancake, cut a bridge in half. It is ten thousand pounds of Paleozoic rock just recently on the move. I look above at the place on the roof of the alcove where this rock used to be. The scar from the break is covered with a thin veneer of fine dirt. This break was imminent. Dirt-laden water from above had been leaking into a preexisting crack for many years before what was once the overhang of the alcove gave way. In this canyon, this could happen any day, anywhere, anytime.

Ten yards up-canyon are rounded boulders the size of compact cars and heavier than full-sized school busses. Rounded boulders. Water moved those stones. Water so big I can't imagine its power except by imagining school busses like leaves floating down a swift-moving stream, all stuffed between canyon narrows less than ten feet wide. The rocks are not limestone, nor are they marble. They are made up of visible crystals, light opaque ones, light transluscent ones, black shiny ones. Not a single crack or fold or swirl can be seen. These rocks are solid. They are hard. They could resist, *had* resisted, the most severe types of erosion. These rocks are granitic. What are granitic boulders doing tucked away in the shady recesses of Marble Canyon?

The granites of the Basin ranges of Death Valley were not in place when the seafloor sediments of the Paleozoic were laid down. The granites are not a basement complex upon which subsequent geologic strata accumulated. There are such rocks in Death Valley, but they are found elsewhere and bear different characteristics. They are much older, Precambrian in origin, and most have been deformed into gneiss. But the granites came later, during a later chapter of geologic evolution, and were intruded into the overlying sedimentary strata from below. Huge bodies of red-hot magma distilled up from the mantle and swelled into the overlying crust. As the magma intruded into the crust, the seafloor sediments of the Paleozoic were bent, pressurized, and cooked. Sandstones became quartzites. Shales became foliated metamorphics. Limestones became marbles. Each place cooked differently; those closest to the intruding granites cooked longer, hotter, metamorphosed more, even intermixed with the granites where the contact occurred, each rock type blurring with fluidity into the next. Far away from the contact zones, the rocks cooked less, retaining most of the characteristics of their sedimentary origins.

Where I stand, just upstream from the Dead Horse–Marble confluence, the rock of the canyon walls looks like limestone. It is gray. It is fractured all over the place. There is little here that suggests the kind of structural integrity that typically comes with metamorphism. I walk up-canyon, towards where the granites came from, looking for marble, looking for the contact zone.

The canyon opens up briefly, then closes in again. This time the rock is noticeably different. It is striped. It is smooth. It is solid, hard, monolithic. It is fantastic. It is marble. I am getting warm.

I keep moving up the canyon. It opens up again, this time for longer, and I begin to wonder if it will close in again. Granite cobbles and boulders litter the canyon floor, mixed with marbleized limestone. Soon whitish rocks begin to appear, composed of nearly pure calcite crystals, exhibiting faint bands reminiscent of forgotten seafloor beds or hydrothermal vent injections. Some are pure white, just crystals, and I can't be sure what they are. The contact zone must be close.

When the canyon closes in again its walls are glittering, crystalline white and beautiful to behold. They are not high, but strong and solid. This is some of the purest, most highly metamorphosed marble I have ever seen. It glints in the low-angle light of winter afternoon. I wonder if Michelangelo would draw stone from this quarry, or if it is too hard, too crystalline to be sculpted into a human form. But over time, perhaps water could do what no chisel could, and smooth this stone into soft, graceful curves. I linger a long while, peering up at distant granite hills, pondering the fine lines of this meeting room.

Dusk falls early down in the bowels of the ancient sea, bringing strange purple light to the walls of the canyon. The cold air settles into the recesses of the narrows, decorating dusk with the slightest scent of moisture. But the sound of waves is even more faint, an elusive memory echoing down the halls of time.

FIVE

Volcanoes and Thunder Lizards

Long before the matchless Sierra Nevada, the earth-toned, striped Basin ranges, or the emerald Coast Ranges, another mountain range stood high and bright in their place. Stretching from present-day Alaska to Mexico, towering over 15,000 feet above sea level, this ancestral range rose amidst plumes of ash and cinders, much as the Andes do today. As Tyrannosaurus Rex stalked its prey in primeval swamps lined with towering tree ferns, these mountains were torn down to low hills. But their roots were hidden, deep beneath the surface of the earth, lying in wait for a chance to rise again.

Mount Rodgers rises like an Egyptian pyramid above the myriad of mountains where the Cathedral and Ritter Ranges of the Sierra Nevada meet. Even from afar, one can surmise that the rock of its heights is dark, broken, more akin to the metavolcanic material of its southerly neighbors than the more solid, gray granite of the mountains to its north. Such rock is not attractive from the perspective of climbing. It means one of two things: either a long slog across unstable talus or a potentially epic climb up treacherous, loose rock. But from the perspective of the geologist, the geographer, the naturalist,

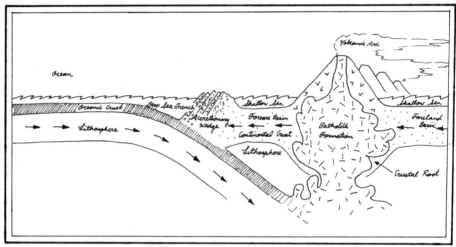

The Subduction Dynamic: Western North America during the Mesozoic Geologic Era

even the merely curious adventurer, it means a firsthand look at the basement of a mountain range that once dwarfed the Sierra Nevada. It means being at the point of contact where the shattered remains of the basement of the Ancestral Sierra were met and uplifted by the uppermost granite of today's Range of Light. It means living the story of the evolution of the mountains of California.

After years of combing the Sierra Nevada, somehow I have neglected the high pyramid of Mount Rodgers. Flanked on either side by mountains higher than it, Rodgers does well at maintaining a low profile. To its south rise the famed twin peaks of Ritter and Banner. To its north rises Mount Lyell, the highest peak in Yosemite National Park, notably hosting the second-largest glacier in the Sierra Nevada. In between Ritter and Lyell there is Rodgers, a beautiful mountain in its own right, spared the attention of its more famous neighbors. Recently it has occupied my thoughts.

For eight weeks now we have traveled throughout the Sierra Nevada. By now the students of my natural history and ecology course have transformed into evolutionary beings. Tanned and taut, we are capable of ascending thousands of feet in a day, despite the burden of the heavy expedition packs that bear down on our shoulders and hips. We can endure hours of the indifferent alpine sun and rejoice in swimming in alpine lakes laced with morning ice. We can eat the same thing day after day, finding joy in our surroundings that compensates for often redundant fare. We take little notice of the beards that grace our chins, or the hair that garnishes our legs, or the smells of consecutive days of living on the ground and hiking for a living. From our camp, a visit to Mount Rodgers seems within our grasp.

I leave camp with Mike Spayd and Blake Lowrey. Mike is a familiar partner, with whom I have both worked and climbed extensively. From Massachusetts, Virginia, Maryland, Alabama, and most recently Wyoming, Mike landed at Prescott College as a student after a transformational experience with the National Outdoor Leadership School. When he found out there was a place he could learn about the natural world while living out in it, he applied to Prescott, got in, and set about making his dreams happen. Perhaps as a leftover from his fraternity days, Mike drinks Budweiser out of a can, almost exclusively. He likes cowboy bars and country music, full-size pickup trucks, and of course fly-fishing, not to mention mountains, rivers, wolves, elk, and wild open country. An aspiring geographer and conservationist at heart, and ever understanding of the lives of working people, Mike views things in ways that are always unique, and usually unpredictable. This summer he is sporting a handlebar mustache.

With Mike and me is Blake Lowrey, representing the best of everything that life and being twenty years old have to offer. Blake is so excited about just about everything under the sun, sometimes I wonder if he ever sleeps. Every morning I wake up and see him sipping coffee, having been awake for hours. Every night I go to sleep knowing he is out there, prancing around in the moonlight. His passion for learning is insatiable. Having him on the course is like inventing the dream student. I wish I could clone him for future use. He is ahead on his work and charged up for a full day in the high mountains.

We set out in the late morning, lightly loaded with food and clothes for the day, knowing we can get water along the way. We move swiftly over the cracked slabs of the Upper Lyell Basin, listening to meltwater streams that gurgle beneath the rocks, emerge temporarily, and disappear again into unknown chambers below. We descend the glacial staircase that is the head of the Lyell Fork of the Tuolumne River, following the young stream down sweeping cascades sliding over wide stone, past blue meadow-lined lakes with soft bottoms of glacial powder. Silent, we keep a quick pace. After a mile and a half of off-trail descent, we meet the John Muir Trail for a short section and follow its dusty, manure-littered, neatly rock-lined lane upward towards the highly trafficked Donohue Pass. We move fast up the trail and soon find ourselves behind a steadily moving hiker heavily laden with a frame pack. His equipment and gait suggest he has been out for a good while. He hears us on his trail and stops to say hello and offer conversation. "Whoa, you guys are cruuuuuuising," he says with a wry grin as he spreads his arms out like airplane wings and moves his body from side to side. I quickly gather from his regalia that he is a long-distance hiker, probably walking south on the Muir or Pacific Crest Trail. I am intrigued by his jovial manner. We introduce ourselves. He says his name is Stoner.

Stoner is thin and a bit lanky, with long, wild, graying hair tamed only slightly by the ponytail he keeps it in. He kind of dances when he talks, even with his pack on, telling us tales of trail-crew camps and free meals and getting hooked up with just about everything. He swears joyfully with every sentence, and soon I notice that we do too. He is hiking to Mount Whitney from Lake Tahoe, a distance of around five hundred miles. I walked the same route in reverse years earlier, so we have much to talk about. Stoner has a hard time believing that we are a class, that this is college, and that I am a professor. When he finally accepts this as truth, he dances in place, in a full circle, saying, "Ahhhhh yesssss, college!" He talks joyfully and extensively about his upcoming resupply in Mammoth Lakes, where he is sure to cruise town in utter ecstasy and eat heaps of carne asada at the restaurant Roberto's, which he speaks of with reverence, dancing as he utters the name. Before we leave him, he tells us about his recent encounter with some horse packers up north. "What's yer name, son?" they had asked him. "Stoner," he said. "Well then, Stoney, take a load off and rest 'er easy awhile," one of the packers suggested. "No," said Stoner, "that's STON-ER!" Obviously pleased with himself, Stoner laughs and dances around.

We say good-bye to our new, elf-like acquaintance and hasten our way up and over Donohue. Stoner quickly becomes an archetypal character in our adventure, and we make up mythical stories about him all day long. Soon we set out off-trail, rounding the outlets of two small lakes just southwest of Donohue, then begin ascending big, granitic talus chunks to an unknown pass above. As I sweat my way up to the pass, I try to picture what the scene will look like on the other side. Somewhere over there is the Marie Lakes Basin, studded with cold blue waters shimmering in the alpine sun. Above the basin rises Rodgers, ornamented with a small bright glacier tucked into its shady northeast recess. As I top the pass, the vision that was in my head spreads out before me.

We drop into the Marie Lakes Basin, working our way down some steep granite benches, our eyes and thoughts set on a small blue lake below, into which a permanent snowfield drops iceberg-like chunks of snow. We work our way down to it, fixed on this miniature Arctic scene. Once there, we crunch our way across the still hard snow, peering into twenty-foot-deep cracks in the surface where the edge of the snowfield breaks away from the main mass. It is falling into the water in slow motion, the cracks themselves partially submerged, slushy, sludgy water filling their deepest corners. None of us is tempted to swim.

As we leave this microcosm of the high latitudes, we fix our attention on Mount Rodgers and the most efficient way of achieving its flanks. We stay high, keeping our course bent west and south, working our way across the scree and talus above the shores of Lake 11,200'+. The rock beneath our feet has changed. Instead of big, light gray granite, we step across smaller, more angular chunks of broken metamorphic material. Less stable than the trusty granite, the metamorphic rubble sinks beneath our steps and easily topples downslope. We seek snow, where we can walk most efficiently and avoid the sliding scree. Once around the lake, we find it. A small glacierette rises steadily from another lake. Traversing it will take us to the high basin below the Rodgers massif. We walk up the white surface, lightly kicking each step into the velvety snow, around and above obvious small crevasses, up to the next tread in the glacial staircase. Nestled there, in the shadow of Rodgers, is a cold, still tarn. Huge piles of broken rock are piled around its circumference, debris pulled down and pushed to a temporary standstill by glaciers in years past.

We circumnavigate the tarn to its inlet—a small trickle of snow-melt water emerging from the heaps of rocks. Around us, the mountain walls rise as an amphitheater, high and steep on three sides. The basin could have been excavated by a giant ice cream scoop. The rock walls are the same dark, broken material we have been walking on, here exhibiting enough structural integrity to form vertical precipices interspersed with long scree and talus slopes teetering at the angle of repose. But the innermost recess of the basin, extending up the vertical northeast face of Rodgers, is different. Here the rock is light gray and strong. It is the familiar rock of the Sierra Nevada, a proud arm of granite intruded far into the overlying metamorphic rock. In fact, it was this very intrusion that metamorphosed the rock on top, way back in the formative years of the range. Here is the point of contact, where the bottoms of the Ancestral Sierran Arc volcanoes met the rising granite of today's Sierra Nevada. The story of both of these mountain ranges is inextricably related.

When Pangea broke up, the whole world was torn to pieces. Before, the continental landmasses had ground their way into mass collision, but now they stretched, ripped, and rifted as convection cells deep within the earth split them apart. As it had been with Rodinia, when the continents rifted, the mantle spewed magma up to try and fill the cracks, but eventually the cracks got too big and seawater came flooding in. It began with the separation of North America and Africa. The Americas rode a convection cell that pushed them west, while Eurasia and Africa scooted east. In between, where the crust of the earth was torn asunder, new crust was formed, and continued to form, as the plates bearing the continents drifted ever further apart. A new ocean was born, the Atlantic, which we have named for the Greek titan Atlas, who bore the weight of the world on his shoulders.

Atlas was the son of Iapetus, a youthful version of him. So was the Atlantic Ocean to the Iapetus before it. As the newly formed Atlantic grew to oceanic proportions, seafloor spreading extended north, rifting Greenland from North America. Seawaters flooded into the rift zone, linking the Atlantic and Arctic Oceans. Eventually this rift zone migrated to the east side of Greenland, severing it from Europe and creating the world's largest island. Meanwhile, the southern margin of North America separated from South America to form the Gulf of Mexico Basin. Over a period of a hundred million years, the face of the earth was changed completely.

Pangea was not built to last. All told, from assembly to disassembly it spanned a few tens of millions of years. And there was never really a stable moment. No sooner than the continental landmasses were snug in place, they began to break apart. The continents backtracked, as if they had minds that recalled the glory days of Rodinia, and so shifted into reverse. But the outlines of the continents were remarkably different than they had ever been before. Chunks of Europe were pasted onto northeastern North America. Greenland was a new shape on the map. The Mediterranean opened. Embryonic India, Australia, and Antarctica began to tug at the land that held them together. As the hemispheres we know today as East and West were born, they diverged at the expense of the massive world ocean that once surrounded Pangea, wrapping well over halfway around the world. As the Americas were pushed west and Eurasia and Africa east, the Atlantic grew and the Pacific was devoured.

Even before Pangea broke, the west of North America had begun to shake and tremble. Once North America had ground its way into Africa and Eurasia, it came to a screeching halt. In its wake, a maverick piece of continental crust was still on the move and continued sliding east towards western North America, overriding and devouring the ocean floor in between. It was like a traffic jam. With North America stopped by its Pangean collision, the incoming piece of continental crust had nowhere to go. The approaching land, known to geologists as Sonomia, collected intervening arc volcanoes along the way and delivered them, along with itself, to the quiet shores of western North America. The effect was violent. Today, Australia is on a similar crash course, headed for Southeast Asia, and the arc volcanoes in between make up the islands of Indonesia. As Australia continues its northward migration, Indonesia will be gathered up and sandwiched in the great collision.

Sonomia hit ground as the Paleozoic Era gave way to the Mesozoic, between 220 and 200 million years ago. It hit with such impact that its leading edge was thrust up to fifty miles east, up and over the crust of North America. The Golconda Thrusts of Nevada are evidence of this meeting. Elsewhere, where Sonomia didn't surmount the West, the sediments that had been laid down in such neat horizontal beds were bent, folded, and broken. Such was the price for a new piece of the American West. Sonomia built much of Nevada and over half of Northern California. The rest was yet to come.

As Pangea broke up, the American West became the hot spot for geologic activity. It was like the earth flipped a switch from off to on. What had once been a place of relative tranquility became the site of land accretions, fuming volcanoes, deep ocean trenches, and large-scale earthquakes. First came Sonomia. Then mountain building began in earnest. It began with the spreading of the Atlantic Ocean basin and the consequent shove of the Americas westward. This promptly changed the plate dynamic between western North America and its western oceanic neighbor from a passive margin to an active one. The oceanic plate, known as the Farallon Plate, collided against the leading edge of western North America. The more dense Farallon Plate began a long career of subduction beneath the more buoyant continental crust of North America. As the Farallon Plate took its submissive dive, the leading edge of North America acted like a snowplow and scraped up the seafloor sediments that had been accumulating on top of the Farallon basement. In some places the "plow" of the edge of North America dug deeper than others, digging into the hard, dark basaltic rock of the seafloor itself and mixing these excavated chunks of seafloor with the sediments above. This mix of sediments and broken seafloor was torn to pieces, piled up, and cemented back together offshore of the continent, thus laying the foundation for the Coast Ranges.

As the Farallon Plate subducted, it scraped against the underside of the crust of the continent, breaking off pieces and taking them down to the depths of the earth. Way down there in the dark heat of the earth's interior, beneath the insulating influence of the overriding continent, the diving Farallon Plate began to melt. Its lighter mineral constituents, such as quartz, muscovite micas, and feldspars, melted first. These minerals solidify at the coolest temperatures, thus they stay liquid the longest, are the most reluctant to turn to stone, and are the first to reliquefy as magma. They are also the least dense of the earth's minerals, and thus the more buoyant. Gravity's pull on them is relatively relaxed, and they are constantly being differentiated outward, towards the surface of the earth. A look at the earth's crust reveals this fact. Underneath the plants and the feet of animals, under the soil and layers of sediment, the basements of all the continents are composed of granitic rocks, or close relatives of granite. Granitic rocks are primarily quartz, mica, and feldspar.

Darker, heavier minerals are more hesitant to melt, requiring the greater heat that more depth has to offer. Being relatively dense, they are less likely to differentiate outward towards the surface of the earth. Amphiboles, pyroxenes, and olivines are among those that do reach the surface, rarely in the quantity that the lighter minerals achieve. They most often appear as the black peppery minerals in granitic rocks, less noticeable to the naked eye in volcanic rocks. Heavier minerals and elements, such as iron, magnesium, nickel, silver, and gold, appear even more rarely on the earth's surface. These are most often picked up by quickly rising bodies of more buoyant magma and "hitch a ride" to the surface. This is why metal ores are often found in association with quartz and feldspar intrusions.

The chunks of crust that the Farallon Plate had stripped off of the underside of North America were already composed of the buoyant minerals typical of continental crust. Pushed down by unimaginably huge tectonic forces, these pieces of crust gave way. They were like balloons filled with air floating on water. If you push them hard enough, they will go under, but once you let go they quickly bob back up to the surface. So did the continental crust that had been caught up in the subduction dynamic. Unable to ascend where the subduction pressure was great, these pieces of crust melted into the semi-molten mix, then re-distilled out beneath the overriding North America, inland from the collision zone. As the distillation process went on, the lighter mineral constituents of the melting basaltic seafloor also began to distill out, joining growing bodies of magma. Pushing against the underside of North America, these bodies of magma began to melt their way through the overlying crust. Moving through vertical miles of continent, they melted the crust around them, and pieces of the surrounding crustal rock fell in and joined the mix. Where the continental crust did not melt, it was cooked and pressurized, metamorphosing the deep Paleozoic seafloor sediments into schists, slates, quartzites, and marbles. As the Farallon Plate continued to subduct, new magma kept distilling out and welling up beneath the old, pushing the molten material ever closer to the surface. Finally it broke through. Where it did, the earth broke open to let it out. Volcanoes exploded across the American West, spewing the innards of the earth across the continent. The Paleozoic seafloor sediments that covered the West split, shattered, tilted, cooked, and otherwise accommodated the new arrivals. The line of volcanoes grew to enormous proportions, over 15,000 feet tall, rising in a smoking wall along the eastern rim of the Pacific Basin, just inland from the subduction zone. All told, the arc of volcanoes spanned a distance of over three thousand miles, from present-day Alaska well into Mexico. The Ancestral Sierra Nevada was born.

The magma kept rising as the Farallon Plate was eaten up by the advancing North America. While much of this molten material broke the surface of the continent, still more of it lay beneath. This reservoir of magma, like the mountain range above it, grew to massive proportions. Insulated by the crust around it, the magma cooled slowly. With time to form, crystals solidified and grew: first black amphiboles, pyroxenes, and biotite micas, then opaque, chunky feldspars, flaky transparent muscovite micas, and large translucent quartz crystals. Granitic rock was formed, the intrusive counterpart of the volcanics of the Ancestral Sierra. This huge body of granite, known to geologists as the Sierra Nevada Batholith (batholith means "deep rock"), became the deeply rooted basement complex of the Ancestral Sierran Arc volcanoes. Related batholiths were emplaced in Eastern California (the Mesozoic granites of Death Valley, responsible for the metamorphism of so much Paleozoic material, are part of this complex), in the Klamath region of Northern California, and in Nevada and Idaho. It was one of the largest granite-forming events in the earth's history.

A trip to the Andes today would reveal much about the countenance of California during the Mesozoic Era. The mountains were immense, the range extensive, and the sea close at hand. In the Andes, as in the Ancestral Sierra, if you could somehow take a pick and shovel and dig down to the basement, you would find granite. Lots of it. There is likely more granite sitting beneath the Andes than there is in all of the Sierra Nevada of today.

The Ancestral Sierra, with its growing basement and deep roots, weighed heavily upon the land of North America. As in most big ranges, the weight of the mountains depressed the land around them, creating basins on either side. To the east of the Ancestral Sierra, facing the interior of the continent, a foreland basin developed. To the west, facing the sea, a forearc basin developed. These were the predecessors of the Great Basin and California's Central Valley. As rain and snow pummeled the heights of the high mountains, streams eroded their flanks, slowly washing the mountains down to the basins below. Here, the sediments of the Ancestral Sierra accumulated, ever deepening even as the mountains matured.

As the Farallon oceanic plate subducted, it acted like a conveyor belt, delivering whatever volcanic islands or bits of continental crust that rode upon it to the western shores of North America. Every time one of these terranes smashed into the continent, the crust rumpled and folded like a compressed carpet along the suture, and the continent grew further westward. These accreted terranes eventually formed the bulk of Alaska, British Columbia, Washington, Oregon, and much of western California, expanding the bounds of North America by as much as 30 percent.

We stare over at the bulk of Mount Rodgers, pondering the stone, dark and light. Rodgers, like Ritter and Banner and the Minarets beyond, was the inside of an old Ancestral Sierran Arc volcano. On the quiet shore of the alpine tarn at the foot of Rodgers, we are standing amidst the shattered remains of the magma chamber that once supplied fresh lava to the neck of a massive volcano. Now the remains of that volcano lie buried deep beneath the fertile soils of California's Central Valley. In places the alluvial sediments that fill the valley are believed to be up to forty thousand feet deep. In a very real sense the contents of the valley are the arc volcanoes turned upside-down. The oldest parts are deepest, while the youngest are closest to the surface. That takes some imagination to piece together in our minds. But the deepest recess of the volcano, its very core, is right before us, outlined as clear as day in the pyramidal shape of Mount Rodgers.

We look for a way up. The most direct route is up the northeast face. It is a vertical climb of well over a thousand feet, up loose and broken rock that offers no protection. Even if we can find a route, we lack the climbing equipment necessary for such a technical ascent. The obvious route is to our left, south, where long, steep fans of scree and talus rise to a broken rocky ridge that continues upward to the summit. In several places the cliffs and sawteeth of the ridge are interrupted and the scree extends all the way up. I speculate that atop the ridge we will find a plateau. While the plateau is serrated and precipitous along much of its northern side due to heavy glacial erosion in the past, I suspect that the sunny south side will be more benign, allowing for fast, easy travel.

We set out from the tarn's inlet and make for the slope. Once we reach the scree and talus, we spread out, creating a wide space between us so as not to climb above or below one another. As soon as we begin climbing, the rocks start moving, sliding out from under our feet and trundling downslope. It is classic scree travel—for every three steps up, the scree beneath our feet sinks two steps down. Beads of sweat across my forehead quickly turn into a steady stream. I flick droplets from my eyebrows to keep the salty liquid from getting in my eyes, but soon it is no use and I just squint and endure the sting of salt. Stepping and breathing in mechanical rhythm, that crazy masochistic side of human nature takes over and I become possessed with the act of ascending. I climb like there is something inside of me I have to burn up, as if pushing hard enough for long enough will clear out the cobwebs and dust of my being and allow for just one moment of pure lucidity. There is no stopping, no rest. Even scree slogs can be ecstatic sometimes.

I reach a prominent gap in the ridge and pull myself up on the steep rock to have a look around. I am elated, feeling my pulse in every corner of my body, eyes wide with the rush of endorphins that swarm and buzz like bees my head. But the view from the ridge is sobering. There is no plateau, no benign ridge terrain that will allow for easy passage. There is only a shattered, jagged ridge. Its convoluted spine extends west, towards the summit. The summit looks more distant than before. Doubt creeps into my mind.

Mike and Blake soon arrive on the ridge. Once they see over to the other side, they both know my plan is smoke on the wind. We look over to the summit and size up the ridge. It is the only option for an ascent. We decide to give it a try, to take it one move at a time, and promise not to get too fixed on the summit.

We approach the ridge with the utmost caution that loose rock deserves. We wind our way around angular teeth, traversing their sides and dipping in and out of the gullies in between. Where traversing is too formidable, we ascend the backs of fantastic gendarmes, rising up and over them. As we make progress, our fear of the rock abates and the climbing becomes easier. We move one section at a time, spreading out and regrouping to look at the route and pick a line. As we climb across the ridge, we recognize that the beauty of the traverse is in the feeling of sustained movement across a seemingly eternal summit. The world drops off on both sides. The exposure is tremendous.

The broken ridge ends gradually, blending into a talus slope of mixed volcanic and granitic material that extends up to the summit rocks. Here, magma that had once welled up freely from reservoirs below solidified in place, choking the volcano by plugging up its source of replenishment. The intruding rock cooked the rocks of the volcanic magma chamber, metamorphosing them. As it cooled below the surface of the crust, the intrusion solidified slowly, forming a thick granitic dike right through the middle of the magma chamber. It is no wonder the dike runs straight through the summit of Mount Rodgers. The granitic material is extremely tough, more tough than the metamorphosed volcanic rock it was set in. It adds strength to its surroundings, rooting them to the more extensive granitic basement below. As the rain and snow of tomorrow lash out at the flanks of Mount Rodgers and tear it down to the sea, its granitic core will be the last of it to remain standing.

The talus teeters and clinks as we step across it and up to the summit rocks. There we sit awhile, letting images of endless Sierran summits imprint themselves on our consciousness. Being there reminds me of the words of an old teacher of mine. To paraphrase him, the thoughts and pictures we take in stay with us for the rest of our lives. It is wise to be conscious of this, and to be discriminatory about how we spend our time. With this truth in my mind, I find no reason to hasten our departure. The picture we are taking into our minds is clear and beautiful.

Forgetting such things as time and space, we linger for a long while. When I finally glance at my watch and become cognizant of the time, I realize we have only two and a half hours to get back to camp. We quickly rouse ourselves and begin our descent.

We dance across the ridge this time. It is as if we are temporarily graced with some small degree of freedom from gravity. What seemed challenging before we now move over with fluidity. Blake and I travel ahead. Mike follows not far behind. We are on a grand tour of the inside of a magma chamber, thrust 12,500 feet above sea level. We hit the scree and run downslope side by side, with a wide berth between us, sending down innumerable chunks of scree and gravel to the basin below, down to the basement of the volcano, to the massive granite of the Sierra Nevada Batholith.

We move swiftly, aware of time and its implications. If the universe is truly expanding, then we will do well to get back to camp sooner than later. After all, wherever we are going might be further away the longer we take to get there. For over an hour we skip and hop our way across talus and glissade down snow and ice, deftly negotiating the familiar terrain with neither sound nor halt. Soon we return to Sierran granite, finally understanding in our bodies how the metavolcanic rock of the whole Ritter Range sits perched as a high roof pendant atop the underlying granite of the Sierra. The talus chunks are larger here, indicative of the strength of granite and its resistance to being broken. We step across twenty-ton pieces four times the size of a man, looking ahead and relying on instinct for swift passage. Then we see something so fantastic it brings us to an unquestionable halt.

At our feet is a nearly perfectly round stone the size of an ostrich egg. In a world of angular, broken talus, this is a strange sight in and of itself. Even more strange, the rock is dark green, slightly sparkling in the afternoon sun. Just next to it, shelved on a flat piece of granite, is another piece. This one looks just like a piece of an eggshell, but it is half an inch thick, a green color similar to that of the round rock. The outside of the shell is gray and granitic, the contact between the gray and green rocks like night and day. The inside, however, is empty. Immediately we can tell the two pieces fit together even without touching them. We look around the area and find a third piece, also like part of an eggshell. I pick up the round stone to see if it fits in the shell. It feels like a cannonball and is as heavy as if it were made of iron. It fits perfectly into the shell pieces.

There is really only one explanation for the rocks at hand, and we all know it though none of us says so at first. We are too smacked with wonder to expound theories. Darker rocks can be found throughout granite if you look for them. Most are pieces of country rock that fell into the molten material as it rose to the surface. Most are slightly darker than granite, ranging from light gray to nearly black, and made up of a mix of minerals rich in amphiboles, pyroxenes, and in some cases olivines. Geologists call such rocks xenoliths. They have been likened to raisins in raisin bread, the granite surrounding them being the bread. But never in my life have I felt something as dense as the rock we have found, or as purely green through and through. Rock that dense comes from deep in the earth. Way deep in the earth. Its crystals are typically small because the great pressure under which it forms does not allow for exorbitant crystal growth. What we have found rarely makes it to the surface. We wouldn't be that far off to say it is as rare as gold. The stone is nearly pure olivine, the deepest, most dense of the crust-forming minerals of the earth. A minor constituent of basaltic ocean floors, olivine is even more scarce in the more buoyant rocks of the continent. Somehow this maverick piece fell into a rising body of magma and was carried upward into the crust. As it was exposed to the world for the first time, the unimaginable pressure under which it formed was finally released. As the spherical rock relaxed, it unloaded, shedding its outer layers like a cracked jawbreaker candy.

Dumbfounded for a while, we remember time and leave the deep rock to its fate. Soon we are skipping across granite again, topping the pass, and descending towards the two glistening lakes that mark our way back to Donohue Pass. Without stopping, we hop talus down the north side of the pass, rounding the first lake and heading towards the outlet of the second. We are really moving now, and doing so with skill and confidence. As we approach the second lake, near where its waters trickle outward amongst darkened rocks, a lone figure appears from behind a boulder. It sees us coming and begins to prance around, arms spread out like a bird. It is Stoner.

He welcomes us with glee, offering tea, coffee, hot cocoa, anything he can possibly come up with out of his pack. We are glad to see him again, feeling like we have gotten to know him even better since we last saw him. Stoner has achieved legendary status throughout the day, and we have stories about him that even he doesn't know exist. Nevertheless, we cannot stay long and have to thankfully decline his multiple offers of hot beverages. We share abbreviated versions of our day's adventures in good spirit. All too soon we say our good-byes and scamper off towards Donohue Pass.

Seeing Stoner again marks our re-entry into *terra familia*. As soon as we hit the John Muir Trail we break into an earnest run. Blake laughs with delight and asks if this is the way we always do it when we climb mountains. We say yes and keep running, tightening our daypacks against our backs to keep them from flopping around. Soon we are in the zone of ultimate concentration, running at an even pace over uneven terrain, moving with the certainty of animals, no distinction between mind and body. It is like skiing downhill: the faster we run, the tighter our focus becomes and the more easily we are able to negotiate the terrain.

Below us is a sea of trees, dark and green, rising from the meandering river and flowery meadows of Lyell Canyon. It is a forest of conifers—whitebark pines, lodgepole pines, mountain hemlocks, and western white pines, whose needles give the High Sierra its characteristic subtle pine scent. We are looking down into a world that is so close yet so different from the glowing alpine zone we have been in for so many days. As we drop down from the pass, we re-enter the world of trees and soft, green, growing things. The feeling of returning to the trees is nearly always soothing to the psyche. The intimacy of close space after stark vastness, fertility after barrenness, softness after hardness, are all laid bare for consciousness to receive and revel in. Returning to the trees after a day in the high mountains is like the calm cool of dusk after a bright day. But long ago, such places did not grace the earth.

The Permian extinction was the most intense crisis life on earth had ever known. When the dust had settled, the earth was a quiet place. It took millions of years for life to bounce back after the fallout, but it did. If not for the devastating effects of the Permian event, most life-forms familiar to us today would never have come to be. There would have been no dinosaurs, no mammals, no birds, few if any flowers, and none of the marine organisms we know today. The old groups of marine organisms, so well preserved in the fossils of Paleozoic seafloor sediments, were eventually replaced by modern forms. New, complex fishes evolved where their primitive ancestors once swam. As the corpses of large Paleozoic amphibians decomposed into soil, reptiles moved into their niches. With waterproof skins, reptiles were able to be out of water indefinitely without risking loss of body fluids. No longer tied to the water's edge, they spread out across the land, diversified rapidly, and radiated into every available niche. These ruling reptiles, called archosaurs, included water-adapted crocodilians, winged pterosaurs, and the land-based dinosaurs. Dinosaurs, the "thunder lizards," developed specialized limbs for walking erect and traveling great distances over land. They were exceptionally successful and became the size-dominant land animals, ruling the continents for over 140 million years. Seed plants became the dominant land plants, and forests of seed-bearing trees grew where tall tree ferns and thickets of horsetails once stood. These forests were made up of cycads, ginkgoes, and the earliest conifers.

For the first time, the scent of some ancestral pine may have spiced the wind. This new abundance of plant life contributed to reptiles' evolution, allowing them to grow to such immense proportions. Life on land flourished and diversified. By the time the mountains of the Ancestral Sierra reached their peak height, there were more species of life on earth than ever before. Forests cloaked much of the land, and warm, wet conditions prevailed. Most of the major landmasses of the earth were centered around the equatorial regions. Evolution enjoyed a heyday as the first mammals and birds made their debut on earth.

WE LEAVE THE SWEET-SCENTED TREES as we leave the trail and jog across the scattered meadows where the Lyell Fork of the Tuolumne River begins. Camp is only minutes away. We are in our backyard. Slowing to a brisk walk, we push on up broken slabs of granite underscored by swiftly moving glacial meltwater. Steeply we ascend a riser of a few hundred feet to a long, narrow tread decorated with a thin, fingerlike lake. We bend to the right, north, up a second riser of benches and ledges. There is no stopping, only the amazing, mechanical, instinctive movement of limbs in response to some primeval force of will. As we top the final riser, camp comes into view like some desert mirage across shimmering slabs of granite. Smiling to myself, I look at my watch. It is 4:45 p.m. At five o'clock class presentations will begin, and we will be there with hot cups of black tea complete with milk and sugar.

SIX

The Stretching of North America

The mighty granite of the Sierra Nevada lay deep beneath the blasting and sputtering cones of the Sierran Arc volcanoes for millions of years. A behemoth of epic proportions lying in wait, the massive reservoir of granite spanned hundreds of miles along the Pacific Rim, its roots extending deep into the crust of the earth, down even to its semi-molten interior. But time would wear away its great overburden and deliver its pieces to the sea. Then, the gargantuan wall of the Sierra Nevada would rise, and steel-gray granite would be exposed, thrust upward and out of its earthly confines to glimmer in the bright light of day. The master Range of Light would emerge from the womb of the world.

The rise of the Sierra Nevada would forever change the countenance of western North America. The range would rise as a contiguous crest, a wall sealing off California from the rest of the continent. It would stand between the Pacific and the interior of the continent, stealing all the snow and rain out of the ocean-borne clouds and leaving the interior a vast, cold desert. It would be shaped and torn by extensive glaciers, sculpted into tortured ridges and basins holding a

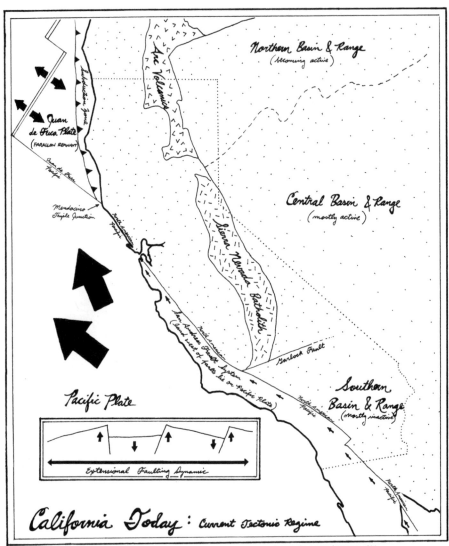

Northern Basin & Range
(becoming active)

Arc Volcanics

Subduction Zone

Juan
de Fuca Plate
(FARALLON REMNANT)

Juan de Fuca Pacific

Mendocino
Triple Junction

North American Pacific

Central Basin & Range
(mostly active)

Sierra Nevada Batholith

San Andreas Fault System
(crust west of faults lies on Pacific Plate)

North American Pacific

Garlock Fault

Southern
Basin & Range
(mostly inactive)

North American Pacific

Pacific Plate

North American Pacific

Extensional Faulting Dynamic

California Today: Current Tectonic Regime

ADAPTED FROM DOTT & PROTHERO 1994

thousand-thousand shimmering lakes. Those snows would melt into rivers and lakes, feeding the thirsty valleys on either side, allowing for some of the most productive agriculture in the world. The range would divide people, first the indigenous tribes of California and later the Euro-Americans that would come to California. It would yield gold in troves, drawing desperate seekers by the tens of thousands. Eventually, a few individuals would penetrate deep into its heart and find there the inspiration and boon of wilderness. This boon would be brought forth from the mountains and fed like wild honey to a culture impoverished of things wild and free.

Thunder Mountain's splintered form captures the first light of day and turns bright and golden. My bleary morning eyes are immediately fixed upon it. I have been looking at its intimidating form for many days now. Finally I am close enough to get to know it better. Within minutes of my awakening, the rosy fingers of dawn begin smudging soft amber light across the impressionable granite precipices of the Great Western and Kings-Kern Divides. Stark, deep blue sky is spread across the west; today is the first of many mornings that is totally clear of lingering, tattered clouds. The gravelly ground between whaleback slabs of glacially rounded and polished granite still smells rich with ephemeral storms, its surface still damp and its flora still intoxicated from the rare dousing of repeated thundershowers it received yesterday. But now the sky is pure blue again. Blue enough to not worry about thunderstorms before noon. Blue enough to not have to get an early start. Blue enough to let heavy eyelids fall to a doze and let the daylight wax.

One hour later I rise and walk out onto the polished granite floor of our high camp, beneath seemingly open skies, the air still and cool, the morning still growing. It is 6:45 a.m. I look over at Mike and find him still snug in his sleeping bag. It looks as though he had the same idea as me. I gather our fire-blackened pan and walk west, towards the looming wall where the Great Western Divide makes its last reach to the north. I search below the sunlit walls for the ribbon of meadow at the shoreline of Longley Lake. There I squat and gather cold, pure water for morning tea. Squinting, I remain there awhile, trying to capture a moment of light on stone. Far off to the east, well behind my shoulders, the vault of the sky crackles and groans, rumbling as if to let all the vastness of the Divide country know that this will be a day of thunder. I turn around slowly, as if meeting a long-dreaded foe, and for the first time notice the brooding mass of sickly gray storm clouds that hang like a heavy doom over the silhouettes of Mount Stanford and Gregory's Monument. The seething conglomeration of energy seems to meet my gaze with a hiss and displays a perfectly timed three-pronged bolt of its electric power. Lightning dances over the far ridges, followed by rolling thunder, long and low like cruel laughter. The blackness boils over and blots out the golden sun.

I return to find Mike stirring in his bed. We soon make hot tea and breakfast, laughing at ourselves first for thinking an early start was unnecessary on such a perfect day, and second for being fools enough to think we could climb such a mountain as Thunder while the sky shuddered and shook. We watch convection cells circulate and moisture accumulate in billowing clouds. There is no doubt. Today it is going to boom.

Humbled, we leave camp with the reasonable intention of exploring the glacial basin connecting the north of Thunder Mountain with the west of Mount Jordan. Nevertheless, as we leave camp I grab my ice axe, and with every passing step I keep my eye trained on Thunder Mountain and its relationship with the developing weather. We move swiftly over wide slabs and soon veer north in the direction of Thunder Mountain. We ascend, negotiating water-streaked granite and soft, cupped snowfields, approaching the rounded divide between the two branches of west upper East Creek. Atop the ridge we encounter huge, rough-hewn talus and soon come to a rest. The view of Thunder and its northern basin has opened wide. Its hulking form stands glowing amidst the shifting light. Its splintered north face widens at its base, curving into high cols on either side of the pyramid. These fall steeply to broad snowfields, sheltered here by the high mass of the Kings-Kern Divide. Undulating, the snowfields fall into the waiting basin below, where a secret round tarn is nestled unassumingly amidst rings of old glacial moraines.

The weather brews, shifts, and changes even as we sit. But these are not tall, bulging thunderheads. The clouds accumulate in girth rather than height, spreading into a wide stratocumulus layer that remains well above the altitude of the highest peaks. Watching intently, for a while it seems that if we concentrate hard enough we can make it go away. But it takes more than two focused minds to prevent differential heating of the earth's surface. After a few minutes with no discernable results, we decide to give up and let the weather happen. We will embrace the weather, rather than fighting it in our minds. Even more firmly than before, we relinquish the aspiration of climbing Thunder Mountain.

We look out at the mountains, in all of their ephemeral illumination and dark, living shadows, and we are inspired. We begin talking about the mountains of the world and all of the explorations we will undertake to find our way into their deepest grooves and most exhilarating ridges. Without argument we conclude that any naturalist or geographer or lover of mountains must make two holy pilgrimages in his or her life. One will be to the mighty Himalaya of Asia, the biggest mountains in the entire world. Here the themes of mountain landscapes, mountain people, and the religious traditions of Hinduism and Buddhism are inextricably intertwined. The second pilgrimage must be to the majestic Alps of Europe, the birthplace of all alpine ideas, and the yardstick against which all mountains have been measured by the Western world. Here too the themes of mountain landscapes and mountain people are interwoven, but with the myths, legends, and histories of the Latin, Germanic, and Celtic worlds. Our thoughts drift to other ranges: the everlasting Andes, second only to the Himalaya in height, covering half the latitudinal span of the globe, and home to one of the world's most extensive and innovative empires; the Southern Alps of New Zealand, sparkling with glaciers and cloaked in dripping Southern Hemisphere temperate rainforests; the high lonesome volcanoes of East Africa, decorated by succulent vegetation; the Caucasus, where Prometheus was bound for gifting fire to the people of the world; the Pamirs of Central Asia, where Marco Polo found relief from the sickness of the world as he made his way to the Grand Khan in China. Portraits of countless ranges appear in our minds, but of all of them, the high Himalaya and the snow-clad Alps stand forward as necessary priorities. In this moment we resolve to go, to undertake those two holy pilgrimages, and soon.

Our talk inevitably finds its way back to the alpine Sierra Nevada, with its thousands of rugged peaks and shimmering lakes and bright snowfields and trailless basins and ridges. Among all the mountain ranges in the world, the Sierra shine like no other. The unique combination of monolithic ambient granite, intense glacial topography, and Mediterranean climate, not to mention immense size, countless lakes, bonsai-like vegetation, and mouthfuls of superlatives, set the Sierra aside as one of the most aesthetically perfect landscapes on earth. We do not doubt that no matter how far we might roam, we will always return to *this* place.

As if in affirmation of our great praise of the Range of Light, we look up to see that a huge blue hole has opened up over Thunder Mountain. We realize that if we were across the basin and upon Thunder Pass, we would have a good chance at making the summit. With all of our imaginative talk about the mountains of the world, we have forgotten the one right in front of us. We set out to gain the pass, and with it, surmount the wall of the Kings-Kern Divide.

We descend the talus quickly, cross the outlet of the small tarn in the bottom of the basin, and begin a long ascent up the velvety snow of Thunder Pass. The snow surface is soft from days of warm summer sun and recent rains, and it is blue and slushy in places. With feet soaked, we keep a good pace up the snowfields, aiming for a gravelly chute just west of the main pass. The chute will bring us higher up the east flank of Thunder Mountain, and it will allow us to avoid the steeper snow at the top of Thunder Pass. Once we reach the base of the chute, we stay on the relatively secure surface of the snow as long as we can, avoiding at all costs the predictably unreliable sand and gravel. The snow slope steepens to fifty degrees, then inevitably tapers out to nothing, funneling us into the upper chute. Reluctantly, we step onto the shifty surface, where we are quickly reduced to groveling on all fours to make our way upward. We gain one step for every four we make, sending sand and scree downslope in crumbling fans. We are two great forces of erosion temporarily unleashed on the flank of Thunder Mountain.

The land is steep and ominous, crowned on all sides by vertical walls of sheer, gray granite. The walls culminate in high summits all around: Thunder Mountain and Mount Jordan looming directly above us, Mount Genevra, the Ericson Crags, Mount Stanford, Deerhorn Mountain, and Polemonium Peak beyond them on either side. And these are connected by ripsaw ridges ornamented with spires, pinnacles, and turrets. Here the mighty glaciers of the Kings and Kern River drainages once backed into one another, ever gnawing away at the high wall between them, as if yearning and groping to tear the wall down. But the divide stood steadfast through the long, cold years of the Pleistocene, as time and time again the ice returned and grew, plucked and scraped, grew and shrank in the sun and spring of ten thousand years, only to melt entirely, then return again for equally as long. Where else in the whole of the Range of Light had the ice not broken through the divides and chewed deeply cleft cols in the high ridges, smoothing their spines in the process? Where else might the journey up and over the bounds of a watershed be so tortuous and all-consuming? We name the river systems of the Sierra Nevada and the divides between them, and none can compare. The Kings-Kern Divide is matchless.

No pass crosses the divide below 12,500 feet above sea level. All involve intricate approaches up hanging glacial valleys, and all of them are filled with sparkling paternoster lakes, ribbon streams, and litters of talus and till. Above these lofty valleys loom the passes themselves: Thunder, Lucy's Foot, Milly's Foot, Harrison, and Forester. They are steep and high, their north faces choked with snow and loose scree and talus up to their faraway tops. Alone amongst the high passes, Forester hosts a footpath, where bold Civilian Conservation Corps crews long ago blasted switchbacks into granite all the way up to 13,200 feet. But all others require close negotiations with difficult terrain: steep, hard snow, precipitous granite cliffs, uncompromising fans of sand and scree.

In 1864 the Divide country was *terra incognito*. Not even Indian trade routes crossed it. The newly formed California Geologic Survey, under Josiah Dwight Whitney, was charged with exploring and mapping the largely unknown Sierra Nevada. Early that summer, a survey party led by William Brewer, also including the topographer Charles Hoffman, set out up Kings Canyon and pushed deep into the heart of the range. The party traveled from Big Meadows up into the Sugarloaf Valley, climbing high points, determining elevation using a barometer, and measuring angular relations among nearby landmarks. Throughout their travels, the looming masses of North Guard, Mount Brewer, South Guard, Thunder Mountain, and Table Mountain dominated the eastern skyline. Assuming these to be the crest of the range, the party steered their course east, up into the High Sierra.

Among the members of this party was a young upstart field geologist named Clarence King. Just twenty-two years old, he was a recent graduate of the prestigious Yale Scientific School. He had come west to find big country and to explore it. Well-trained, determined, short, stocky, and with indomitable physical stamina, King was well suited to the task. He had convinced Brewer to include King's two trusted comrades, James Gardiner and Richard Cotter, both young and able. Together, the three of them made up the volunteer constituency of the survey team.

Camped below the peak that would soon bear his name, Brewer set out early one morning with Hoffman to try the summit. With hands and feet, the two senior members of the party made a difficult but successful ascent, becoming the first people known to have stood on the pale summit rocks of Mount Brewer. As they looked out at the extent of the Sierra Nevada before them, the men were slack-jawed. The peaks spread out to the north, east, and west horizons, hundreds of them, broken into insurmountable cliffs, dissected by deep, forested canyons, daunting to even the sturdiest of explorers. Then Brewer realized the truth. He did not stand on the crest of the range, but rather the crest was split in two. Where he and Hoffman stood was the northern end of a Great Western Divide. Across the deep canyon of the Kern River, an eastern crest stood even taller and more proud, a thousand feet higher than the summit of Mount Brewer. From where they stood, Mount Brewer's massive granite cliffs extended south as a tormented wall, forming a formidable barrier between them and the high crest of the range far beyond.

Brewer and Hoffman returned to camp late. With tired, sweat-encrusted faces, they told their triumphant yet tragic tale to the young volunteers. King later recalled, in *Mountaineering in the Sierra Nevada*, that while Hoffman showed sketches of the eastern crest, Brewer expressed his belief that "to cross the gorge and ascend the eastern wall of peaks was utterly impossible."

King must have tossed and turned in his bed all night, unable to accept Brewer's verdict of impossibility. By morning he was set. He approached Cotter with a plan. Together, they would gain Brewer's consent and make a foray into the *terra incognito*. King's choice of companions was not without careful thought and consideration, as he later wrote: "Stout of limb, stronger yet in heart, of iron endurance, and a quiet, unexcited temperament, and, better yet, deeply devoted to me, I felt Cotter was the one comrade I would choose to face death with, for I believed there was in his manhood no room for fear or shirk."

Brewer's choice was not an easy one. He was, after all, responsible for the lives of each member of the expedition. He seemed particularly fond of King, however, and while he was protective of his young assistant, he was responsive to King's charisma and to his persuasive words. In the end, he consented, under the guise of intent to learn more of the *terra incognito*. Immediately King and Cotter set out making preparations: "We laid out a barometer, a compass, a pocket-level, a set of wet and dry thermometers, note-books, with bread, cooked beans, and venison enough to last a week, rolled them all in blankets, making two knapsack-shaped packs strapped firmly together with loops for the arms, which, by Brewer's estimate, weighed forty pounds apiece."

The next morning, all five members of the survey party made their way up Brewer Creek, breaking treeline and passing cold lakes on their way up to the high shoulder of Mount Brewer. They passed through the prominent col on Brewer's southwest ridge and continued along the cliff-bound lakes at the crest of that high pass. Talus followed as the party ascended to the shattered saddle southeast of the peak. There, looking out at the broken Brewer wall, King experienced a profound moment of doubt. Before him lay the sleeping dragon of uncertainty. Behind him was the warm, soft bed of complacency. He found hope in the eyes of Cotter, who seemed resolute and up to the task. There they said good-bye to Gardiner, Hoffman, and Brewer, unsure if ever they would see them again. All the men wept.

As the alpine wind dried their eyes, King and Cotter set out to traverse the Brewer wall. They rose from the saddle, surmounting the peak now known as South Guard. From its gravelly, rounded back they descended to the vicinity of Longley Pass. The grandiosely corniced pass offered a window to the south and east. As they peered out in this direction, King and Cotter descried another wall, a high divide running east-west, culminating in monstrous peaks, connecting the high eastern crest of the range with the Great Western Divide on which they stood. The divide they saw that day was the Kings-Kern. To get to the eastern crest, they would have to overcome this huge mountain barrier. Blocked by unnegotiable pinnacles on the Brewer wall, they descended Longley Pass by rope and sought camp for the night.

As they approached the Kings-Kern Divide, King and Cotter scoped out a small granite bench and made their bivouac for the night. There, King experienced a rare moment of transcendental lucidity, realizing the capacity for both beauty and death in the raw nature of the high mountains: "After such fatiguing exercises the mind has an almost abnormal clearness: whether this is wholly from within, or due to the intensely vitalizing mountain air, I am not sure; probably both contribute to the state of exultation in which all alpine climbers find themselves. The solid granite gave me a luxurious repose, and I lay on the edge of our little rock niche and watched the strange yet brilliant scene":

> All the snow of our recess lay in the shadow of the high granite
> wall to the west, but the Kern Divide which carved around us
> from the southeast was in full light, its broken sky-line, battle-
> mented and adorned with innumerable rough-hewn spires
> and pinnacles, was a mass of glowing orange intensely defined
> against the deep violet sky. At the open end of our horseshoe
> amphitheater, to the east, its floor of snow rounded over a
> smooth brink, overhanging precipices which sank over two

thousand feet into the King's Canyon. Across the gulf rose the whole procession of summit peaks, their lower halves rooted in a deep somber shadow cast by the western wall, the heights bathed in warm purple haze, in which the irregular marbling of snow burned with a pure crimson light. A few fleecy clouds, dyed fiery orange, drifted slowly eastward across the narrow zone of sky which stretched from summit to summit like a roof. At times the sound of waterfalls, faint and mingled with echoes, floated up through the still air. The snow near by lay in cold ghastly shade, warmed here and there in strange flashes by light reflected downward from drifting clouds. The somber waste about us; the deep violet vault overhead; those far summits, glowing with reflected rose; the deep impenetrable gloom which filled the gorge, and slowly with vapor-like stealth climbed the mountain wall extinguishing the red light, combined to produce an effect which may not be described; nor can I more than hint at the brilliancy of the scene under full light, and the cold, deathlike repose which followed when the wan cliffs and pallid snow were all overshadowed with ghostly gray.

A sudden chill enveloped us. Stars in a moment crowded through the dark heaven, flashing with a frosty splendor. The snow congealed, the brooks ceased to flow, and, under the powerful sudden leverage of frost, immense blocks were dislodged all along the mountain summits and came thundering down the slopes, booming upon the ice, dashing wildly upon rocks. Under the lee of our shelf we felt quite safe, but neither Cotter nor I could help being startled, and jumping just a little, as these missiles, weighing often many tons, struck the ledge over our heads and whizzed down the gorge, their stroke resounding fainter and fainter, until at last only a confused echo reached us.

King and Cotter spent a frigid night on the bare granite of the alpine Sierra, nestled there in the northeast cirque of Thunder Mountain. Teeth chattering, the two explorers held onto each other for life, barely dozing as the temperature dropped continuously throughout the night. When dawn broke on the high summit of Mount Jordan, they roused themselves and checked the thermometer. It stood at two degrees Fahrenheit. Chewing on frozen venison and sipping from the canteen they had, thankfully, kept between them in the night, they padded their pack straps and set out to climb the divide.

King and Cotter met hard, frozen snow and soon found climbing difficult. As the snow steepened and their steps faltered, they unsheathed Cotter's huge Bowie knife and carefully cut steps into the snow surface. Fearing a fatal slip, they carved their steps deep and wide. When they reached the top of the snowfield it was still shady morning on the north side of the divide. There they confronted vertical cliffs, stretching upward to the sunlit sky. No route seemed to penetrate the mass of granite before them. King wrote of the moment: "It would have disheartened us to gaze up at the hard, sheer front of the precipices, and search among the splintered projections, crevices, shelves, and snow patches for an inviting route, had we not been animated by a faith that the mountains could not defy us." Undeterred, they started up, Cotter taking the lead. As they ascended, they looked down at the route they had come up, unable to fathom a descent by the same way. Eventually, climbing became the only option. From a ledge bound by sheer, featureless stone, King threw his rope and lassoed a spire thirty feet above. They climbed one at a time, hand over hand, up and over the crux of the divide.

History is unclear about just where King and Cotter made their legendary ascent of the Kings-Kern Divide. Neither King's romantic accounts nor the history books that tell his story are decisive. Thunder Pass would not have posed such a formidable barrier as King's account suggests. It is likely, therefore, that they ascended east of that low point in the divide, perhaps between Peak 13,231 and Mount Jordan. King's account in *Mountaineering in the Sierra Nevada* goes on to describe the knife-edged ridge atop the divide, "so narrow and sharp that we dared not walk, but got astride, and worked slowly along with our hands, pushing the knapsacks in advance, now and then holding our breath when loose masses rocked under our weight." From there, the stunning view of the Kern Plateau was opened up to them. Kings writes, "The view was so grand, the mountain colors so brilliant, immense snow fields and blue alpine lakes so charming, that we almost forgot we were ever to move."

The young intrepid explorers of the 1864 California Geologic Survey eventually left the ridge, suffering a fantastic and hazardous descent onto the Kern Plateau. They successfully explored the main crest of the Sierra Nevada, making a notable first ascent of Mount Tyndall to survey the highest peaks of the range. The two returned from their adventure to tell the tale, though by then Cotter's boots had disintegrated and his bloody feet were wrapped in blankets. King's account of his and Cotter's famous ascent of Mount Tyndall, forever glorified in prose, quickly became a classic piece of mountaineering literature.

I STAND UPON THE CREST of the Kings-Kern Divide and look out upon the granite country of the Sierra Nevada. Over 60 percent exposed rock, the high country is mostly bare, near naked to the eyes of the beholder. From Thunder Pass, the granitic rock of the Sierra takes on such an array of forms as would beguile any armchair geologist. Along the high crests it is splintered into a million vertical joints, forming pillars, battlements, and fierce turrets. Water, ever at work, freezes in the cracks, prying off often huge pieces of long stable rock and casting them down to the slopes below. These pieces, once shed from the noble heights, are heaped into strewn piles of huge, broken talus, sharp and angular. As the slopes spread out like massive aprons to the wide basins below, the granite takes on a different form: broad, flat, polished in places by glaciers long past, reflecting the bright glare of the sun. A closer look at the polished surface of the granite would reveal dark, rounded xenoliths like leopard spots or flies suspended in amber. Around them are swarms of lighter-colored feldspar and quartz, forming web-like intrusions into the otherwise uniform color and texture of the bedrock. Prominent joints are visible, running roughly south-southeast to north-northwest. With a little imagination, I can recall the main axis of the range. These joints run parallel to it. They also parallel the main axis of the Central Valley, the Coast Ranges, and the coast itself. Suspicious. A second set of prominent joints runs perpendicular to this master set. Together with the prominent vertical joints of the crest, the entire alpine Sierra is broken into huge rectangular blocks of varying sizes. My thoughts drift further west than my eyes can see, to where the range slopes down towards the Central Valley, where the granite blocks are huge, monolithic, and unbroken. They bear names like Angel's Wings, the Whaleback, Charlotte Dome, El Capitan, and Half Dome. Time has worn away their irregularities and revealed their secret spherical cores. Granite cools from the outside in, forming concentric spheres of natural weakness. Nature will exploit these whenever she can. From my vantage point the more broken rock typical of the main crest is most visible, extending far to the east, even to the high, frost-smashed needles of the Whitney group.

I have never seen more granite in a single gaze in any place in the world. I recall so many places in the High Sierra where I can say the same thing, and few places anywhere else in the world where I could even come close. The contenders for the most extensive granite mountain landscapes line up in my mind: Patagonia, southern Greenland, Baffin Island, the Mont Blanc massif, the Karakoram, the Wind Rivers, Mount Katahdin. Only a handful of places on the globe make inroads into my consciousness. We are sitting on top of the foundation of one of the most extensive mountain ranges the world has ever known. Here is the basement complex of the Ancestral Sierran Arc volcanoes. Here is the heart of one of the most extensive complexes of granite ever distilled from the earth's mantle and emplaced in the crust. But how did this vast subterranean formation break the surface? What happened to the fifteen-thousand-foot mountain range that once stood on top of it? How and when did the granitic Sierra Nevada of today raise its broad shoulders above the land?

Seventy million years ago the long-reigning dinosaurs cruised the land in the shadow of the fuming Ancestral Sierra Nevada. The range had long been built, and the tectonic processes that contributed to its rise were still in full effect. But North America was centered around the equatorial regions at the time, and warm, wet rains fell down on the mountains and quickly ate away at their flanks. Erosion rates during this warm, wet Cretaceous Period were accelerated as everywhere the processes of chemical weathering, so common in warm climes today, tore landscapes down and brought them closer to the sea. The Sierran Arc fought a losing battle to maintain its lofty peaks, holding its own, but barely. The mountains were wearing away faster than they were rising. If something were to happen and the tectonic forces that caused their uplift were to cease, they would quickly wash away to their surrounding basins.

Far away in the newborn Atlantic, new ocean floor was being created as the crust rifted apart. Below this spreading center, somewhere deep in the earth, a profound convection cell was driving the process. Around seventy million years ago, the convection cell surged, and the conveyor belts that split the Atlantic in two began to drive faster. As magma welled up along the Mid-Atlantic Ridge at an unprecedented rate, the seafloor spread rapidly, pushing the landmasses of Europe and North America apart at a quickened pace. Around the bend, in western North America, this meant even faster devouring of the Farallon Plate, the remains of which still separated North America from the larger Pacific Plate. The Farallon Plate had been subducting at a steep angle for tens of millions of years, diving into the semi-molten interior of the planet, melting, partially distilling back up, intruding into the overlying crust, extruding back out of the crust, and throwing up mountains all over the place. As North America's westward movement increased in speed, the subduction angle of the Farallon Plate decreased to accommodate the swiftly overriding continent. Instead of diving, the shallow-angle subduction caused the Farallon Plate to actually underride North America. Because of the decreased subduction angle, the Farallon Plate no longer dove deep enough to reach the semi-molten asthenosphere, and thus it ceased to melt, ceased distilling back upward, ceased intruding into the crust, and ceased extruding back out of the crust. Mountain building in the Ancestral Sierra was shut down. The rains fell, and the mountains washed away.

The two plates passed each other like trains in the night, North America above, westbound, the Farallon Plate below, relatively eastbound. But the friction between the two plates was incredible. Inland from the subduction zone, east of the suture zones of California's accreted terranes, thick sequences of sediments still lay as a veneer atop the crust of North America. Atop basement rocks were piled Paleozoic sandstones, shales, and limestones. Atop these were Mesozoic sediments of the same kinds. All told, these sedimentary sequences piled up thousands of feet thick. Not yet completely settled and rigid, still retaining some degree of elasticity, these thick sequences withstood the tremors beneath them as the Farallon Plate underrode the continent. Rather than buckling and folding under pressure, they swelled and arose as a cohesive unit of sequential horizontal layers, bowing upward like a layer cake to form the Colorado Plateau. Further eastward, however, inland from those primeval beaches of the Paleozoic, seas had not licked the land so often, and sediments had not accumulated so evenly or abundantly. Here, the underlying pressure had grown too great. The crust of the continent buckled, bent, folded, and broke. In a prolonged violent spasm, the beginnings of the Rocky Mountains were shaped.

Geologists know this tremendous event as the Laramide orogeny. It was the most recent phase of the same great Cordilleran orogeny that began way back in the midst of the Mesozoic Era. The Laramide event spanned the end of the age of reptiles and the beginning of the age of mammals. It both closed the Mesozoic Era and opened the Cenozoic, culminating around forty million years ago and relaxing five million years later.

While the Colorado Plateau and the Rockies rose, the Ancestral Sierra crumbled, decayed, and was washed away by equatorial rains. To the west, the remains filled the forearc basin of what would become the Central Valley of California, while to the east they filled the foreland basins that would become part of the Great Basin. Over the next fifty million years, erosive forces reduced the high peaks of the Ancestral Sierra to a system of undulating uplands. As the overburden was worn away, the granitic basement which had for so long underlain the arc volcanoes was gradually exposed. By thirty million years ago, the California coastline lay along what is now the western foothills of the Sierra Nevada, indented by an elaborate system of swamps, lagoons, and bayous. The deep sediments of the Central Valley lay beneath a shallow sea, bound to the west by a series of islands that would become the Coast Ranges.

On top of the freshly exposed granitic basement of the Ancestral Sierra, the roots of a handful of old arc volcanoes still stood. These roots, cooked, pressurized, and metamorphosed by the rising magma that eventually cooled to become granite, were lifted as if on pedestals, and they stood perched atop the basement complex as the highest peaks in the worn-out range. Eventually these metamorphosed volcanic cores would form some of the highest summits of the range, including such infamous peaks as Mount Dana, Mount Gibbs, Mount Rodgers, Mount Ritter, and the Black Kaweah.

Thirty million years ago things changed yet again. The surging convection cell that drove the Atlantic spreading calmed down, and North America slowed in its westward migration. The Farallon Plate resumed its status quo subduction beneath the leading edge of North America, and mountain building action returned to the west coast. The first rumblings of the return were felt in the Northern Sierra Nevada, where violent volcanic explosions blasted their way across the landscape. Originating from vents near the present-day crest of the range, these eruptions blew out entire cubic miles of rhyolite and ash, blanketing the exposed basement granites with a new overlying layer up to a thousand feet thick. These volcanic layers are best represented in the Sweetwater Range, east of the main crest of the range. As these initial eruptions subsided, they were soon followed by less violent but equally catastrophic eruptions. Andesitic lava oozed from the vents along the crest, mixing with mud and water to form thick, steaming flows that spread out across the rounded uplands and gradually encased them in yet another layer of volcanic material. These flows covered the entire northern half of the range and sprawled south past Sonora Pass to northern Yosemite.

For millions of years the Farallon Plate had separated North America from the Pacific Plate. Deep beneath the boundary between the Farallon and Pacific Plates was a convection cell, similar to the one beneath the Mid-Atlantic Ridge. The Pacific and Farallon Plates were just like the two sides of the Atlantic, and with each passing moment of geologic time the two plates spread further and further apart. While the Farallon Plate moved southeast, ultimately to be gobbled up by the encroaching North American Plate, the Pacific

Plate moved in the opposite direction: northwest. Like all divergent plate boundaries, the Farallon-Pacific seam was not a smooth one. No single brush stroke on a map could trace its complex details. It was, rather, cracked and broken into a long series of edges, angles, and corners. Twenty-five million years ago, most of the Farallon Plate had been devoured by North America. Only tattered remains kept the westbound continent from contacting the northwest-bound Pacific Plate. Then, finally, a last remain of the Farallon was swallowed up. North America and the Pacific Plate met and collided. The shaping of modern-day California began.

At first, only one small corner of the Farallon-Pacific seam touched North America. It was like an elbow pointing eastward at the approaching leading edge of North America. Once the continent touched the point of the elbow, the Farallon Plate was divided into two remnants. The northern remnant became the Juan de Fuca Plate, and the southern became the Nazca Plate. Both of these Farallon remnants continued to subduct, following the same pattern of mountain building that had given birth to the Ancestral Sierran Arc volcanoes. The remnants melted into the semi-molten asthenosphere, distilled back out, intruded into the crust, and extruded out the surface, eventually forming the Cascades in the north and the Mexican volcanoes in the south. But in between, the Farallon Plate was totally gone. With no plate left to subduct, mountain building was shut down. As more and more of the northern and southern remnants subducted, they were consumed. The gap between them widened.

Where North America and the Pacific Plate met, the tectonic regime shifted abruptly. The two plates had a similar westward agenda, which meant no subduction of the Pacific Plate and consequently no arc volcanism. But the Pacific was not just going west, it was going *north*west. When the two plates met, the leading edge of North America slightly overrode the Pacific Plate, which, as it tucked under westernmost North America, grabbed a hold of the continent and began tugging it northwest. Now, instead of convergence and subduction, the Pacific Plate began a new agenda: continue northwest at all costs, ripping, stretching, and dragging the continent along with it.

For the last forty to fifty million years, the underriding Farallon

Plate had protected the underside of North America from the semi-molten material of the earth's interior. As North America slid over the Farallon Plate and finally devoured it, the underside of the continent came into direct contact with the mantle. The intense heat of the mantle caused the rigid crust of the continent to soften and become elastic, much like peanut brittle or taffy would if warmed. Because of this, when the Pacific Plate began tugging at North America, the continental crust was able to stretch rather than rip open.

The stretching of North America is believed by many geologists to have begun in what is today southern Arizona, inland from the point where the Pacific Plate first contacted North America. As the contact zone widened, so did the zone of direct contact between the continent and the mantle, and so did the zone of stretching. The crust was stretched an additional 10 to 15 percent of its original width, pulling most of California 165 miles west in the process and twisting the southern extension of the basement granites towards the southwest. As the crust stretched, it thinned to between twelve and nineteen miles in thickness and became some of the thinnest crust in the world. As the crust thinned, the hot, semi-molten material of the interior was brought even closer to the earth's surface, causing the thinned crust to bow upward. Eventually the strain was too great. The crust cracked and broke along a series of lateral faults, forming a system of huge, long blocks. As extensional faulting continued, some of these blocks down-dropped, sinking lower into the asthenosphere, while others tilted up as if on a hinge, some leaning towards the east, others to the west. As the Pacific Plate pulled the continent northwest, the blocks migrated in that direction, sliding past each other along the lateral fault systems that separated them. Each block neatly paralleled the another, and also ultimately the north-northwest to south-southeast orientation of the contact between the North American and Pacific Plates. Here, the most famous of the lateral fault systems, the San Andreas, was created. West of the San Andreas system, a small piece of North American crust sits on top of the northwest-bound Pacific Plate. East of the San Andreas is the North American Plate.

The crust of North America opened up like an accordion. As the accordion pleats spread, a distinct Basin and Range topography resulted, presently evidenced by over a hundred north-south-trending mountain ranges all across the American West. In California, these include the White, Inyo, Warner, Cottonwood, Panamint, Argus, Granite, Avawatz, Amargosa, Grapevine, Funeral, Greenwater, Nopah, Bristol, Providence, Old Woman, Sacramento, Turtle, Sheep Hole, Palen, Big Maria, Whipple, and Chuckwalla Mountains, among others. In fact, the Basin and Range Province of the American West contains more distinct mountain ranges than anywhere else in the continent.

Eventually the broken crust opened up so much that the sea flooded in. By ten million years ago the lateral fault system along the edge of Mexico tore open into a wide rift. West of the rift the crust moved northwest in accordance with the dominant paradigm of the Pacific Plate. As this movement continued, the ocean waters of the Pacific poured in to form the Gulf of California. As extension continues, the peninsula of Baja California will eventually become the island of Baja California.

All this time, the deep basement granites of the Sierra Nevada lay low and quiet. By nature, the basement granites were like a once heavily laden barge now relieved of their burdensome cargo. Like the barge, without the weight of their cargo the granites should bob up and float higher on the water. The common analogy is that the crust floats atop the semi-molten asthenosphere much like ice floats upon water. If you look at an ice cube in a bowl of water, a portion of the ice is above the water's surface, but most of it is below. The ratio of how much is above to how much is below remains the same, regardless of the size of the ice cube. If you were to cut away a portion of the ice above the surface of the water, the extra buoyancy pressure exerted from the subsurface portion, or root, would cause the cube to bob up to achieve equilibrium. Unload the barge and it will bob up. Step out of a canoe and it will float higher. Remove the ice cap from Greenland or Antarctica and the underlying land will rise. Erode a mountain range and it will rise again, and again, and again.

This principle, whether applied to ice, boats, or the crust of the earth, is called isostasy. Accordingly, the process of rebound, or "bobbing up," that follows a release in overlying pressure is called isostatic rebound. Isostatic rebound is the earth's way of working towards ideal flotational balance among the different parts of the lithosphere. While the ideal balance for ice is around 1:10, the ratio for the crust of the earth is 2:8. This means that fresh, new mountains ten thousand feet high have roots forty thousand feet deep; mountains fifteen thousand feet high have roots sixty thousand feet deep; and mountains twenty thousand feet high have roots eighty thousand feet deep. That's the theory. In reality, there are so many other factors at play that the numbers rarely add up perfectly.

For a hundred million years the roots of the Ancestral Sierran Arc volcanoes had been depressed by the high mountains that stood upon them. As the mountains of old wore away, the roots became over-deep, and they were then weighed down by thick sequences of sediments, both west and east. Because the erosional processes were gradual and not catastrophic, the sediments didn't break like rigid solids but rather bent like plastic. Even over the top of most of the granite, sediments covered the basement rocks, strapping them down like huge elastic bands, preventing the roots from rising up into immense granite mountains and achieving isostatic equilibrium. The roots, which were destined to become the Sierra Nevada, were repressed. Only a force of tectonic magnitude could break the tension and allow the granite to rise.

Extensional faulting changed the landscape dramatically and suddenly, snapping the elastic hold of the restraining sediments and breaking California into pieces. With the formation of the two north-south-trending fault systems—the San Andreas to the west and the Owens Valley system to the east—the land on either side of the Sierra Nevada collapsed as the crust was stretched, becoming the Central Valley to the west and the Owens Valley to the east. The immense granite of the Sierran root was finally freed from its restraints and, like an ice cube, it bobbed upward.

In a geologic blink of an eye, the Sierra Nevada rose thousands of feet, to nearly its present height. Uplift began nine to ten million years ago in the Southern Sierra, and the mountains rose northward as the Farallon slab gap grew wider. As the gap opened, the triple junction of the Farallon remnant, the Pacific Plate, and the North American Plate, known to geologists as the Mendocino Triple Junction, migrated north at a rate of around six centimeters per year. As the gap widened and the junction moved north, the book was closed on subduction and associated arc volcanism and opened to the dynamic of crustal ripping, stretching, and uplift of associated fault-block ranges. When uplift began in the Southern Sierra, the region was faulted on both the east and the west sides. The Southern Sierra therefore rose boldly and uniformly, as both flanks of the range were freed from the weight of adjacent valleys and their deep, long-accumulated sediments. Faults also developed within the range itself, as is evidenced by the twin crests of the Mount Whitney region and the Great Western Divide, separated by the Kern River Canyon.

As the range rose northward, the crust did not break along its western front. Here, the deep sediments of the Central Valley acted like a counterweight pressing downward on the range as it rose, keeping the western slope of the range low, its overall uplift less than the depth of its root would suggest. As a result of this repression of uplift to the west, the eastern crest compensated and rose dramatically, more than the depth of the root dictated. Here, clean faults broke the range. As the Sierran crest rose, the adjacent eastern blocks sunk as grabens. This complicated uplift dynamic gave the Northern and Central Sierra Nevada the long, gradual west slope and the steeper eastern escarpment that is characteristic of the region today.

It took less than five million years for the entire range to rise. By five million years ago, at the close of the Miocene Epoch, the Sierra Nevada was a broad, plateau-like range topographically resembling the White-Inyo Ranges of today. The average elevation of the Miocene Sierra Nevada was greater than that of today. Maximum elevation, however, was lower. Few who know and love today's Sierra Nevada would have recognized these mountains without their characteristic jagged peaks and deeply carved valleys. The range was quarried and raised, but yet to be shaped and sculpted.

ATOP THE KINGS-KERN DIVIDE, Mike and I reflect on the story of the rise of the Range of Light. Looking up at the torn ridges on either side of us, we pay homage to our predecessors. I look longingly out onto the expansive Kern Plateau, flooded with a tide of trees up from the low-lands. But my attention is quickly drawn to the raised, monstrous, flat-topped form of Table Mountain. I scan its horizontal profile from east to west, across the tabletop to the intimidating sawtoothed arete that connects it to the gothic cathedral of Thunder Mountain. Above the heights of Thunder Mountain's elusive peak, the sky is gray, but not roiling. Its underbelly is smooth as slate, not bulged and torn. Neither lightning nor thunder has shown any sign of presence for many an hour. I push the shaft of my ice axe into the snow. It will serve as a marker indicating the upper opening of the chute. Without a word, we start up the southeast ridge.

At first the climbing is a chore, and the rock broken and loose. As the slope angle increases, so does the structural integrity of the rock. Soon we are surmounting large blocks stacked atop one another, a giant, steep staircase to the top of the mountain. We watch carefully as the clouds thicken south of Table Mountain. They seem to be moving to the west of us. I eye them with suspicion as they slide across the sky. The weather holds.

We reach the south summit without difficulty. Before us stand proud blocks of strong granite, forming a formidable summit ridge and spanning the few hundred feet between us and the summit proper. The granite is clearly broken into square-shaped sections, and prominent cracks run at right angles to one another, vertical and horizontal. I quickly begin scanning these lines for a route across the summit ridge, knowing that although the clouds have not yet broken, our traverse to the summit and back will have to be a fast one. Mike begins scouting a high route while I look lower on the ridge. I spy a narrow cleft in the ridge, between the south and middle peaks. Some airy steps across the face of the ridge, followed by a short pitch of long downclimbing moves, bring me into the cleft. Mike hangs back. I can feel his hesitation. He yells across the significant mass of silent stone that now separates us. "I don't know about this one. I don't know about making these moves efficiently if and when we need to." He has a point. I think fast.

"I'm not worried yet. We've had no sign of electricity for hours. I think these clouds still have a while to go before they burst." I look at the notch I am in, wondering if it would provide shelter if things really did get bad. Mike starts negotiating his way across the ridge. I watch as he steps confidently onto a foothold and it crumbles and breaks beneath him. He recovers gracefully, but he is obviously shaken. He bends down and retrieves the broken piece of rock and holds it aloft in his hand.

"This is it. This is my sign," he says. "If you're going to go, you'd better do it now." There will be no discussion about this. Mike's decision is final and I know it. I am torn. I know his offer is sincere and he doesn't want his decision to affect my confidence, but inevitably it does. It doesn't seem right to continue without him. Mike's hesitation is founded on a near-death experience with lightning two years ago. While making an evening ascent of White Mountain Peak, he was pinned down by a violent thunderstorm that sent ground currents through his whole body. In that gray and purple dusk, blue sparks of electricity danced on the brim of his hat while the world buzzed and the question of life or death hung in the air. I can see the memory of it in his eyes. The fear is contagious, even though all of my knowledge of weather tells me there is nothing to fear right here, right now. I stand there for a few minutes trying to get myself together.

I find myself making the first steps of the traverse to the summit with great fear and hesitation. Both of these emotions soon surrender to the certainty of movement and the exhilaration of being alive in such a place. Time pulses like a cosmic heartbeat. I step delicately across narrow ledges, making my way over to the base of the North Summit. The last fifteen feet up to the top of the summit block are vertical. A wide crack marks the way, stuffed with a head-sized chockstone about halfway up the crack. I begin climbing, working my feet up to where I can grab the chockstone. It is loose. I get scared and downclimb back to the ledge below the crack. Anxious, I scout around in search of an alternative route to the top. Around a corner to the west, I find a tall off-width crack that rises to the upper summit block. Using foot jams and arm braces, I work my way up the crack about ten feet, then hesitate. Off-widths and chimneys are my favorite kind of climbing, but fear has crept into my heart and I am certain I don't want to die up here. I downclimb again. As I land back on the ledge, a drop of rain strikes my cheek. It is a sign, but a sign to depart right now or a sign to get my head together and take a few steps closer to the firmament? I muster my nerve and return to the chockstone crack. This time, instead of trusting my weight to the loose stone, I work my way up just left of the main crack, using smaller holds but good ones to pull up and onto the summit. My hands rest upon the top only for seconds. I realize that this is a false summit and that the true summit is up another fifteen feet of vertical granite. Rain falls down and onto my face.

I retreat quickly. The hesitation I felt approaching the mountain has evolved into determination to get off the mountain as soon as possible. What seemed like daring moves on the ascent are comfortably dulled by necessity and the knowledge that I have already done them once. The drama factor is quelled by pragmatism. I am spooked and it is time to go.

Once I am across the ridge, the rain stutters and stops. I thank it for inspiring an efficient return. I look up at the burgeoning sky, where gray orbs shift and billow over the looming dentate ridgelines of the Kings-Kern Divide. The bellies of clouds gestate patiently. Deep in the afternoon, they will birth droplets of rain and pea-sized balls of hail, bringing granite to life as water and stone mingle in a mysterious alchemy and a sweet aroma fills the high alpine air. Breathing deeply, I set out down the broken blocks and oversized talus of the southeast ridge. Below, atop Thunder Pass, I will find Mike, and together we will find our way back over the wide world of granite of the Kings-Kern Divide.

SEVEN

The Bulwark of the West

At the edge of North America, in the Big Sur country of the Santa Lucia Range, the land falls down, tumbling in undulating grassy slopes to the churning brine of the everlasting sea. Waves, borne west across the shimmering blue vastness, curve and curl, rank upon rank, gnashing and eating away at the crumbling plenty of the land. Always taking, always shifting, sifting, the sea gouges blowholes in headlands and cuts them into bridges, arches, sea stacks, then tears them away. Undermined, the steep terrain of the mountains, so hastily consolidated and uplifted, quickly breaks, slips, and slides downslope, taking its vegetation along for the ride. The wall of the mountains is immediate, rising like the broad shoulders of an ancient sea god, now cloaked in the soil and green things of the earth, often veiled in white wispy clouds fresh off the sea.

Steep canyons penetrate the flanks of this rugged country. These are inroads for the influences of the sea in an otherwise impenetrable mountain barrier. These canyons are not the result of slow and steady erosion but of rushing streams quickly cutting into soft stone as the mountains heave their way upward. The canyon waters deliver the silt, sand, and stone of even the highest peaks down to the salty sea. But the water flows in two directions here. While freshwater streams gush into the ocean, warm summer air is cooled by cold, upwelling ocean waters. As the air cools, its moisture vapor content condenses out, creating low, coastal fog. Westerly winds blow the cool fog up-canyon, filling up the deep ravines with thick, brooding mists. Tall trees down in these shaded recesses capture tiny water droplets from the fog, collecting them on their thirsty leaf tips. Drip by drop the water falls to the forest floor, feeding the needy root systems of cathedral-like redwood groves. The canyons hold the fog in. The redwoods creep upslope only so far, bound by the summer moisture the fog provides. Above the thick alluvial soils of the canyon bottoms, they mix with pepper-scented bay trees, tall, straight tanoaks, and big-leaf maples. Above the fog zone turkey vultures soar, wavering slightly in the blistering sun, riding thermal updrafts over rolling grasslands, tangled chaparral, and open oak woodlands. The summer sun leaves the slopes dry and crackled, a tinderbox for a blaze if one should strike. The silent vultures look intently for food, listening always to the booming sound of surf on stone far, far below.

Beneath the mosaic of growing things, green, brown, yellow, and every color of flower sprouting from the imagination of the earth, beneath their corrugated root balls and smooth white root tips, beneath the brown loamy soils of humus, air, sand, and clay, the bedrock of the Big Sur country stands in massive piles and heaps and squeezed wedges, itself a mosaic of rocks, a patchwork quilt of disparate parts, an aggregate of stone hailing from different places and different times. There are granites stolen from the Sierra Nevada and conveyed to the coast along lateral fault systems. There are scraped-up seafloor sediments mixed with residual, broken pieces of seafloor basalt, all stuffed and crammed together to form crumbly schists, greenstones, and cherts. There are stiff, exotic chunks of crust from the subtropical regions, stacked upon each other and heaped into piles of gneiss, marble, amphibolite, quartz diorite, tonalite, and granodiorite. Overlying all of these rocks is the thin veneer of the present—the sediments washed down from today's Coast Ranges that haven't yet made it to the sea, deposited in the nooks, crannies, and secret folds of the landscape.

The Big Sur country of the Santa Lucia Range is but one small link in a system of coastal ranges that spans western North America all the way from Mexico to Alaska. To the south the coastal mountains become the peninsular ranges of Baja California, including the Sierra de la Giganta, Sierra de Mulegé, Sierra de San Borja, Sierra de San Pedro Mártir, and Sierra Juárez. North of the U.S.–Mexico border, the coastal mountains become confused with the Transverse Ranges, but most sources agree that the Laguna and San Rafael Mountains are definitively coastal. In Central California, the Santa Lucia Range dominates the coastline, while the Diablo Range parallels as an inner coastal range. North of San Francisco Bay, the mountains splay out to numerous sub-ranges, often unnamed, including the Kings Range, before they bend around the complex Klamath Knot and continue up through Oregon and Washington. There, the coastal mountains build into the wet, forest-flanked glaciated masses of the Olympic Mountains. Beyond, the coastal mountains attain still greater height and grandeur in the Pacific and Kitimat Ranges of British Columbia, and the Saint Elias, Chugach, Kenai, and Aleutian Mountains of Alaska. There are enough mountains along the coast to fill a page.

These ranges are the bulwark of the West, forming some of the steepest coastal slopes in the world, sheltering the continental interior from the immediate maritime influences of the Pacific Ocean. On their western flanks, they host deep, dark, dripping redwood and temperate rainforests and cold gray glaciers to the north, while to the south the mountains are cloaked with drier woodlands and coastal chaparral. Whether in the Olympics or the Lagunas, the east sides of the Coast Ranges are substantially drier, separated from the effects of the sea by at least one ridge. Moving inland, the rain-shadow effect created by the Coast Ranges becomes more pronounced, and plant communities are drier still. In California, this effect is extreme enough to allow for wet redwood forests against the coast, while the Central Valley of the interior is a parched grassland. Even in the comparatively drenched and shivering Olympics of Washington, the west side of the range soaks in a deluge of well over two hundred inches of rain a year, while the east side receives a mere thirty.

The wall to the west is broken in only a few notable places. San Francisco Bay cuts California's Coast Ranges in half, separating the southern ranges from those in the north. The bay, along with the Sacramento and San Joaquin River systems that drain into it, is the only fluvial outlet for inland waters to drain to the sea. If not for this outlet, the Central Valley would fill up with water like a giant bathtub until it breached the coastal rampart in some lesser place. To the north, the next significant gap is the Columbia River watershed, where the substantial Columbia delivers inland waters from the northern intermountain states to the Pacific. Further north is the Puget Sound, where the Pacific itself makes inroads into the continent. Beyond are the wild mountains of coastal British Columbia, so convoluted that only two writhing roads cross them from east to west.

The Santa Lucia Range of Central California has the steepest coastal rise in the contiguous United States. Here, the wall of the Big Sur country rises up out of the foamy sea and attains heights of over 5,000 feet just three miles inland from shore. Cone Peak stands atop this rise, commanding a grand view of the surrounding mountain landscape. For a hundred miles in length, from north of San Luis Obispo to Carmel, and twenty miles in width, the Santa Lucias stretch out their ragged form. Although the highest summits of the range never exceed 6,000 feet, the relief of the range is impressive. The landscape appears tortured, twisted, upthrust prematurely, caught between grand but opposing forces. Ridges rise in bent masses and plummet abruptly into steep, dark ravines inhabited by cold, quick streams. At first the assemblage of ridges and valleys seems totally contorted, but as senses settle into the Big Sur aesthetic, the initial chaos gives way to discernable patterns. The distinct line of the Coast Ridge stands out, rising from the sea in a continuous blockade, paralleling the northwest-southeast-trending edge of North America. From its uppermost heights, deep canyons are carved into the west slope by an abundance of rainwater fresh off the sea. But those waters spend only a short time on land before rushing madly back to their source in loud cascades, merging with the ocean at sandy pocket beaches nestled secretly in coves surrounded by high, dripping cliffs. The creeks that inhabit these canyons are many, bearing names such as Mill, Kirk, Hare, Limekiln, West, Vicente, Devils, Big, Rat, Dolan, Lime, Hot Springs, Anderson, McWay, Partington, Torre, Lafler, Grimes, and Graves, among others. Separating each of these canyons are high spur ridges that branch off perpendicularly from the Coast Ridge, running northeast-southwest, connecting the Coast Ridge to the Pacific by way of steeply descending, undulating hills. But there are notable exceptions to this pattern. In several places the Coast Ridge is preceded by broad, flat coastal headlands, exhibiting a striking contrast in form when juxtaposed to the vertical relief of the adjacent mountains. This topography is exemplified by the terraced landscape around Pfeiffer and Cooper Points. Inland from the Coast Ridge the topographical pattern follows the norm. The main ridges and river valleys roughly following the northwest-southeast orientation of the coastline, buttressed and separated by perpendicular spur ridges.

The formation of the Santa Lucia Range, like that of all the coast ranges of western North America, began with the westward migration of North America and the consequent subduction of the Farallon Plate. Inland from the subduction zone, the Ancestral Sierra were extruding while their associated batholiths were intruding. But west of the major mountain building, where the leading edge of North America scraped violently against the top of the subducting Farallon Plate, seafloor sediments, basalt, and material from the edge of the continent were all bent and broken, heaped up and crammed together into a rude and indiscernible mix of rock, sand, and mud. As the continent pushed its way west, successive layers of this material were plowed up on each other in massive wedges, or slabs. It was like taking a piece of hard, flat stone and pushing it along the top of a bed of mud. Eventually, the mud stacks up against the front of the stone and the constant pressure pushes the mud up and over the stone's leading edge. More pushing results in more mud on top of the stone, the newest mud always at the leading edge while the oldest mud is pushed further and further back on the stone. In the case of the subduction dynamic, the main action was always at the contact between the edge of North America and the top of the subducting Farallon Plate. As each new wedge became active, it pushed the older layers back inland, and they became inactive.

Wedge after wedge of material was scraped up off the subducting seafloor and pasted onto North America. But this was not the only way the continent grew westward. Sitting upon the subducting seafloor were plateaus, volcanic island arcs, and other assorted micro-bits of crust. As the Farallon Plate subducted beneath North America, it acted like a conveyor belt, delivering these previously offshore terranes to the collision zone. One after another they stacked up against the leading edge of the continent, mixing and mashing against the slabs of the accretionary wedge, building into mountainous islands and eventually land-locking the ancient sea that covered the Central Valley. These newly accreted terranes formed a patchwork of heterogeneous land against the relatively homogenous land of the interior. The origins of the terranes varied greatly, but ultimately they came from the west. They contributed to the formation of not only California but also much of Oregon, Washington, British Columbia, and Alaska.

Then the Farallon Plate was swallowed up. The Ancestral Sierran Arc volcanoes sputtered and stopped. The last of the accreted terranes of the west smashed up against the coastal country, shook, rumbled, and grew quiet. A final slab of the accretionary wedge was sliced off the top of the Farallon Plate before the plate disappeared into its offshore trench and slid under North America. Perhaps for just a blink of an eye in the life of the earth, the West was still.

At the tail end of the Farallon Plate, where it rose from some forgotten oceanic ridge, was the vast and foreign Pacific. It grew opposite the Farallon and spread its dark basaltic plain to the northwest, groping ever towards Alaska and distant Asia. As it joined North America and tucked under the exhausted leading edge of the continent, a new plate boundary was born. It was here that the Pacific Plate tucked itself under the leading edge of North America, grabbed hold, and pulled, and the San Andreas Fault system was born.

While this led to extensional faulting inland, at the coast the pull of the Pacific Plate was felt differently. Here was the actual plate boundary, the real hot seat for geological action. But the boundary did not appear neatly at the actual coastline. Instead it formed just inland and broke California in two. West of the San Andreas, the Pacific Plate, now including the Central Coast, Southern California, and Baja California, began sliding past North America on its north-westerly journey to Alaska. The movement of the Pacific Plate relative to North America averaged around 1.5 inches (3.8 cm) per year. Along the seam the pressure built up and the crust tore and shook in tremendous earthquakes. Thus the convergent boundary of North America and the Farallon Plate was replaced by the oblique lateral boundary of North America and the Pacific Plate.

As soon as the Pacific Plate butted up against North America, it began delivering new chunks of crust to California. These new pieces came from the southeast, riding the Pacific as it moved northwest. They came from as far south as the tropics, slowly but surely conveyed northwest at speeds measured in inches per year. Granites from the Sierra Nevada were pulled along fault systems as the southern tip of the great range bent around to the west, succumbing to the tug of the Pacific Plate. Eventually these chunks of granitic crust moved across the Garlock system and made it to the San Andreas. Once at the coast, they too began scooting northwest. A look at a physical map of the west coast of North America tells the story of what happened next. Eventually the central coast and pieces of southern California will tear away from the continent, looking much like Baja California does today.

The basement of Big Sur is made up of rocks from both before and after Pacific Plate contact. The older rocks of the accretionary wedge and associated accreted terranes form what geologists call the Nacimiento Block. This block is part of a larger formation of similarly formed rocks that extend all the way up the coast of California, called the Franciscan Complex. These rocks formed under high pressure and relatively low temperatures, which partially metamorphosed seafloor sediments, basalt, and material from the continent into blue schists, greenstones, and cherts. These rocks are typically crumbly and erode easily, forming relatively low-lying topography. In Big Sur, the Nacimiento Block is bound to the east by the prominent Sur-Nacimiento Fault, which parallels both the coast and the San Andreas system for 180 miles. The fault itself is believed to be reminiscent of the Farallon subduction zone—a crustal scar left as evidence of previous convulsions. The rocks of the Nacimiento Block form the basement of the Southern Santa Lucias, as well as the conspicuously low-lying coastal headlands around Lopez Point and the region of Pfeiffer and Cooper Points and Point Sur.

Sandwiched between the Sur-Nacimiento Fault and the San Andreas system to the east, the mountains rise steep and high. Here are the exotic terranes of the tropics and the Sierran granites. As an aggregate, they make up what geologists refer to as the Salinian Block. Many of these rocks were intensely metamorphosed under conditions of extreme heat but relatively low pressure (opposite conditions than the rocks of the Nacimiento Block), forming gneiss and marble. These metamorphics stacked up alongside mixed granitic rocks of Sierran and exotic origins, such as amphibolite, quartz diorite, tonalite, and granodiorite. These rocks, hard and resistant to erosion, form the rugged mountainous topography typical of the Santa Lucia Range.

Ever since their conception, the rocks of both the Nacimiento and Salinian Blocks have been continually covered with sediments as sea levels fluctuated, lands rose, and rivers ran over them. These relatively thin veneers of sandstones, shales, and conglomerates have since eroded off of the raised country and are best preserved in the valleys and folds of the range. They vary in age greatly, some bearing fossils from the old days of subduction, others laid down seventy million years later, just before the land rose up and out of the sea.

As the Pacific Plate slid past North America, the residual pressure between plates was just enough to squeeze out the land between. Stuck in the middle of two of the biggest plates on earth, the Santa Lucia gave way to the pressure and bent, folded, and broke, piling into a chaotic mess of coastal mountains. Around five million years ago the mountains reached their present height, and subsequent years have seen a continuing battle between uplift and the accelerated erosion that is the bane of all mountains. Will the Santa Lucias grow still higher, or wash away to the sea? For now they are subject to both fates at the same time, at once appearing youthful in their vigor and vulnerable in their haste.

EIGHT

Birds, Bees, Flowers, and Trees

Every spring Big Sur explodes with color and song. The rich, thick, green mantle of winter, nourished and encouraged by months of cool, fresh rain, gives birth to such a profusion of wildflowers as is seldom seen on the earth. Hundreds of thousands of brilliant orange poppies illuminate the grassy slopes, sometimes so thick the green of grass between them all but disappears. Shimmering, purple sky lupines sugarcoat hillsides with their buttery, honeylike scent. Blue dicks and blue-eyed grass make more subtle inroads into the open meadows. Elegant morning glories weave their way through coastal scrub, decorating the tiny, sweet-scented, purple flowers of California lilac and the orange-sherbet-colored trumpets of the sticky monkey-flower. Where the sage smells of the coastal scrub give way to the drier upland chaparral, our lord's candle sends up tall, lantern-like flower stalks from its succulent rosette of leaves, and astringent yerba santa graces the passerby with its purple funnel-form blossoms. Bright scarlet paintbrushes burst forth from between shrubby oaks, mountain mahogany, and manzanita ornamented with thousands of sweet, tiny white and pink urns. Beneath the canopy of oaks, pines, maples,

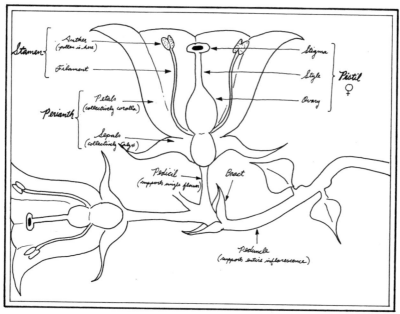

Stamen:
- Anther (pollen is here)
- Filament

Pistil ♀
- Stigma
- Style
- Ovary

Perianth:
- Petals (collectively corolla)
- Sepals (collectively calyx)

Pedicel (supports single flower)

Bract

Peduncle (supports entire inflorescence)

A Flower

madrones, and bays, the purple-streaked petals of the Douglas iris unfold from its lanceolate leaves, as white, pea-shaped, nectar-filled madrone flowers fall from above and litter the ground. Still deeper in the forest, in the dim light beneath the towering redwoods, secretive trilliums open their buds, followed by star flowers and pink-striped redwood sorrel. Nearby, the streamsides are blessed with nodding crimson columbines and waxy orange lilies. Everywhere the Big Sur country is electrified with vibrant hues and intoxicating aromas.

The intensity of color is only matched by that of song, as innumerable birds chime in for the dawn chorus. From the deepest branches of sprawling oaks, tiny house wrens throw back their heads and chattery cascades of notes pour out, prolific in length, volume, and frequency. Each time a cadence comes to its end, the house wren closes its beak, wide-eyed, in seeming disbelief of what just issued forth from its little self. Then the next inspiration arrives, bubbles up from its tiny throat, and bursts out. The house wrens are accompanied by vireos, warblers, tanagers, towhees, and grosbeaks as the woodland and chaparral communities express spring through sound. They awaken early, when the cool air still hangs low and calm and sound is not disturbed by the shifting winds that follow sunrise. They sing from four-thirty until the first yellow shafts of morning sun make it over the crest of the ridge, each bird species having its own special time to rise up in particularly boisterous song. On cloudy mornings and even during light rains, they sing right through sunrise and into the day, and the dawn chorus can last for many hours.

They come from the lowlands. They come from the south, from the tropics of Central and South America. They come from far and wide and converge on the Big Sur country. Not because of its wondrous views or fresh ocean air, nor for the sunny days of spring or the cool late rains. They come for a much more simple reason. They come for food. Every spring, as the buds of poppies and lupines burgeon and break open, so do the hundreds of millions of eggs of countless species of insects. They swarm the place, fevered with spring and the promise it brings. Butterflies and moths, beetles, flies and mosquitoes, bees, wasps, and ants, dragonflies and damselflies all take to the air and earth in search of the rich abundance of the season of rebirth. Drunk on nectar, they fall prey to the larger winged hunters, and the birds gorge themselves and their hungry young on the fat six-leggeds. The insects come for the flowers. The birds come for the insects.

I sit on the grasses of Boronda Ridge in the Landels-Hill Big Creek Reserve, surrounded by a dozen eager faces, a spray of impossibly orange poppies before us. Four straight days of rain have kept us tentbound for too many precious hours of too many spring days; as I look at the circle of faces around me, they seem to be glowing in the warm sun, full of bliss just to be alive and on this flower-spattered grassy slope overlooking the wide Pacific. I begin class with what I hope to be a profound statement: "If not for flowers, we would never have been." Then I begin to tell a story.

The tale begins three and a half billion years ago with the origin of life, prokaryotic unicellular heterotrophic bacteria, living off of dead organic matter and half-realized amino acid chains. It continues with primordial dinoflagellates ingesting but not digesting autotrophic cyanobacteria, eventually giving rise to some of the first eukaryotes, cells with their genetic material tucked into a nuclear envelope. This ingestion of cyanobacteria led to the development of chloroplasts, which would allow autotrophs to not only produce their own food but actually store it. Soon primitive algae made the great leap from unicellular to multicellular and diversified into the red, brown, and green algae of today. The story goes on.

Next algae left in dried-up pools and along intertidal zones developed strategies to live on land, and the first true plants sprouted in the dry and bright terrestrial sun. In time they developed vascular systems and grew upward, taking advantage of vertical niches for the first time. Eventually the gamble of multigenerational spore-based reproduction was phased out in favor of pre-fertilization among parent plants, and the first seed plants spread their larder across the ground. As some of these seed-producing plants became increasingly dependent on animals to disperse their seeds, they developed tasty dressings around their previously naked seeds. These dressings were often fleshy, fruity, or nutty, undoubtedly tempting for the animal passerby. But not only did these new plants seduce animals for the purpose of seed dispersal, they also sought to lure them in for pollination. While the naked-seeded plants depended on the wind for this essential step in their reproductive cycle, the dressed-seeded plants sought a more reliable, predictable pollination method. Their leaves evolved into brightly colored petals, nectar-filled pistils, and pollen-tipped stamens. They developed stripes and spots to guide winged pollinators to their sweet prize. Flowers bloomed across the world.

We bend over the shining corollas of the poppies, using fine-tipped tools to separate the delicate, intricate inner workings of the flowers, examining reproductive parts closely with hand lenses and even a six-inch-diameter steel-rimmed magnifying glass. Our heads are all so close together that we speak in hushed tones as we inspect the stigma, style, and ovary of the pistil, and the filaments and anthers of the stamens. We discuss the botanical terms used to describe flowers, words like "perfect and imperfect," "regular and irregular," "superior and inferior," all unabashedly biased in our cult worship of flowers. Questions begin to roll off of people's tongues like biological music to my ears. Where do flowers come from? Why are they so colorful? Why do they smell so good? How does pollination work?

It was the zenith of the age of reptiles, the end of the Mesozoic Era, when the thunder lizards had attained their greatest array of diversity. The post-Pangea spread of continents arranged themselves neatly around the equatorial regions, and warm rains poured down across the land. Atmospheric carbon dioxide levels are believed to have been slightly higher than today, and the overall productivity of the earth was unprecedented. A thick, juicy mantle of tropical and subtropical vegetation cloaked the land. In this rich, fertile time, those wind-pollinated, naked-seeded gymnosperms that developed specialized relationships with animal pollinators and seed dispersal agents were favored by natural selection. Their male and female parts developed ornate decorations and food incentives to lure animal pollinators in, and their seeds developed sumptuous fruit around them. The animals came, and the plants prospered, passing these successful new traits on to subsequent generations. Flowers opened up in all corners of the continents, broadcasting their success through bright colors and sweet aromas.

For hundreds of millions of years the spore-producing plants had been sending out trillions of spores and losing the vast majority of them to the elements. This worked because of the sheer numbers of spores that were produced, and the relatively small amount of energy investment put into the production of each spore. Nevertheless, success rates were low and reproduction was far from guaranteed. There was also little insurance of cross-fertilization, and many plants ended up self-fertilizing instead. Sexual reproduction, involving the fusion of gametes and the exchange of genetic material, improved in leaps and bounds with the development of seed-producing plants. Seeds, although also capable of being self-pollinated, were at least pre-fertilized and then dispersed, by wind or animals, far away from their parent tree. The evolution of flowering plants brought with it additional insurance against self-pollination, by guaranteeing that specific pollinators that would personally carry pollen from plant to plant. Plants also developed other strategies to prevent self-pollination, such as not opening their pistils at times when they are producing pollen, and staggering their time of bloom so that genetically related individuals bloom at different times. This greatly increased the genetic diversity of flowering plants, thereby increasing the genetic variation in populations and allowing them to evolve quickly into a multitude of forms. Unfavorable recessive genes that subjected plants to disease or weakened them in other ways were more easily phased out, and diverse, healthy, adaptable populations resulted. Pollinators insured this.

Flowers offered nectar as a lure for pollinators. This incredible concoction consisted primarily of fructose sugars and water but also included amino acids and proteins, organic acids, phosphates, vitamins, and enzymes. Certain flowers, such as orchids, even developed bonus ingredients to intoxicate their animal dependents. As the sweet aroma of nectar filled the Cretaceous air, small, able animals were drawn to the flowers. Insects had been around in small numbers since the Paleozoic Era, but they did not diversify until they found flowers. Perfect for the job of pollination, insects soon developed specialized relationships with flowers. As insects buzzed about in search of nectar, they rubbed up against pollen-tipped stamens, and as they reached deep into the pistils of neighboring flowers for their precious sugar water, they inadvertently deposited some of the pollen into the tubular pistils. Pollen grains that made it down into the ovary of the flower fertilized the ovary, and fruit and seed began to grow. The pollen of the angiosperms, unlike the powdery stuff of their gymnosperm predecessors, was sticky, and it became stickier with the years as stickiness proved successful. A look at such pollen under a microscope reveals its secrets. It is not round like a ball at all. It looks rather like a star or a spiky burr, the tips of which eagerly latch onto any textured surface.

Nectar was not the only lure for pollinators. Flowers developed increasingly colorful and decorative parts as advertisements for their tasty prize. Petals evolved and diversified into the oranges, yellows, blues, reds, purples, and whites that bring spring to such life as we know today. But simple color was not all that evolved. Many flowers developed specialized markings, spots or stripes to act as landing guides for certain insects. Flowers even developed ways to communicate whether or not their nectar reservoirs had already been tapped, by either changing color or dropping their petals entirely. With time, exclusive relationships developed and particular groups of flowers and insects became codependent on one another for pollination and food. With such reliable insurance of pollination for flowers, and a steady food source for animal pollinators, both types of organisms were extremely successful. This was symbiotic mutualism at its best; both flowers and animals benefited at the expense of neither. It was a coevolutionary launchpad. Over time, the flowering plants, the angiosperms, swept across the land, displacing tree ferns and gymnosperms along the way. Insects diversified and specialized into the beetles and bugs, butterflies and moths, mosquitoes and flies, and bees, wasps, and ants we know today.

The diversity of flowers on earth reflects the diversity of pollinators, and vice versa. Some remarkable relationships have resulted from over a hundred and thirty million years of coevolutionary specialization. Through investigating the color, size, shape, odor, time of bloom, and texture of its pollen, a keen observer can tell much about a flower and its animal dependents. Bees, for example, do not see reds. The flowers bees visit tend to be blue, purple, white, or yellow. Because bees can hover in place, the size of bee-pollinated flowers can be variable, though most often their shape is open (except in the case of lupines, which bees love!). Bees are attracted to mild, sweet odors. Pollen, often the primary lure for bees, and a necessary element in the building of hives and the manufacture of honey, must be sticky. As bees are most active in the day, bee-flowers are most often diurnal bloomers. Yellow composites are classic bee-pollinated flowers.

Butterflies and moths look for different floral features. Color and size are of less importance than shape: the retractable proboscis of the lepidopteran species allows them to access specialized tubular and funnel-form flowers, such as phloxes, that other pollinators can't get into. As nectar is the primary objective of butterflies and moths, these flowers are overwhelmingly sweet. Their pollen, like that of all animal-pollinated flowers, is sticky. While butterfly-pollinated flowers bloom by day, moth-pollinated flowers bloom by night. Some flowers take advantage of both types of lepidopterans and stay open around the clock. Beetles and bugs, often carrion feeders, seek large, open, brown, green, and purplish flowers that smell musky or rotten, such as wild ginger or fritillary. Mosquitoes and flies, being opportunists, will take just about anything they can get.

Insects are not the only animal pollinators of flowers. No one can ignore the whirring of hummingbirds and the bright ruby flash of a gorget as a male bird dives, screeching, and hovers in place. Hummers are drawn almost magnetically to red. Hummingbird lovers know this and have been known to wear red hats or even red climbing helmets to allow for up-close inspection of these quick, tiny creatures. With their long, slender bills, hummingbirds can access all but the tightest tubes in their search for nectar. They most often favor flowers that are tubular or funnel-form, horizontally oriented, sweet smelling, and any shade of red, orange, or purple.

The only intentional mammalian pollinators are bats. While other mammals certainly contribute to pollination by rubbing up against flowers and moving pollen around, some bats actually feed on nectar. Being among the largest pollinators, bats require large, often funnel-form flowers with sweet, musky odors. As bats are primarily nocturnal and rely more on echolocation than sharp-sightedness, bat-pollinated flowers bloom at night and are typically white or pale cream in color.

Other flowering plants appear not to produce flowers at all. Their flowers include only the bare essentials, pollen-laden stamens and empty pistils, all positioned for maximum exposure to the wind. Because these plants, which include grasses, sedges, and rushes as well as oaks, maples, and many others, are wind pollinated, they have no use for showy petals and energy-intensive nectar.

With flowers came new food sources to the world. First was nectar, the preferred energy source for so many small winged animals with high metabolic rates. Insects diversified and increased dramatically in numbers, themselves providing a new and abundant food source for animals higher up on the food chain. The development of fruit also made the energy of plant productivity available to more animals. Such large, concentrated energy packages as fruit had never before been available on earth. The development of these readily available calorie concentrates had far-reaching implications because they contributed greatly to the widespread development of warm-blooded animals, such as birds and mammals. Flowers diversified. Insects diversified. Dinosaurs found sweet magnolias mixed in with their green fodder, and themselves diversified into more new and different forms. Birds and mammals flourished on insects and fruit and themselves blossomed into new and different forms. Human beings were still only a remote possibility, but a growing one. The great tree of life grew and branched ever more, and greater levels of complexity, activity, and intelligence grew at the tips of these branches.

MY STUDENTS AND I ARE mesmerized by flowers for hours, crouched intently around their graceful corollas in an attitude of reverence and genuine curiosity. Besides the fiery poppies, fields of sky lupines nearby beckon us over for a visit. We marvel at the complexities of their banners, wings, and keels and their hidden sexual parts only to be revealed by certain pollinators. Blue-eyed grass and blue dicks introduce us to the monocots, with slender, parallel-veined leaves, root bulbs, and flower parts in multiples of three. As dusk falls, we collect our hand lenses, field guides, water bottles, and abandoned sandals and jackets, and head through the mixed woodland back to camp. Enthusiastic talk of flowers continues, some poetic, some scientific, some esoteric, as we prepare and eat supper. Night falls on the fields and woods.

As insects and flowers experienced their coevolutionary orgy and birds and mammals found food to sustain their rapid metabolisms, dinosaurs, though more diverse and greater in number than ever before, were approaching the end of their dominion. The high peaks of the Ancestral Sierran Arc volcanoes were quickly washing away in a slurry of equatorial rainwater. The Atlantic seafloor spreading had increased and North America was moving westward faster than ever. Deep beneath the surface of the continent, the Farallon Plate slid between the underside of North America and the semi-molten asthenosphere, scooting eastward against the grain of the overriding continent. The Rocky Mountains began rising in contorted protest. The Colorado Plateau began to bow upwards. Then catastrophe struck, and somehow the world went cold and dark. Life withered, froze, starved, and died.

Any living thing incapable of coping with a prolonged period of cold and darkness perished in the great Cretaceous extinction. On land, the recently evolved flowering plants experienced massive die-offs, along with their more primitive relatives, the gymnosperms and ferns. Overall plant productivity fell sharply, cutting the base of the food pyramid drastically and causing extinctions all the way up to the top. Dinosaurs and their winged counterparts, the pterosaurs, at the apex of the food pyramid, suffered the far-reaching effects of the Cretaceous event the most. Unable to secure the massive stock of resources necessary to sustain their large bodies, and unable to produce their own body heat, the largest perished first, toppling like fallen kings to the cold, dusty earth. Not even the smallest of the dinosaurs made the Cretaceous cut. Not one group of the thunder lizards caught so much as a glimpse of the Cenozoic Era to come. Other reptiles fared better, particularly those of small size who could hibernate for long periods of time. Lizards, snakes, and most amphibians were relatively unaffected. Somehow turtles and crocodilians made it through. The mammals of the Cretaceous Period were all small in size and had the added security of being able to produce their own body heat as the global temperatures became erratic. Although their warm-bloodedness required that they eat more to sustain their body temperature, they were small enough and thus their needs meager enough that they made it through the event relatively unscathed, though the marsupials suffered more loss of species than the newly evolved placental mammals. Birds, with their recently developed capacity for flight, were most easily able to find new and ephemeral sources of food. Like mammals, they were warm-blooded and able to survive cold periods. Although we know little of them from the fossil record, it seems as though they made it through the Cretaceous extinction with little catastrophe.

In the sea, the effects of the Cretaceous event were felt even more. The tropical groups suffered the greatest, unable to adapt to the changing climatic conditions. As on land, the extinction of planktonic organisms at the base of the food pyramid caused the mass extinction of hundreds of species higher up. Brachiopods, mollusks, echinoids, fish, and ammonites all suffered. As the web of life collapsed, the higher reptilian predators disappeared.

Paleontologists, geologists, meteorologists, ecologists, oceanographers, biologists, zoologists, and astronomers, not to mention poets, philosophers, and pop science fanatics, have seldom gathered their efforts together as they have in the attempt to discover what was behind the great Cretaceous extinction. The fossil record shows two things plainly. Most obvious is the profound disappearance of so many species of life. Less obvious are the high concentrations of iridium, rare in rocks of the crust but not uncommon in deep volcanic rocks and meteorites. Once these deposits were recognized, geologists found them all over the world, in clear abundance along the boundary between the Cretaceous Period, when the Mesozoic Era ended, and the Tertiary Period, when the Cenozoic Era began. The coincidence seemed uncanny. Little doubt remained that either profound volcanic activity or the sudden impact of a massive meteorite contributed to the Cretaceous extinction, creating huge clouds of atmospheric dust and blotting out the sun. But such a catastrophic event was not the only indication of worldwide changes. Studies have shown that ocean waters had begun cooling as much as two hundred thousand years before the alleged volcanic and/or meteoritic event. Sea levels were also on the decline, and inland seas across the globe were drying up.

To this day, there is no certain explanation for the Cretaceous extinction. While some scientists look for ancient meteor craters in the Yucatan, others are discovering evidence of huge-scale volcanic activity associated with the Indian subcontinent's migration across hot spots in the Indian Ocean. The answers to big questions are rarely simple. But the results of big events are often decisive.

AS MY STUDENTS DRIFT OFF to their tents, I gather my sleeping bag and pad and head out for a starlit bivouac on the open ridge. The thought of waking to fields of flowers and the distant deep blue of the ocean easily draws me away from our camp. I listen to the rhythmic sounds of the night insects as I nestle into the drying

grasses and inhale the fresh scent of evening dew. I pick out con-
stellations and invent my own as the earth slowly spins beneath
the wide ceiling of stars. My mind turns to simple thoughts. It is
early April. I am in Big Sur. Down there is the Pacific Ocean. I
am on the surface of a boiling planet. The planet is spinning at a
thousand miles an hour. How come there is no wind? I am being
recklessly hurled around a massive nuclear reactor, the sun, and the
whole solar system is hurling around in the spiral arm of a galaxy
named for the simple necessity of mother's milk. Is the galaxy being
hurled around the center of the universe? There is no center of the
universe. Everything is the center at the same time.

A shriek arises from the woods. It sounds like bloody murder. I
have only heard that shriek a few times in my life, and every time, it
sends an eerie chill up my spine. I can feel my hair stand up on end.
I know what it means. In the woods somewhere nearby, one of the
most highly evolved predators in the world is making its kill. A mix
of awe and fear sweeps over me. My stomach sickens. It is only a few
tens of yards away. Does it know I am here? If I stir too much, will
it come looking for me? I am trapped in my sleeping bag, alive but
wrapped up like a mummy. A mummy. Living dead. I feel a sense of
helpless dread. I know what is coming.

As if summoned by my fear, a black silhouette emerges from the
woods and walks directly towards me. It moves without a sound,
sliding through the thick, dark air of night with grace and ease, like
living ink. A long tail flickers behind its svelte form, the only indication that it too might be nervous. Or maybe it is just sensing my fear
with that tail. Does it know I am scared? Is it aware of how absolutely
vulnerable I am? What is it thinking? I can hardly breathe. A mountain lion stands twenty feet away from me.

Of all the terrestrial creatures in the world, few inspire such archetypal awe and fear as the big cats. Few other mammalian predators
are so decidedly carnivorous. While bears, foxes, dogs, and even
wolves mix their bloody meals with grubs, berries, and other vegetable matter, the cats eat only one thing: flesh. And they like it
tender and juicy, the fresher the better. They are well equipped to
exploit this precious, limited resource. Their weaponry exceeds that

of all other terrestrial mammals. A quick look at a cat skull tells a simple story. True molars, those teeth used for grinding vegetable matter, are absent. Their incisors, those teeth used for snipping vegetation, are tiny. But their carnassials and canines, those scissorlike and spikelike teeth used for slicing, ripping, and tearing flesh, are huge and especially highly developed. Their claws are like those of no other mammals. These hooked devices retract into cartilaginous sheaths, protecting them from everyday wear and tear, keeping them dangerously sharp for when it counts. As most people can attest, even the smallest housecat is capable of thrashing out a mess of blood with those claws if it is provoked. I've seen a hundred-pound dog flee in terror from the prickly batting of a relatively tiny domestic feline.

I grew up with cats. After thirty years of observing their stealthy moves, I have developed a considerable amount of respect for these ultimate hunters. Several felines I've employed for mousing have threatened to decimate songbird populations in the vicinity of my cabin. I have repeatedly installed warning bells on my cats to prevent such carnage, but it's only ever a matter of days until a cat figures out how to stalk with the bell on, and not a single jingle is ever heard again. It weaves its way through the bushes, slinking along noiselessly. When within range, it stops completely, crouched low amidst the vegetative cover. Spying its unwary prey, it lowers its head intently, and its hips begin to sway ever so slightly back and forth. Then it pounces. I watched one of my cats clear a distance of eight feet in a single bound. It knocked its prey senseless, simultaneously breaking the unsuspecting victim's neck. My cat emerged from the shrubs with a juvenile white-crowned sparrow in its bloodied maw. A practiced adult will almost always emerge with a prize.

Cats didn't evolve overnight. They are the product of many tens of millions of years of mammalian evolution. Mammals first evolved from primitive synapsids, the mammal-like reptiles that roamed the earth two hundred and fifty million years ago, during the late Paleozoic Era, and included such groups as the fin-backed *Dimetrodon*. The synapsids developed several mammalian characteristics that they would eventually pass on to their successors. Unlike reptiles, they had specialized teeth, which would eventually develop into the incisors, canines, carnassials, premolars, and molars of modern mammals. Their skulls also underwent changes, culminating in the mammalian development of a singular jawbone to which strong chewing muscles could attach. Fossil evidence suggests that some of the synapsids may have had hair and may have even been warm-blooded. By the Tertiary Period, the archosaurs, of which the dinosaurs are most famous, displaced the synapsids and began their long dominion over the world. Far from an evolutionary dead end, the synapsid lineage evolved into small, subtle, opportunistic mammals that could make a decent living in the ecological shadow of the dinosaurs.

After the Cretaceous extinction, when the atmospheric dust cleared and the carcasses of the dinosaurs decomposed into the bowels of the earth, the small marsupials, similar to today's opossums, and placental mammals, similar to today's shrews, crept out of their holes and emerged to a bright and empty world. With the dinosaurs gone, the mammals explosively radiated into the realm of the thunder lizards, growing to huge body proportions and filling every available niche. The recently evolved placental mammals fared better in the new world than their more primitive cousins, the marsupials, and except for places like Australia and perhaps Antarctica, which separated from the other continents before the development of placental mammals, the marsupials were largely displaced. The ecological release was profound. In just fifteen million years, from the beginning of the Cenozoic Era into the Eocene Epoch, mammals evolved into such diverse modern forms as whales, bats, carnivores, primates, rodents, and rabbits and grew to the size of today's African elephants. Here was evolution's answer to the Cretaceous extinction.

The primitive carnivores that stalked the continents of the Eocene Epoch eventually gave rise to the bears, raccoons, ringtails, weasels, dogs, and cats of today. Among these groups, cats are unique in that nearly all members of the family Felidae are morphologically identical. Aside from color and size, all cats, with the notable exception of cheetahs, look the same. *Felis concolor*, the dreaded predator of North America, known in different parts of the continent as the mountain lion, panther, puma, catamount, and cougar, is essentially a housecat of epic proportions, with all the expertise, temper, and violent capabilities of its smaller domestic counterpart.

Felis concolor once roamed the continent far and wide, far up into northwestern Canada, across all of the United States, through Mexico, and deep into South America. Today it is all but gone from most of its original territory. Humans have not only hunted *Felis concolor* outright but have also hacked its food base out from under it by destroying and fragmenting its territory. Agriculture replaces wild plant food and steals from the hoofed mammals, cutting their populations to mere fractions of what they were in the past. Those populations that do remain are stressed for space and food and show up in backyards or dead on highways as humans further encroach upon their habitat. *Felis concolor*, at the top of the food chain, feels the pressure of human expansion a hundredfold. Perhaps unwilling to compromise their undeniable dignity, they slip into the shadows of night. The sight of a mountain lion in the wild is so rare that one in a lifetime is worth writing about.

Big Sur is one of those uncommon places in the world where mountain lions seem to be everywhere. Black-tailed mule deer, the preferred food of the mountain lion, are plentiful throughout the Santa Lucias and provide a food base substantial enough for a large population of predators. In the Landels-Hill Big Creek Reserve, along certain trails I've seen lion scratchings in the forest litter every hundred yards. Cat scat is almost as common. Historically, homesteaders trying to make a living in this rugged country killed off cats by the dozens. Arbeus Boronda, a homesteader around Big Creek in the early 1900s, killed up to fifty mountain lions in a single year. Although their numbers have been greatly reduced by hunting, the mountain lions enjoy a high degree of protection in the Landels-Hill reserve, which is buffered from any kind of development by the Ventana Wilderness, and further by the Los Padres National Forest. Researchers working in the reserve set up tripwire-triggered cameras in the night and post dozens of photographs of surprised-looking mountain lions on their cabin walls. John Smiley, the reserve manager, doesn't let his kids out of the house at night.

I lie there paralyzed. *Felis concolor* just sits and stares at me. I want desperately to move, but I'm afraid of what *Felis* might do. Besides, as I lie on my stomach, my arms have fallen asleep folded beneath my chest. I can barely even move my fingers. My shoulders feel like stumps with lifeless appendages hanging from them. Minutes feel like hours. I know I have to stand up or roll over if I want to regain the use of my arms. I wonder what *Felis* thinks of me. I am sweating.

I muster my courage and roll onto my side, then quickly roll back onto my knees and come up to a kneel. *Felis* is gone. My arms grow hot and start to tingle. Ten feet to my left the meadow ends and abruptly gives way to thick shrubs. *Felis* is in there somewhere. I listen intently and can't hear a thing except my own labored breath. I can feel my pulse in my fingers. I free my arms from my sleeping bag and begin feeling around for my headlamp, keeping both my eyes fixed on the shrubs. *Felis concolor* almost always takes its prey from behind. I'm not going to give it that chance. Unsure of what to do, I follow my instincts. With my headlamp shining on my head, I unzip my sleeping bag and stand up with it wrapped around my body like a cloak. I start singing loudly and flapping my arms around, trying to make myself look big and fearsome. Without diverting my eyes from the shrubs, and without stopping singing, I stoop down and grab my pack and my pad and begin waving them around too. Anyone watching would think I've gone mad.

I walk slowly across the meadow, past the shrub hedge, singing and flapping my arms along the way. Between me and camp is the wooded thicket *Felis* came out of earlier, and to get to my class I have to walk through it. The faint silver light of the stars fades to inky black shadows as I pass through the boughs of trees. *Felis* could be anywhere. I am as helpless and vulnerable as I was on the day I was born. After a few tens of yards I emerge from the thicket to a small grassy clearing fringed by a few manzanita bushes. Below me, down a small hill, just thirty yards away, is my class. They are all nestled into their sleeping bags, a few in tents but most sleeping out under the stars in a loose group. The thought of them all so near is comforting. For some reason I think I am close enough that *Felis* will leave me alone. I set down my pad and sleeping bag and begin to settle in. Within minutes, I sense something in the thicket. I turn to look, and the dying yellow light of my headlamp illuminates two large, green eyes. *Felis* is out there. Whether it is stalking me or returning to its

NINE

Pleistocene Passion

Shasta. Snowing again. Tentbound. September storms unload nearly a foot of wet snow on us, pasting tent flies to tent walls, the snow sliding down steep nylon and piling into heaps in the critical space between the ground and the bottom of the fly. I awaken to moist and sticky warm air and beat my gloved hand against the sagging tent. Snow reluctantly lets go of its purchase and slides to the ground. I carefully unzip the back door and stand up, blinking in the indigo of night, snowflakes the size of my thumb falling like feathers onto my waiting eyelashes. I relieve myself. Crouching back inside of the tent, I become disturbingly aware of the reek of the confined air. It has been snowing like this for the last five days.

Beside me, my co-instructor David Lovejoy and our teaching assistant Mike Spayd sleep soundly. I say soundly because they both make sounds. Mike's ruckus approximates the sound of a small sawmill operation. David's resembles some huge, low-groaning, gurgling mammal in deep hibernation. After five days I've grown used to it. I get horizontal and somehow tune out the cacophony. Sleep eventually returns.

A Glacial Landscape — ADAPTED FROM GRAYDON 1992

We awaken to a window in the weather. We rally our students and set out to explore California's longest and most respectable glacier. Once roused and our bellies full of hot coffee, we walk out onto the new snow, through shafts of sunlight that seem enthusiastically to penetrate the gray cloudscape smudged across the day sky. We leave our camp, just below the Bolum Glacier on the north flank of Mount Shasta, and traverse across ice-cored morainal material and onto snowfields deeply sun-cupped by the long months of summer. We crunch our way across glasslike lenses of firn spiegel, traveling north and east, up and over the jumbled mess of ridge, volcanic debris, and moraine that separates the Bolum Glacier from the body of ice we are looking for. Sweating up alternating sections of snow and rock, we keep our heads up and our eyes to the northeast, hoping for a view of the glacier to come. Low-lying clouds have found their way into the next drainage and they swirl there like spirits. We can only speculate what the ice underneath looks like.

We pick our way down the piles of rock and snow, bent on arriving atop the next heaped moraine, which must border the glacier. Down and back up the moraine, we gather together on its loosely consolidated top. The swimming whiteness before us tears open, and tails of clouds look like tattered gauze adrift on the wind. In between, blurry black stripes and broken blocks of blue ice emerge and slowly sharpen into focus. At first we can only see parts, fleeting glimpses of the larger glacier at hand. Gradually the clouds part and reveal the full length and girth of the Whitney Glacier. It pours off of the north side of the Shasta, dropping into a confined notch bound on either side by deep brown cliffs, just below the Shasta-Shastina saddle. It swells out of this restricted place with all the violence of a flash flood frozen into ice.

The glacier before us looks like the aftermath of a hundred train wrecks. Blocks of ice the size of boxcars are stacked atop one another, crumpled and bent, broken and cracked, folded and sandwiched as the momentum of millions of tons of ice tries to squeeze through and flow over the underlying topography. As this contorted mess carves its way across the rock of the mountain, it undermines the cliffs on either side, sending tons of broken rock trundling down the increasingly steepening slopes and onto the moving surface of the ice.

People call glaciers rivers of ice. Yes, they follow predetermined drainages and often behave much like their liquid counterparts, but there is little suggestion of the liquidity of fluvial motion as we look out at the groaning surface of the Whitney Glacier, none of the gentle, tranquil nature of water. This is no river, be it a whitewater river or not, and calling it a river of ice would make about as much sense as calling a river a glacier of water.

A short but technical definition of "glacier" reads something like this: "a moving body of ice of terrestrial origin, formed by compaction and recrystallization of snow." This concise definition points out the structure of a glacier (snow and ice), the process by which it is formed (compaction and recrystallization), and how it functions within the greater landscape (by movement). All of these criteria are met by snowfields except for movement. A true glacier, unlike a snowfield, is a dynamic, moving body of "living ice." The creation of such a body of ice requires two things: cold and precipitation. Enough cold that the bulk of the precipitation falls as snow and the resulting ice stays frozen, and enough precipitation in the form of snow to exceed melt-off.

During the Pleistocene Epoch, both the Cascades and the Sierra Nevada were situated perfectly for heavy glaciation. They were close enough to the ocean to get plenty of precipitation and high enough in elevation to have cold temperatures. In the cold, stormy climate of the Pleistocene, larger glaciers grew along the Sierra-Cascade axis than in any other area of similar latitude in the continent. The Coast Ranges, in comparison, held relatively few glaciers. They had plenty of precipitation but lacked cold temperatures, due to their maritime position and relatively low elevation. The Basin ranges to the east also held few glaciers. Here there was plenty of cold but not enough precipitation, due to the rain-shadow effect of the Sierra-Cascade axis.

We organize ourselves into two roped teams of five, tie into evenly spaced butterfly knots, step into our crampons, and walk out onto the ice. Once on the glacier, we move like two snakes, one after the other, twining our way through gaping crevasses. Ahead and above us, the glacier bends over an undulation in the bedrock topography. But the drop is too steep for the glacier, and the upper, brittle ice is not plastic enough to stretch over the fall. Instead it is cracked and broken, like a dry scab on a bent elbow, like a Slinky going downstairs. It is broken into towering blocks of cold, hard ice, looming above us, monstrous, drawn with swirling foliation lines in all shades of white, gray, black, and blue. Dirt covers the blocks in patches, shadowing portions of their angular form. These have fallen down the drop one after the other as the glacier has slid its way downslope over time, the blocks themselves migrating in crashing succession, piling into hundreds of stacked, tilted, smashed seracs on the surface of the glacier below. Some have fallen headfirst into open crevasses, filling the blue void with black-streaked broken blocks crammed awkwardly between the frozen walls.

There seems to be more open space on the surface of the glacier than there is closed, more yawning crevasses than there is solid ice. We continue upward, against the flow, making our way across a body of living ice on which every apparent feature evidences the fact that gravity is pulling the glacier off of the mountain. The only thing that keeps it up here is the dozens of feet of new snow that fall on Shasta every year, feeding the glacier at its upper end as gravity tugs at it and its lower end melts into oblivion. The whole glacier is experiencing a continual migration downslope. As with all glaciers, the rate of movement constantly changes with the slope angle, with the temperature of both the air and the ice, and with the bedrock topography and structure of the underlying landscape. Typically, mountain glaciers like the Whitney flow at a rate varying from ten to a thousand feet per year, translating roughly from a fraction of an inch to several feet per day. Movement is usually slow and gradual, especially in large polar glaciers, but in summer months temperate and equatorial mountain glaciers can move perceptibly in an hour's time and occasionally surge, flowing up to a hundred feet per day. Surges, often a response to climatic fluctuations, were likely frequent in the Cascades and the Sierra Nevada during the Pleistocene. They are best documented today among the glaciers of coastal Alaska and the European Alps, where surging Alaskan tidewater ice has been known to create epic sea waves, and rapidly advancing valley Alpine glaciers have taken out entire villages. The small glaciers found in California also reflect climatic fluctuations and are even more sensitive to minute changes, due to their small size. They may advance in some years, while in others they may recede, or experience no movement either way. Here, even just a few years of the wrong conditions can turn a living glacier into a stagnant snowfield.

Glaciers, like rivers, move faster towards their middles and relatively slow along their sides. They are also like rivers in that their velocity varies with depth, and as a glacier flows over a knob in its bed, it must accelerate and thin, just as river water accelerates and becomes more shallow as it flows over a boulder. The deeper, metamorphic ice, at depths of greater than a hundred and fifty feet, responds to this by either elastic or plastic deformation, essentially stretching around the obstruction. But the upper ice has much less pressure on it and is brittle. Here the ice cracks, forming deep crevasses in the surface of the glacier. These crevasses can exceed a hundred feet in depth, though the crevasses of small California glaciers are rarely so deep. For most of the year the yawning crevasses of all glaciers are covered with snow. Woe to the mountaineer who is unwary of such things.

As we weave our way towards the middle of the glacier we spot several boulders two meters in girth, perched like erect mushroom heads atop three-foot-high stems of blue ice. They are table rocks. If they were significantly smaller, the effect would be opposite. Being darker than the snow surface, they would absorb more insolation than the snow itself, heat up, and sink into the ice like hot chips in ice cream, creating the deep pockmarks typical of late-season glacier surfaces. But these boulders are too big. Not only do they shade the snow but they are so thick that they actually insulate it from the heat of the sun. As the surface of the glacier melts differentially, these rocks are left standing on pillars of ice.

As the day waxes into late afternoon, we begin to wind our way back the way we came. On our way back to the moraine, we edge out onto a narrow peninsula of ice that separates two of the deepest, widest crevasses I have ever seen. We stay roped together and file out onto the peninsula, forming a straight line along its upslope edge. We all lie down on our bellies, wriggle to the lip, and peer down into the abyss.

The crack is several hundred feet in length and forty to fifty feet wide. It is so choked with fallen seracs and ice debris that I can discern no bottom. Some of the blocks of ice in the bowels of the crevasse must be sixty feet down. I look up at the back wall of the crevasse and read the complex story of the movements of this metamorphic ice. The top layers are horizontal, representative of successive snow years. Excepting their whiteness, they look just like the sedimentary layers of the Grand Canyon. Below these even top layers are more lines, metamorphic foliations in the glacial ice, more complex the deeper they occur. These lines are drawn inward from the lateral moraine at the edge of the glacier, then sink near the crevasse into a deep synclinal fold. It appears that the plastically flowing ice at some time sunk into the gap of some ancient crevasse, and it still bears the script of such a story. Even deeper down are graceful layers of flowing, folded ice interspersed with neat calligraphic bands of black debris, both synclinal and anticlinal—evidence of hundreds of years of undecipherable action. Still deeper, a giant fallen serac protrudes from the abyss—a cryptic standing stone of silent ice.

The glaciers of Shasta hint at the expanse of ice that once covered much of the mountain country of California. Now what is left of the mountain glaciers of the world teeters on the edge of oblivion. Winter snows are fewer and summer warmth greater. The ice gives itself back to the sea. In the heart of the Sierra Nevada I found myself haunted by a sense of biological longing for the ice. Small cumulus clouds advanced in rows, distilled from a distant salty sea, borne on chapping winds curling around the high brows of the mountains. Once, twice the white aggregates of moisture droplets tore open and apart and spread into widening webs, each strand stretching, snapping, and dissipating. Shadows played across the parched ledges and gravelly flats around and above the shore of Ice Lake, over archipelagos of tree islands spattered across the crumbling slopes, over snowfields twinkling only slightly in their last days on earth, as the last vestiges of the seaborne white blossoms of fine water eclipsed the sun momentarily before continuing their flight northeast, to the desert, and to their oblivion.

Everywhere I go the glaciers are dying. They sprout surficial meltwater streams from subsurface moulins and the streams gush blue water so cold it looks as thick as syrup. The snouts recede and unfamiliar rocks are left exposed to the persistent summer sun. Snowfields that for decades occupied northeast hollows are entirely gone. White spots on the map are reduced a hundredfold, now mere trimmings of once vast snowfields. It's like returning to a beach to find that the sand has disappeared, taken away by tidal rips to some undefinable place—not moved or changed, but altogether gone. Wet meadows dry up, and dry meadows give themselves up to gravel flats as widely spaced cushions and rosettes replace emerald grasses and seemingly succulent wildflowers. Trees seem to march upslope and young recruits are seen on high sites where no adults have been for a thousand years. I trust that I need no thermometer to inform me that average July temperatures are well above the fifty degree isotherm. Every day I go shirtless and walk across the slabs in sandals, and even the nights bring only a slight chill. The land has a thirsty feel that a winter or two of heavy snowfall can no longer slake. The cirques howl as they are emptied, stone hollows where ice once dwelt. Taking in the last vestiges of a time that is passing, when I drink the meltwater of the mountain glaciers, I raise my cup to my lips and feel truly cold water, kryal water, enter into and move through my innards. Perhaps reluctant to ever be so warm, it cools me from the inside out before surrendering to my internal fires. I muse that I could give it all back to the ice and make it grow again.

For a glacier to remain living ice, its replenishment, or accumulation, must exceed loss, or ablation, over time. Accumulation rates can vary a lot depending on the proximity of large, storm-giving bodies of water. But one factor is unchanging. It's got to be cold. Cold enough in the winter for precipitation to fall as snow. Cold enough in the summer for the ice not to melt its way into oblivion. Today, with the notable exceptions of the Patagonian Ice Cap and a few of the ice caps in Norway, we see the same thing the worldwide. The ice is in retreat. And human-induced global warming is the reason why.

The story is much the same in all the mountains of the temperate latitudes: the Sierra Nevada, the Cascades, the Olympics, the Coast Ranges of British Columbia and Alaska, the Rockies, the Alps, the Caucasus, the Hindu Kush, the Pamirs, the Tien Shan, the Karakoram, the Himalaya—all in the Northern Hemisphere—and the Southern Alps and Andes of the south. Nearly all the mountains of the temperate latitudes are changing. Their glaciers are wasting away, ablating, dying. The polar regions are not exempt, and in fact feel the most pronounced effects of global warming. The North Atlantic Current, responsible for the moderate climates of Ireland, Great Britain, and Scandinavia, is reaching ever further north, sending fingers of warm water in between East Greenland, Iceland, and the Svalbard Archipelago, melting pack ice and releasing cold, fresh water into the North Atlantic. This deviation of ocean currents, in combination with outright melting of Arctic sea ice due to increased air temperatures, suggests that the permanent sea ice that mantles the Arctic Ocean will be gone within decades. Since 1979 the ice has diminished by 20 percent. In 2002 Russian icebreakers found *open ocean water* at the pole. South, the West Antarctic Ice Sheet calves off state-sized tabular icebergs into the cold waters of the Ross and Weddell Seas. The Larson Ice Shelf, a prominent feature of the Antarctic peninsula on most maps of the Southern Continent, broke apart in 2002 and is now mostly out at sea, monstrous fragments of detached ice, some bergs in excess of two hundred miles long. As a result of so much melting of ice, the earth's surface reflects less light, and temperatures rise still more, exacerbating the situation. Ocean waters once covered with ice now warm and expand, their volume augmented by the freshwater once bound up in the ice. Sea levels are rising several inches per decade.

In New Zealand, like so many other mountainous places in the mid-latitudes, mountain glaciers are in retreat, leaving behind house-sized chunks of once living ice as the glaciers withdraw into more sheltered hideaways up-valley. Left behind, these bodies of dead ice often linger for decades or more, covered with debris that protects them from the disintegrating intensity of the modern sun. Like sand- and gravel-coated plow piles in a shopping center parking lot, often these forgotten leftovers lie lifeless for long periods of time after their surroundings have melted away. Larger islands of dead ice will last longer, given their large volume and the relatively low surface area through which they are subjected to the wasting effects of the sun. Gradually, over tens, even hundreds of years, they become shrunken and broken, drop by drop, left like standing stones, glistening and dripping in the sunlight, their coating of blackened debris only partly hiding the blue, mysterious ice of their interior. Dead ice saturates and bears down on the underlying earth, depressing the gravels and sands that underlie it and simultaneously filling the depression with meltwater as the ice wastes away. As if in an effort to capture itself before total disintegration occurs, the ice melts into its own private kettle lake, often turquoise, jade, or sapphire, untainted by the nearby milky, frothing meltwater stream that deposits rock flour and sand in a multiplicity of braids.

High up on the steep hanging walls of the glacially excavated valley, tributary glaciers that once fed valley glaciers such as the Tasman, the Dart, the Fox, and the Franz Josef, among hundreds of others, not to mention the Whitney of Mount Shasta, are left hanging on lofty perches as their master destination drops out from under them and wastes away to the ocean. The hanging glaciers now flow right over the brink, successive seracs of mobile ice calving off and trundling downslope a thousand feet, obliterated, smashed to pieces, pulverized in their attempt to reach the no longer existent master glacier below. Their fragments melt away and are carried downstream in the slurry of meltwater. As the ice continues to ablate, these will become hanging valleys and host free-falling waterfalls, the fluvial equivalent of hanging glaciers.

It was a summer climb in the Southern Alps that convinced me of the impending demise of temperate mountain glaciers. My climbing partner and I made the mistake of crossing the Bonar Glacier on the flank of Mount Aspiring in the middle of the afternoon. We slogged through mile after mile of ankle-deep slush and water for the entire distance from the Shipowner Ridge to the French Ridge, scorched by the afternoon sun reflected off of the ice's surface. We had chosen to climb Aspiring early in the day, and we were happy to have had hard snow along our route to the summit. Then we paid the price: many times the distance and many times the hours on mush, across scores of surficial streams, blue runnels all headed into crevasses and ultimately over the hanging walls of the Bonar Plateau, down horsetail hanging waterfalls to the flat bottom of the West Matukituki Valley. The Bonar, once linked to the vast valley glacier of the Matukituki, is now an island of ice, isolated on a high alpine perch as the tide of trees and sticky growing things slowly rises, shrinking the shoreline of the island and ever wasting away its edges. In the mountains of California, even the islands themselves are drowning, becoming tiny, ever more isolated, ever more often reduced to permanent and eventually ephemeral snowfields.

The chronology of the events that culminated in the Pleistocene Ice Age has not yet been deciphered and is the subject of hot debate among geologists and climatologists alike. Nevertheless, there is a story to be told.

Over one hundred million years ago, while insects and flowers experienced an evolutionary orgy and a growing shadow foreboded the doom of the thunder lizards, the whole earth experienced a prolonged spell of relative warmth. Throughout the characteristically warm, wet Cretaceous Period, most of the continental landmasses were gathered around the equatorial regions of the globe. This allowed warmer ocean waters to circulate around the planet. At the poles, these dark masses of ocean waters were less likely to freeze, due to continued circulation as they absorbed and captured a tremendous amount of solar radiation and distributed it around the globe. This situation perpetuated an ice-free global climate. Temperature gradients between the equatorial regions and the poles were much less steep than today, and the planet experienced a warm, moist period of relatively few temperature extremes.

Around forty million years ago, during the Oligocene Epoch of the Tertiary Period, the warm-wet dynamic of the Cretaceous began to change. Antarctica was skating towards the South Pole. The landmass, lacking the heat-holding capacity of water, cooled things off significantly and began accumulating ice. Soon the ice itself mirrored heat back out to the atmosphere, and one of many feedback loops led to the encasing of Antarctica in glacial ice. As the continents continued their drift away from the equator, things cooled down even more. As polar ice caps built up, sea levels dropped. As sea levels dropped, land bridges between continents were exposed, cutting off Arctic Ocean waters from warmer waters to the south. These isolated waters got colder and colder, freezing into an ice shelf that eventually covered the polar regions to the north. Mammals ruled the world. Woolly mammoths and giant ground sloths made their debut.

As the continents approached their present positions, ocean basins that had been expanding since the breakup of Pangea reached their maximum volume, and the fixed amount of ocean water on the planet couldn't quite fill them up. The result was still lower sea levels and more exposed landmass. As this was happening, worldwide uplift of land surfaces occurred throughout the late Cenozoic Era, including the Himalaya, Alps, Austral-Pacific Ranges, and Andes, not to mention the many ranges of the North American Cordillera. These major uplifts, among many other factors, may have resulted in wide-scale climatic change, altering air circulation and rock weathering rates across the globe. Increased rock weathering required an increase in carbon dioxide consumption, thus decreasing the greenhouse effect and reflecting less heat back to the earth. The result was global cooling. As the planet cooled, the poles were influenced by climate change dramatically while the equatorial regions remained relatively stable, and air and water began to shift around to compensate, ultimately leading to stormy weather all across the globe. Snow and ice came down over the poles and high mountains, collecting and compacting over many years to form the huge glaciers of the late Pliocene and Pleistocene Epochs.

The ice grew. A third of Eurasia and half of North America were inundated. By three million years ago, at the close of the Pliocene, the first glacial ice appeared at the mid-latitudes, including the mountains of California. The Ice Age slowly wrapped itself around more and more of the earth's surface. This was not the first large-scale glaciation of the earth. Evidence in Africa and South America indicate that large-scale glaciation occurred in the Paleozoic as Gondwanaland rode over the South Pole on its way to becoming part of Pangea.

Before that, Rodinia held substantial glaciers of its own as parts of it encountered polar latitudes. Conclusion: stick a continental landmass over a pole and things get chilly.

Between fifteen and twenty glaciations are thought to have occurred throughout the Pleistocene Epoch, each averaging about one hundred thousand years long. Average global temperatures during these glaciations were five to fifteen degrees cooler than during interglacial periods. Although evidence is scant concerning the earlier glaciations, it is believed that they were of about the same extent as the more recent glaciations. Between each glaciation were warmer periods during which the glacial ice melted, wholly or partially. During these times, Pleistocene conifer forests rose up the flanks of the mountains, squeezing the alpine areas up to even higher elevations, only to be chased down by the alpine tundra as the climate cooled once again. During cooler periods, when it would seem that the alpine habitat would expand the most, glaciers covered the landscape, again contracting the alpine habitat to the highest unglaciated peaks and plateaus. Thus the alpine country of California fluctuated greatly, even as the mountains continued to heave upward throughout the Pleistocene.

Since the end of the last major glaciation, around ten thousand years ago, the climate in the mountains of California has continued to fluctuate in correspondence with the greater climatic fluctuations of the planet. The warming period of eight thousand to six thousand years ago (called the "climatic optimum" by climatologists) wiped the region completely clean of glacial ice. Treelines rose significantly during this time, though soil development was slow in the wake of the glaciers. The climatic optimum did not last long, however, and was followed by a series of four small-scale glacial advances beginning around fifty-eight hundred years ago. The most notable (and most recent) of these was the Little Ice Age of 1350 to 1850, during which all of the remaining glaciers in the mountains of California, and many that have since ablated, advanced significantly. The Little Ice Age was caused by increased atmospheric circulation, which shifted the polar front southward by five to ten degrees, allowing wetter weather to bombard western North America. As temperatures worldwide averaged one to two degrees colder than at present, snow levels dropped three hundred to five hundred feet throughout the Northern Hemisphere, causing glaciers across the globe to grow and sea ice to expand. A warming trend in the mid-1800s brought a close to the Little Ice Age, and glaciers all over the world retreated rapidly.

Recent years have been no exception to the rule of climatic fluctuations in the mountains of California. Tree-ring studies in the alpine zone indicate that the last century has brought both severe drought (1910–1934) and a long period of relatively high precipitation (1937–1986) that has been exceeded only twice during the last thousand years. The Sierra Nevada in particular is still in a period of a high precipitation anomaly, though droughts within this period may partially disguise this little known fact. Climate change over the last two thousand years, including the recent global warming of the late twentieth and early twenty-first centuries, may be attributed to the amount and quality of insolation in the alpine Sierra—due in part to the fluctuations in celestial mechanics. Other influences may include volcanic activity, global air circulation, and shifting landmasses.

Time has brought many changes to the land, as the interplay between that which is occurring beneath the surface and that occurring above it determines what is happening on the surface at any given time. For the mountains of California, this has meant change ever since their birth. Since then, the land has seen conifers, ice, bare rock, soil, bright-eyed wildflowers, and countless walking and flying creatures, all chased in and out of the top of the ranges by the winds of change. A few million years may well bring the return of both forests and ice to the region, then a return to fell fields, lakes, and flowers as one of many concentric cycles completes itself once again. But let there be no doubt, when people speak of the Ice Age as a thing of the past, they are mistaken. The Ice Age is now. We find ourselves in the midst of one of several interglacial periods, but the factors contributing to the Pleistocene Ice Age are still very much at play. We have renamed the geologic epoch that ended with the latest retreat of the continental ice sheets and began with the emergence of human agricultural societies, but perhaps we should still be using "Pleistocene" to refer to the present time period. "Holocene" is arguably just a fancy, anthropocentric name for "current interglacial." Geology has little to do with agriculture, and the next advance of the ice will not halt at the edge of human habitation. We have only to see what role human-induced global warming will play in the larger scheme of things, whether we have altered the climate enough to significantly alter the rhythms of the Ice Age, or whether, a million years from now, such global warming will be but a hiccup in the grand scheme of things. In the meantime, we would do well to hope for the latter.

AFTER SOME HOURS of exploring the broken back of the Whitney Glacier, hunger drives us from this awesome place. We sift our way through scattered bits of storm, passing clouds as they pass us on our journey back to camp. As we draw nearer to home, the familiar sight of our tents is obscured as weather falls upon the north side of the mountain. We find the slight impression of nearly lost foot-prints and we retrace them to our waiting stoves, kettles, and tents. As we prepare water for tea, we look back and find that our tracks are already gone.

TEN

With the Coming of the Ice

During the Ice Age the slate was wiped clean. Not only was the geologic landscape reshaped, but almost all life was erased. Rock, soil, plants, and animals were indiscriminately pushed out, and deep beneath the mantle of ice the landscape was remade. In the Sierra Nevada, this mantle spanned up to 275 miles, from the Feather River Canyon in the north to the Kern River Canyon in the south. Emanating from this contiguous ice cap were scores of valley glaciers that flowed down the drainages of the main Sierran crest. Along the West Slope these valley glaciers were massive, tens of miles long and thousands of feet thick, sculpting such marvels as Kings Canyon, Yosemite Valley, and Hetch Hetchy. Along the eastern escarpment, the glaciers were shorter and steeper, those to the north flowing out onto the basin floors east of the range, those to the south truncating above the basin bottoms.

When the glaciers retreated a new land emerged. The Sierra Nevada mountains, raised but not yet shaped prior to the Pleistocene, were now gouged, sculpted, fluted, their valley bottoms flattened and valley walls steepened, their peaks raised and ragged. What were once rolling upland plateaus and V-shaped valleys were transformed by glacial erosion into jagged aretes, pyramidal horns, excavated cols, theater-like cirques, hangings valleys, and immense glacial staircases embroidered with countless paternoster lakes, ribbonlike streams, and plummeting waterfalls. Even the fine details of the landscape bore testimony to the ice's power of change. As bedrock was exposed, it was polished and ground to a high sheen by rocks and dust cemented into the undersides of overriding glaciers. Etched into the polished rock surfaces, the glaciers left their signature as grooves, chatter marks, scratches, and striations, all indicating the direction of flow and eventually pointing to the ultimate destination of the glaciers: downslope, to the sea. In response to the removal and relocation of so much material, as well as the removal of the overbearing weight of the ice itself, the range rebounded isostatically, causing the most recent uplift of the Sierra Nevada. Although the mean elevation of the range had been reduced by so much glacial erosion, the maximum elevation increased through isostasy. The east-west profile of the range was exacerbated. The eastern crest had experienced the most glacial erosion and thus experienced the most local isostatic compensation, while the west slope received the additional weight of the glacial deposits and virtually no isostatic compensation.

While postglacial landscapes reoriented themselves to the primeval spring, living things also reorganized, engaging in some of the most fantastic migrations the world has known. Among these species were human beings.

The human species grew up in the Pleistocene. It may be no small coincidence that the earliest fossils of human ancestors date back to around the time of the first great glacial advance. Over the past three million years, humans and human ancestors have dealt with Ice Age conditions on a daily basis and made a decent living while doing so. The genus *Homo*, to which we belong, sprang out of the evolutionary tree in the very midst of the Pleistocene Epoch and later evolved into its full glory while ice repeatedly inundated much of the Northern Hemisphere. We developed technologies to hunt big game and deal with the cold. We snuggled together and cooked over fires, napped the finest stone points of the times out of silica-rich rock, wore the hides of animals, painted, sang, and laughed. When seas were particularly low because so much water was locked up in the ice, we crossed land bridges and found new, wide lands teeming with game. Such changing times demanded ingenuity and flexibility. Every time the climate changed and the ice advanced or retreated, those people who survived did so by moving or figuring out new ways to live with the prevailing conditions. In this way, we grew up with the ice.

Interestingly, human evolution began in the tropics. Ten million years after the Cretaceous extinction, the first tree-dwelling primates made the fossil record. These small, agile mammals developed opposable thumbs that enabled them to climb more efficiently and eventually allowed primates to use and manufacture tools. They also developed wide-angle stereoscopic vision, which allowed them to perceive depth with an accuracy never before achieved by mammals. They cruised the forest with precision. Around thirty-five million years ago, deep in the tropical forests of the Americas, New World monkeys evolved from more primitive ancestors and began their long career of swinging through the trees. Simultaneously, Old World monkeys evolved in similar tropical regions of Asia and Africa. During this time a third group diverged, which included the common ancestors of all apes. Gibbons and orangutans diverged from this common lineage early on. Between five and nine million years ago, the remaining African apes split into three distinct groups, which became the gorillas, the chimpanzees, and the homonids.

The homonids quickly distinguished themselves from their gorilla and chimp relatives by developing an upright posture. The common misconception of humans evolving from gnarly, hunched-over man-apes is bunk. Fossil evidence shows quite clearly that human ancestors were walking fully erect by at least four million years ago. In size and appearance these early homonids closely resembled chimpanzees, standing around four to five feet tall, likely hairy, with sloped foreheads, heavy brows, and prominent jaws. But in posture and gait they were more or less just as upright as humans are today. Their brains were a fraction of the size of ours.

These primitive homonids, called the australopithecines after their genus, *Australopithecus*, evolved simultaneously with the pronounced period of global cooling that preceded and carried through the Pleistocene Epoch. In response to such dramatic climate change, the once dense tropical forests of Sub-Saharan Africa began to thin and eventually gave way to broad grassland and savanna. While the ancestors of today's chimpanzees and gorillas followed the forests as they retreated, the australopithecines developed more opportunistic strategies, employing their newly freed hands to use crude bone and stone tools, and their erect posture and stereoscopic vision to see out across the plains. Herds of newly evolved hoofed mammals reproduced prolifically and radiated into new niches as the grasslands on which they depended spread across tropical and temperate regions worldwide. As their numbers swelled and they swarmed the plains, a new hunter stepped out onto the field.

The australopithecines grew in stature. We must speculate that the ability to solve problems and the faculty for associative learning became increasingly successful in a world of flux, because fossil evidence shows that while our ancestors got bigger, their cranial capacity also increased relative to their body size, thus allowing for bigger brains. At least three australopithecines emerged from the tree of life. *Australopithecus robustus* was a large and, as its species name suggests, robust vegetarian with highly developed molars for chewing vegetable matter (some authorities place *robustus* in a separate genus, *Paranthropus*). *Australopithecus afarensis* and *Australopithecus africanus* were both omnivores, more opportunistic, and not surprisingly, more successful. The famous fossilized remains of "Lucy" are those of a female *A. africanus*. It is likely from her lineage that we have sprung.

By two million years ago, Lucy's children had advanced significantly. The early australopithecines evolved into the first species to bear the same genus name as humans. *Homo habilis* roamed Sub-Saharan Africa. These human ancestors grew taller and smarter and began manufacturing their own crude tools. As the great continental ice sheets waned and waxed and the climates and communities of the earth continuously shifted, *Homo habilis* was eventually succeeded by *Homo erectus*: even bigger, smarter, and more sophisticated. *H. erectus* roamed the earth from one and a half million years ago until less than half a million years ago. During that time this revolutionary species covered a lot of ground.

Homo erectus was the first human ancestor to leave Africa. We speculate that the technological advances of evolving homonids led to increased success, and increased success led to increased populations. Without a growing resource base, the competition for a fixed amount of resources would have increased, leading small groups of *H. erectus* to wander increasingly far and wide in order to avoid such competition. Equipped with larger brains, stone and bone tools, increased cooperation and communication, and perhaps even limited use of fire, *H. erectus* began a series of migrations that would eventually lead humans to every inhabitable corner of the earth.

Homo erectus quickly spread across subtropical Eurasia to such disparate locations as Europe, the Middle East, China, and Java. Without the advanced use of fire, the development of sewing and tailoring technologies, and the further development of the voice box that would allow for the cooperative hunting necessary to take down Pleistocene megafauna, *H. erectus* was limited to warmer climes.

Less than half a million years ago, the human species *Homo sapiens* made its debut on planet Earth. No definitive date can be given to this period in evolution because no paleontologist can pinpoint that instance in the evolutionary spectrum where we became diagnostically human. There are fossil remains that are decisively *Homo erectus* and fossils that are decidedly *H. sapiens* and everything in-between, which are decidedly undecided. In fact, we have debated over what it means to be human for about as long as we have called ourselves human, and to no end. It has been argued that a representative of the *H. erectus* species, shaved and groomed of course, could sit down to dinner in a coat and tie and attract only a few sidelong glances. From a genetic perspective, only time and/or distance could isolate *H. erectus* and *H. sapiens* from each other for long enough for them to be unable to produce viable offspring. But even this criteria for speciation is not diagnostic. *Canis lupus* and *Canis domesticus* (wolves and domestic dogs) reproduce successfully, as do *Canis latrans* (coyotes) and *C. domesticus*. *Ursus maritimus* and *Ursus arctos* (polar bears and brown bears) can also reproduce successfully, as can countless other named species of mammals, birds, reptiles, arthropods, fishes, mollusks, annelids, plants, protists, and bacteria. The definition of a species, though written otherwise in countless scientific texts, might best read like Evelyn Hutchinson's definition for an ecological niche: "a multidimensional hyper volume in space and time." With everything in the universe in a constant state of flux, defining the boundaries of a species is like naming individual clouds. In moments they are no longer recognizable. In hours they are gone completely.

Paleontologists first identify humans somewhere around a third of a million years ago. The characteristics include a still greater relative brain size, an enlarged, rounded skull, and a specialized voice box. Big brains allowed us to think even more critically and solve more complex problems. Enlarged skulls gave a house for such a brain. Specialized voice boxes allowed us to communicate in complex, sophisticated sounds, and they increased our capacity for cooperation. Big brains were better than small brains and more brains were better than one.

Homo sapiens evolved differently in different climates. In the tropical and subtropical regions, humans attained the physical characteristics most of us share today. In the temperate and subpolar regions of Eurasia, however, a more robust, stocky version of *H. sapiens* evolved in response to the colder, more erratic conditions there. These were the Neanderthals, *Homo sapiens neanderthalensis*, the original human inhabitants of Eurasia. The Neanderthals were a sophisticated group of humans. They lived in tribes, practiced religion, buried their dead, communicated vocally, manufactured specialized stone tools, and likely laughed and daydreamed much as we do today. If there is any doubt of their human intelligence, we would do well to remember that their brain size was 10 percent larger than ours.

It was the slighter version of *Homo sapiens* that developed the even more sophisticated tool kit that eventually enabled humans to spread across the globe. While Neanderthals were sheltering from winter in caves and keeping warm around their fires, *H. sapiens* elsewhere were developing elaborate stone points, axes, and scrapers, atlatls, sewing awls, and eventually bows and arrows. Meanwhile, with *H. sapiens'* increased dependence on cooperation and communication for survival, the voice box further developed to its modern level of complexity. These technologies and evolutionary innovations allowed

H. sapiens to survive in a wider range of environments. The result was a second major migration, or rather series of migrations. *H. sapiens* either subsumed, outcompeted, or destroyed the Neanderthals in Eurasia. They furthered this by moving into the subpolar regions north of around 55 degrees, a move only made possible by the invention of precision sewing awls and tailored clothing. This put modern *H. sapiens* further north than Neanderthals had ever inhabited. But the most significant migration occurred in the south. In the north, the continental ice sheets accumulated and advanced, culminating in North America as the Wisconsin glaciation of sixty thousand to twenty thousand years ago. As the ice sheets bulked up for this last great hurrah, they drank up so much seawater that many continents and islands were temporarily connected by land. *H. sapiens* living in Southeast Asia were able to make land crossings or short sea crossings all the way down the Malay Peninsula to Sumatra, Java, Bali, Lombok, Sumbawa, Sumba, Sawa, Roti, and Timor. From the shores of Timor they would for the first time look out across what appeared to be open ocean, unable to descry the massive uninhabited continent of Australia over the horizon. How it happened we can only guess. Perhaps some fishermen were swept out to sea and found themselves washed ashore in Eden. Maybe some bold early explorer speculated the presence of land and sailed out into the unknown in search of it. We know for certain that the journey required boats, and a significant amount of expertise to master sophisticated craft. No such use of boats was to be repeated for another thirty thousand years.

The human colonization of Australia was a collision of epic ecological proportions, seconded only by the subsequent human colonization of the Americas. In both cases, the land and all of its life, having never known the human animal, were ill-adapted to the continual disturbances of human presence. In the case of Australia, the continent had been disjunct from other land since the early evolution of mammals. Marsupials had made it there before Australia was sundered from Gondwanaland, but placental mammals had not. Marsupials had radiated into every possible niche, evolving into cat-like marsupials, bearlike marsupials, and deerlike marsupials, growing to the same huge proportions as mammals did all across the globe during the late Cenozoic Period. Flightless birds stood ten feet high and weighed hundreds of pounds, their lack of defenses evidence of the dearth of predators. The human animal walked among these zoological spectacles and they did not flee in fear. The hunting was good. Within a few thousand years humans radiated to all corners of the continent. Simultaneously, most of the Australian megafauna went extinct.

Humans reached into Siberia by around twenty thousand years ago. Once they were able to make a successful living there, they spread across northeastern Asia in search of land and game. As the last great glacial advance waxed, the land bridge spanning the Bering Strait spread to over a thousand miles wide, allowing for mass migrations of land animals between the Old World and the New. By fourteen thousand years ago, as the ice sheets waned and seawater lapped up on the shrinking shores of the land bridge, humans made their way across. Whether they followed game or some primordial call, they found, as humans had done in Australia thirty-five thousand years before, land and life totally oblivious to human presence.

Humans found the tundra of western and central Alaska free of ice and trodden by the feet of migrating megafauna. As the ice sheets continued to wane, an ice-free corridor opened between the eastern edge of the Cordilleran Ice Sheet, which was centered in the mountainous regions of the western part of the continent, and the Laurentian Ice Sheet, which was centered around Hudson Bay. This ice-free corridor provided a migration route into the interior of the continent—a direct route to the Great Plains, teeming with wild game. It was a replay of Australia. In less than a thousand years humans reached Patagonia. Within a few thousand years after human contact, most of the Pleistocene megafauna of North America went extinct.

By ten thousand years ago, all the habitable corners of the globe were occupied by *Homo sapiens*. No other single, large animal species on earth has ever been able to survive in such a wide variety of habitats and circumstances. The radical climatic changes associated with the Pleistocene not only opened niches by causing many specialized species of the stable Cretaceous Period to go extinct, they also resulted in the kind of dynamic disturbance regimes that favor opportunistic species. Equipped with opposable thumbs and an upright posture, early humans developed the potential for tool use. Stereoscopic vision allowed us to perceive depth to a high degree and made us a formidable predator on the widening plains. Ever-increasing brain size gave us the ability to solve problems, communicate in increasingly sophisticated ways, and spread out across the globe. Continuing climatic shifts opened up new lands, and with tools and fire we explored over the farthest horizons. From the rainforests of the Zaire to the deserts of Tibet to the storm-blasted rock of Tierra del Fuego, humans have adapted to landscapes and learned to laugh and tell stories about it. If not for the coming of the ice, there would have been a different story to tell.

A person who drinks water from the ice will feel a change, as if the very coldness and purity of the water ignites some near-forgotten genetic memory, reawakening three million years of the Pleistocene past during which humans and glaciers waxed simultaneously across the planet. The blasting cold wind and milky braided streams send memories of mammoth and spear, of long journeys on foot, of gathering closely around fires, of open spaces and room to roam, of being joyous at seeing the few people you do, of working hard to live and living fully because of that, and of dying of completely natural causes. For some, the ice invokes a longing in our blood, and ever after, when we are reminded of it we seek to be near it, to bear witness to the past out of which we were created. Over hundreds of thousands of years we made a way of life synonymous with the Pleistocene. A Pleistocene species, an Ice Age species, we wait now patiently for the ice to return. It is familiar. It is, quite literally, in our blood.

I GET A NOSTALGIC FEELING in my solar plexus when I'm in glaciated landscapes. The Alps, the Southern Alps, Scotland, Norway, the High Arctic, Maine, the Sierra Nevada. As I am flying over the Greenland ice sheet on a clear day, something way down deep inside of me perceptibly moves. It's a genetic calling. It says, undeniably, *"Go home."*

ELEVEN

Fire from Within

I stand out on the north shore of Mono Lake amid snow flurries in May. Mike Klapp, friend, employee of the Mono Lake Committee, connoisseur of the Mono Basin, and fellow exuberant lover of life, stands out here with me amid the sagebrush and desert peach. We draw a circle around us, following the horizon in a grand panorama. Mike points out every landform out there and I take notes. To the north and west is the Sierra Nevada, founded in the Mesozoic and uplifted in the late Cenozoic. The rusty orange and brown forms of Dunderberg, Dana, Gibbs, Lewis, Parker, and Wood betray the Ancestral Sierra Nevada that once stood on the granitic foundation of the range. The Sierra continues south, past the Ritter Range to the faraway forms of Mount Morrison and Bloody Mountain. The Range of Light takes up a lot of space in the panorama, and we are only looking at a small fraction of the total extent of the range. But east of the Sierra, and closer to us, the character of the landforms and the story they tell change dramatically. Wilson Butte. The Aeolian Buttes. The Inyo Domes. Mammoth Mountain. The Mono Craters. Glass Mountain. Cowtrack Mountain. Paoha Island. Negit Island.

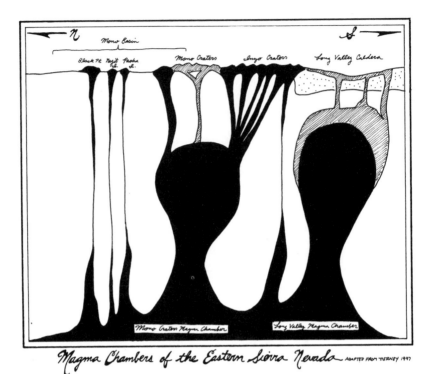

Magma Chambers of the Eastern Sierra Nevada ADAPTED FROM TIERNEY 1997

Black Point. Here are some of the youngest mountains and associated landforms on the planet. They are still rough-cut, still in the making, ready to explode at any time. Every single one of them is volcanic.

BENEATH THE THINNING CRUST of the West, the semi-molten material of the asthenosphere welled up close to the surface, melting more and more crust and forming magma chambers on the verge of bursting. Where the crust broke into faults, forming the down-dropped grabens and tilted horsts of the Basin and Range, the magma came out, spewing basalt flows, raising andesitic cones and rhyolitic plug domes, heating groundwater to form hot springs, sending incinerating explosions across the land, and blasting pyroclastic material as far afield as Nebraska.

In the morning I will set out on my own and go find those places. Our breath forms small, ephemeral, swirling clouds as dusk falls and the air temperature plummets. Soon my fingers feel like stumps and my pencil flails across my three-by-five notepad. Mike and I wander through the aromatic shrubs, past his recently dug pit toilet (of which he is immensely proud), and back to the ramshackle trailer he bought for a dollar just weeks ago. Golden slanted rays of sunlight penetrate the dissipating clouds that hang over the mountains. The shafts come down like spotlights from the heavens, illuminating the high desert landscape with an almost Arctic light. Brief but precious minutes pass.

Back at Mike's trailer we rejoin friends and make preparations for a supper of shepherd's pie, Dutch oven–style. Arya Degenhardt, old friend and Mono Lake Committee employee, joins forces with Emily Muschinski, visual artist and printmaker extraordinaire, and Isaac Nadeau, even older friend, good soul, naturalist, and fellow cosmological ponderer, to chop colorful vegetables and potatoes, knead bread, and prepare the coals for our feast. Once the pie is filled and the oven on the coals, we gather around the warmth and light of the fire as the cloak of night falls cold and dark.

Isaac and I each have a harmonica in hand, and we find ourselves improvising songs, trading off riffs, crooning and shouting ad lib lyrics up to the darkening sky. Soon Mike reveals his own harmonica prowess and unobtrusively comes in with his cupped, bent notes and improvisational cries. Eventually Isaac and I stop completely and just watch Mike go.

Music fades to the quiet of night. The last scraps of the day's clouds dissolve into a thousand silver stars and the glistening arm of the Milky Way. We move on to stories, each of us sharing a different culture's story about the stars. As our pot pie bakes to perfection, we hear about how Coyote burnt his nose by peeking into a secret jar and accidentally letting the stars out. Hummingbird uses her needle-like bill to pierce the black cloak cast over the sky and let the light back in. Elbereth places the stars above Middle Earth to light the world for the wakening elves. When an hour has passed, we eat well and do so thankfully.

I sleep hard and have dream after dream of stars and explosions. At dawn, I lie in the shrubs, watching the pink light of morning dapple its way across the high peaks of the Sierra Nevada, then brighten to gold, then white, and slide down the mountain flanks and across the floor of the Mono Basin to overwhelm me. But even at this early hour a wreath of clouds hangs over the midriff of the mountains, and I know that snow will soon come.

It is afternoon when I drive south towards the Long Valley. After a late morning of snow flurries and cold winds I find my courage in two cups of hot black tea, and I am anxious to get out into the field and be alone with rocks for a while. Before rising up over Deadman Summit, which divides the watershed of the Mono Basin from that of the Owens Valley, I turn left on an obscure dirt track and follow it towards the Mono Craters, through the increasingly dense shrubs, towards the conspicuously out-of-place forms of the Aeolian Buttes. Once I am within a half-mile of the buttes, I park the car and set out on foot across the desert.

As I walk through the desert peach, rabbitbrush, sage, and cliff-rose, the wind throws sand particles into the air and I am pelted with innumerable grains. Looking at the contorted, Salvador Dali–style forms of the buttes, it is not hard to imagine how they got their name, or by what processes they achieved such shapeliness. Aeolis was the Greek god of the winds, and he seems like a persistent presence here. But while their name betrays the process by which they are being destroyed, it says little of their genesis. As I draw nearer to the buttes I am struck by their composition. They appear to be made up of stacked, successive layers of molten ash, the bottom layers laid down first, and the top layers last. They remind me of castles made of wet blobs of sand, or massive, towering cow patties. A freshly broken surface reveals bands of alternating dark and light material such as would be found in metamorphic rock, with tiny but visible silica crystals and pebble-sized chunks of pumice suspended in the mix throughout. The tuff at the base of the hill seems different than that above. The former resembles gneiss in coloration and banding but is far less solid and more crumbly. The tuff higher up, however, is buff-tan and orange in color, less banded, and even more crumbly. I speculate that the lower rock has been partially metamorphosed, or at least more structurally consolidated, by the added pressure and heat of the rock above.

Molten ash means only one thing: an explosion. It means an explosion big enough to blow rock to smithereens, heat it to the point of liquefaction, and blast it up and out of the earth. Gravity takes care of the rest, pulling the pyroclastic material back down to earth. As it rains down, the molten ash fuses and piles up. Some of the Aeolian Buttes are forty feet tall. That means a lot of molten ash.

With the stretching of North America came the development of magma chambers close to the crustal surface of the American West. As molten material oozed its way into the surrounding crust, it acted much like the plutons of the Mesozoic Era that coalesced to form the Sierra Nevada Batholith. The magma started relatively mafic, with a mineral composition similar to basalt or andesite, or their intrusive counterparts gabbro and diorite. As the crust melted into the magma chamber, the mix became increasingly siliceous. As it became more siliceous it became less dense and more buoyant. As it became more buoyant it rose still closer to the surface, and the feedback loop continued.

Unlike the plutons of the Mesozoic Era, which found their exits through the Sierran Arc volcanoes, the magma chambers of today find their release through the widening faults associated with Basin and Range extension. As the crust of western North America stretches and breaks, magma chambers below send up plumes along these points of weakness, filling the cracks with magma and pasting the thinning crust back together. But when the magma hits the surface it gushes out. If the magma is basaltic, with relatively low viscosity, it flows. If it's andesitic, it sputters and oozes. If it's rhyolitic, with a relatively high viscosity, it clogs its own vents, pressure builds up, and like a pot of boiling plaster with the lid on too tight, eventually it blows.

As the Basin ranges and the Sierra Nevada rose, magma from beneath flowed and oozed out of the normal faults that developed along the mountain front. A drive north through the Owens Valley shows the evidence. North of Independence, black basalt flows reach down to the valley floor. At the base of the mountain front, their sources stand exposed as orange, brown, and black sputter cones, perched classically atop the faults that run the length of the east side of the Sierra. To the west the picture is much the same. Cones and flows decorate the long bajada between the valley bottom and the escarpment of the White Mountains. North of Bishop the scene changes quite dramatically. The cones and flows give way to the expanse of the Bishop Tuff formation, a layer of molten ash hundreds of feet thick that extends from just north of town all the way up and over the Sherwin Grade. It covers nearly every square mile of ground for a few hundred square miles. The vastness of the Bishop Tuff makes the Aeolian Buttes seem puny and insignificant. Whatever explosion caused such a huge amount of rock to be blown out of the earth and superheated to temperatures high enough to liquefy stone must have been truly immense in scale. In fact, the stories of the Bishop Tuff and the Aeolian Buttes are the same. The Buttes are a disjunct section of the larger tuff formation, separated during the Pleistocene by the erosive forces of the valley glaciers that issued forth from the eastern Sierran front. The glaciers scraped away the relatively soft tuff and deposited its remains in the then swollen waters of Mono Lake. Because of the lay of the local topography, the Aeolian Buttes were spared this fate, and they now stand as the last remnant of the Bishop Tuff in the Mono Basin.

By three million years ago, as the first mountain glaciers of the Pleistocene mantled the nearby Sierra Nevada, a massive magma chamber had worked its way into the underside of the crust beneath what is today the Long Valley. At first the magma found its way out via vents on the northeast side of the valley, and basalt extruded and flowed in successive layers to form Cowtrack Mountain. Within half a million years the magma had grown increasingly siliceous in composition, and andesitic eruptions ensued. Another half a million years and the magma chamber was mostly rhyolitic, and a series of violent eruptions began that built Glass Mountain. But the buildup of siliceous magma was too great, and the release at Glass Mountain was not enough. The pressure built until the earth broke.

The Long Valley magma chamber blew itself inside-out 730,000 years ago. The explosion was equal to six hundred Mount Saint Helens eruptions. Ash—one hundred and fifty cubic miles of it—blew out of the earth and rode on prevailing westerly winds as far east as Nebraska. Closer at hand, an incinerating blast equal in power to the entire world's arsenal of nuclear arms seared the surrounding land with temperatures exceeding thirteen hundred degrees Fahrenheit. All life was annihilated. Long Valley itself collapsed into the resulting void in the crust as layer upon layer of burning ash rained down and welded together, accumulating in Long Valley itself to thicknesses in excess of three thousand feet. For three hundred and fifty square miles around, the earth was blanketed in tuff up to six hundred feet thick.

The relief was only temporary. The chamber awoke again, 130,000 years later. Basalt extruded from vents along the San Joaquin River and blocked the water's flow. The San Joaquin, which had drained to the east long enough to erode a prominent gap in the Sierran crest, was rerouted to the west. The basalt cooled uniformly from top to bottom, forming the stunning columns of Devils Postpile. By four hundred thousand years ago, Mammoth Mountain had begun to rise as increasingly siliceous magma blasted its way out of the chamber, piling up in heaps of quartz latite atop already deep layers of volcanic debris. Rhyolitic material found vents and blew out to form the Inyo Domes. The earth shook, opened, and groaned.

"Power," I think, "beyond my imagining," as I finger the pumice-flecked slag heaps of the buttes. The power of a hundred million years of geomorphic processes all condensed into a single, catastrophic event. The power to destroy all life in a single day. The power to shape a mountain landscape in a geologic blink of an eye.

With sand on my lips I descend the hill, looking down and admiring the transient veneer of vegetation patterns overlaying the land. The darker green cliffrose is more abundant on the low-angle slopes, giving way to the lighter, dusty silver-green of sage and rabbitbrush on the basin flats. Further towards the lakeshore, I speculate these will give way to the halophytes, salt-tolerant plants such as greasewood and saltbush. To the east, dark Jeffrey pines dot the gray pumice scree slopes of the Mono Craters. West, towards Highway 395, a conspicuous green swath of grassland several miles square invades the sagebrush, spreading out like an apron along the flat below Williams Butte. Decades ago, when the Los Angeles Department of Water and Power began buying up lands to monopolize the water rights of the Mono Basin, resentful landowners irrigated their land in hopes of a higher-dollar sale. The landowners got the money they wanted and L.A. got the land. At least that's how the local legend goes. The echo of the Long Valley eruption is but whisper on the wind, a faint foreboding suggestion of what brews beneath our feet. People go about their lives. Eventually the timelines of geology and human experience intersect.

I leave the Buttes and head north, hoping to find such an intersection between geologic and human time. I set out for Panum Crater, the smallest and youngest of the Mono Craters, thought by some to be the youngest mountains in North America. A cold wind whips around the basin, drying and chapping my hands and cracking my lips. I find desert peach shrubs in bloom and stop to admire the sweet fragrance of their many small blossoms as they fling their aroma out to the wind. Soon I find myself walking on a crunchy mix of pebble-size pumice, rhyolite, and obsidian, and I realize how much can be observed about the texture of rocks by the way they feel beneath our footsteps. Pumice feels like hard styrofoam and almost squeaks when it rubs against itself. Obsidian is like walking on old broken bottles dulled at the edges by time and wear. Rhyolite is somewhere in-between. I become fixated on the sound: crunch, crunch, crunch.

I am ascending the debris ring of an explosive pit that just six hundred and forty years ago would have completely incinerated me, my car, and all the desert peach, sage, cliffrose, and rabbitbrush for at least ten miles around. Panum Crater is undisputedly the youngest of the Mono Craters, the most recent in a series of explosions that began a hundred thousand years ago and could resume any day. Just as occurred in Long Valley hundreds of thousands of years before, an analogous magma chamber moved in beneath the Mono Basin around a hundred thousand years ago and has been blowing the place up ever since. The Mono Craters were among the first to blow, and they also include some of the most recent volcanic landforms.

When a new dome like Panum is born, subsurface rhyolitic magma begins to extrude through a vent, but the viscosity of the material is so great that its fluidity is compromised and the magma plugs up the vent. It takes the pressure of trapped gasses and additional magma to make the vent blow. When it does, there is no time for gasses to escape from the magma. Pumice, which is rhyolitic material puffed up with gasses, explodes violently from the surface of the crust. This initial blast sends debris flying outward from the vent, forming a neat raised ring of pebble-sized pumice and other pyroclastic material around the epicenter of the explosion. These debris rings may be several miles wide and several hundred feet tall.

The debris ring is but a precursor of more violent action to come; the explosions that form them, while providing an outlet for pent-up gasses, rarely mark the end of an explosive cycle. As more magmatic material builds up beneath the clogged vent, eventually the pressure becomes great enough that the magma breaks through the crust and begins to push upward in a thick, sticky mass. The image has been likened to a toothpaste tube when the lid has been left off too long, the hole caked and clogged with dried, hardened paste. Enough pressure and enough squeezing and the toothpaste will break through, pushing out the plug as it extrudes. The material on the outside of the plug cools the fastest, and if it cools fast enough and it is pure enough, it will solidify to become obsidian, volcanic glass, the extrusive counterpart of quartz, nearly 100 percent pure silica.

The distinction between obsidian, pumice, and rhyolite, while readily made in a laboratory or defined in text, is rarely so discernable in the field. As I ascend the crest of the ring and drop into the vicinity of the plug, huge angular chunks of rock, ranging from fist-sized to car-sized, come into view. The plug looks like industrial wreckage. The contrast between these forms and the barren but soft sweep of the debris ring is sharp. I climb up and onto the plug, passing head-sized chunks of black glass along the way. On top, I am surrounded by obsidian, pumice, and rhyolite, and everything in between. The rock is banded and welded into waves and stripes, each rock type blending into the other with no clear division, showing with both force and grace the limits of our human categories. I can point to obsidian. I can point to pumice. I can point to rhyolite. But these are no more fixed than are species, no more permanent than the stars in the sky. In between obsidian, pumice, and rhyolite is the truth, so hard to see but ever present. The truth is that everything we perceive is part of a hundred spectrums, and the knowledge of a thing comes with understanding those spectrums.

The obsidian of Panum Crater was like a gold mine to the native Paiute that inhabited the basin. They quarried the stone by heating it with fire and pouring basketfuls of cold water over the surface. The abrupt change in temperature caused the obsidian to contract and crack. The Paiute exploited these cracks to quarry large chunks of raw material. Matchless in its use in the manufacturing of stone tools, essential for survival and an indispensable part of most aspects of daily life, high-quality obsidian was the closest thing the Great Basin tribes had to currency. Obsidian was found locally in abundance, but elsewhere in California obsidian in as pure a form as could be found at Panum Crater was hard to come by, and thus the material wealth of the Great Basin cultures came to be coveted by all the Indians of California.

Asian nomadic hunter-gatherers migrating into the lower forty-eight reached California by ten thousand years ago. The earliest immigrants found the land empty of people and enjoyed the rich abundance of California with room to spare. Here was a true wilderness, a land that for hundreds of millions of years had been devoid of human presence. Nature soon became the home of culture. Wave after wave of Amerindians found their way into the region. They came from almost every linguistic group found in the Americas, including Algonquin, Athabascan, Penutian, Hokan, Uto-Aztecan, and Yukian, and thus had affiliations with other tribes as far-flung as northeastern Canada, Alaska, and South America.

Those immigrants that made their way west of the Sierra Nevada found a land of plenty and soon bore the fat of abundance. The streams swarmed with trout and salmon. The woods and fields teemed with wild game. Golden grizzlies ambled through the fertile grasslands of the Central Valley beside herds of tule elk and pronghorn. Enormous flocks of migratory waterfowl darkened the skies for days as they migrated. The western tribes learned how to leach the tannic acid from acorns and were thus able to access a food source of sufficient abundance to make western California the most densely populated region of North America north of Mexico. These western tribes were numerous, each with its own cultural identity and often language. They included, in part, the Shasta, Wintu, Yahi, Yana, Maidu, Miwok, Mono, Yokuts, Tubatulabal, Kitanemuk, Fernandeño,

Tongva, Acjachmem, Luiseño, Cupeño, Kumeyaay, Chumash, Ohlone, Esselen, Salinan, Wappo, Tolowa, Karuk, Whilkut, Hupa, Chimariko, Wiyot, Nongatl, Bear River, Mattole, Lassik, Sinkyone, Kato, Wailaki, Yuki, and Pomo.

The Sierra-Cascade axis, a divide between watersheds, weather systems, geologic provinces, and plant communities, was equally a divide between human cultures. East of the divide were the broad horizons and open landscapes of the Basin and Range, bearing little resemblance to the rich land to the west. The Uto-Aztecan tribes that made these lands their home did so with ascetic grace. Scarcity was the rule, and the scarcity of life-sustaining natural resources meant low populations and widely dispersed tribal groups. To the north were the Northern Paiute and the Washoe. In the Mono Basin the Mono Paiute made their living. South were the Owens Valley Paiute and the Panamint Shoshone. Each of these tribes counted their members in the hundreds, and together their numbers added up to a few thousand at most. Population of the western tribes, for comparison, is estimated to have been at least three hundred thousand individuals prior to Euro-American contact.

The eastern tribes had obsidian that had no match in the west, and they had it in abundance. Although no tribes had permanent settlements in the higher reaches of the Sierra, both eastern and western groups ranged into the high country during the summer in search of pine nuts, game, and other seasonal fare. Trade between the east and west became a regular affair, and the Paiute of the east traded obsidian and pine nuts for acorns, fish, and animal skins from the Miwok, Maidu, and Tubatulabal to the west, among others. Seasonal encampments were established along major trade routes at Walker Pass, Piute Pass, Mono Pass (southern), Mono Pass (northern), Sonora Pass, Ebbetts Pass, Carson Pass, Donner Pass, and many places in the lower mountains further to the north. Many a Paiute sat by a sparkling alpine lake working obsidian into fine points while waiting for trade partners to arrive. The best of the obsidian came from Panum Crater. The hundreds of thousands of obsidian chips and shards strewn across Mono Pass, Parker Creek, Helen Lake Pass, the Kuna Crest, and the Donohue Pass vicinity are testimony to its dispersal. Similar piles of worked stone can be found on most of the passes in the range. Panum glass made it everywhere.

As the sun sinks behind the clouds along the Sierra crest, I am entranced by the swirls of inter-blended rock. I ponder how much of Panum's core has been carried off by Paiutes in years past. I wonder where their favorite quarry was before the relatively recent eruption of Panum, and what they were doing when it erupted from out of the ground. I bound down the slope of the plug, step back onto the pebbles of the debris ring, and crunch my way back to its low-angle outer slope. Beyond spans the basin in the waning light of evening. I watch as mountain bluebirds catch insects on the wing, flashing their colors in the shifting glow.

I RETURN TO MY FAMILIAR CAMP SPOT on the north shore of Mono Lake and settle into a warm sleep beneath the unseasonably cold sky. As my eyelids grow heavy, nighthawks dart like Australian boomerangs through the purple colors of late evening. They make sharp turns like bats as they hunt their winged insect prey.

In the morning the clouds that have for so long invaded the Basin skies have finally departed, and brilliant blue stretches out across the ceiling of the world. The snow-encrusted earth finally melts away to May's best warm sun and fresh wind. I lie in my sleeping bag for an hour just listening to the ruckus of gulls near the lakeshore half a mile away. The sound of the gulls invokes in me a strong nostalgia for the sea, and memories of boats and tides rise like fish into my consciousness. But there are no boats out there on the wide, glassy, oily, salty, alkaline waters of Mono Lake. There are no discernable tides. There are no fish in waters so heavily laden with minerals. The gulls are feeding on endemic brine shrimp that number in the trillions and alkali fly larvae that number in the hundreds of millions. The inland sea that Mark Twain called "the Dead Sea of California" is one of the most biologically productive places on earth. The distant cries of gulls are testimony to this fact. But my attention is quickly diverted. My purpose is in discovering the dynamic landscape *around* the lake.

I am lying on a huge expanse of dark brown sand and gravel that extends for miles in all directions. The pebbles that make up the gravel are rounded at their edges and do not show evidence of once having been larger rock that was then broken into such pieces. This stuff formed as pebbles. The surfaces of the rocks are covered in tiny pits and pockmarks: vesicles formed by gasses that escaped while the rock formed. There are no discernable crystals. With the evidence at hand—dark, vesicular rock with no crystals—it is not difficult to come to the conclusion that this is basalt. As I look around, the source of the debris is obvious. A few miles to the west, Black Point rises as a broad plateau standing several hundred feet above the surrounding basaltic plain. I get up and pack my things to go there.

As I begin my ascent of the south slope of Black Point, the pebbly basalt beneath my feet turns to soft, black sand. I trudge upward, losing a full step for every two I take as the sand collapses beneath my weight. I find myself in familiar company as I gain the flank; widely spaced sagebrush, desert peach, and rabbitbrush are joined by cliffrose. Here and there I observe milkvetch, trumpet phacelia, and paintbrushes, all in bloom. The day's wind has not yet arisen, and suddenly no-see-ums seem to be everywhere. I am distracted by swarms of them on my face, lips, eyes, and nose, and in my hair, ears, and shirt cuffs. Violet-green swallows enjoy a feeding frenzy above me, cruising through the air with admirable efficiency and mobility. An anxious desert cottontail flees upslope before me, zigzagging from bush to bush in a classic display of evasive agility.

Halfway up the slope I notice that the sand is changing color, fading from dark brown and black to a softer, lighter brown. As this trend continues, it becomes evident that some other rock type is contributing to the mix. Soon I find a fist-sized chunk of smooth, rounded granite, obviously smoothed and polished by ice or water. As I continue, this conspicuous granite find is complemented by others of similar origin, as well as angular pieces of sedimentary rock that match the color of the new sand. As I approach the top of the hill I encounter outcrops of this sedimentary material: coarse, light brown sandstone with fragments of rounded granite, basalt pebbles, and even small pieces of pumice suspended in the sandy matrix. As I crest the hill, the sedimentary outcrops come together and form a sandstone cap eighty feet thick in places. I ask myself, "What is all this sandstone doing on top of this recently erupted volcanic plateau?"

Throughout the dramatic climatic fluctuations of the Pleistocene and the accumulation and ablation of glaciers that characterized this time, the Great Basin was a huge catchment system for trillions of gallons of glacial meltwater. While the glaciers of the west slope of the Sierra-Cascade axis drained out to the Pacific via the San Joaquin and Sacramento River systems, the glaciers east of the divide drained into the terminal basins of the Great Basin. From here the Pleistocene waters, just like the waters of today, had no fluvial outlet to the sea. While today the input of water is small enough that evaporation prevents the basins from overfilling, during the Pleistocene this was not the case. As the glaciers repeatedly retreated in torrential slurries of meltwater, the basins filled, and a vast system of lakes formed throughout the Great Basin. The largest of these Great Basin lakes was Lake Bonneville, of which the Great Salt Lake of Utah is but a small remnant. Bonneville itself, during the height of its glory, had a surface area over ten times that of the Great Salt Lake, and a volume many times more than that. But Bonneville was not the only huge lake that wet the basins. Most of the major valleys of Nevada, southeastern Oregon, and eastern California hosted such waters. Pyramid Lake of western Nevada is a remnant of the once larger Lahontan Lake. Summer and Abert Lakes of southeastern Oregon are remnants of Pleistocene Lake Chewaucan. The Pleistocene Mono Lake, eight hundred vertical feet higher than today, overflowed into the Adobe Valley to the southeast, which in turn overflowed into the Owens River watershed to the south. As Owens Lake swelled to a depth of two hundred feet, it also overflowed to the south, into the China Lake Basin. As China Lake overfilled it flooded into Searles Lake. Once Searles Lake filled to a depth of around six hundred and sixty feet, it began dumping water into the Panamint Valley to form Panamint Lake. Panamint Lake eventually drained into Lake Manly of Death Valley, the last step down in the long succession of dumping grounds that ultimately found the bottom of the Great Basin at Badwater, the lowest point in the continent.

The bottom of the Pleistocene Mono Lake, like the bottom of any of the Great Basin lakes of that time period, would have been the collection basin for massive amounts of a wide variety of sediments. During glacial advances, the growing glaciers of Rush Creek, Parker, Bloody, Lee Vining, and Lundy Canyons would have come right down to the lake itself and calved blue icebergs into the cold waters of Mono. The granite of the Sierra Nevada, quarried and moved by the glacial ice, was encased in those icebergs, and these rocks fell out of the melting ice and found temporary resting places at the bottom of the lake. During glacial retreats, rushing meltwater brought vast quantities of sand, gravel, and cobbles down from the mountains and deposited these sediments in the lake. They swirled through the cloudy lake water and eventually settled out on the floor. Meanwhile, explosions in the vicinity of the Mono Domes hurled pyroclastic debris all over the basin.

The lake bottom sediments that cap the basalt indicate that Black Point was built by volcanic eruptions that occurred prior to the last glacial retreat, when the waters of Mono were still high enough to submerge Black Point completely. Geologists have dated the rock of Black Point at around 13,300 years old, approximately the same time as the Sierra Nevada's Tioga glacial advance. The eighty vertical feet of sediment that accumulated between then and the time the lake waters receded below the upper slopes of Black Point are testimony to the volume of sediments that were moved and deposited as the glaciers ebbed and flowed.

I follow the prominent ridge of the sedimentary cap northward, in the direction of Lundy Canyon, spooking a few jackrabbits from their daytime hiding spots as I walk along. As I look east over the cap, I am struck by the series of wide cracks etched deeply into the sandstone surface. I have heard before that there are fissures atop Black Point, but I have no idea what to expect. The most prominent cracks run parallel to one another, roughly north-south, with smaller perpendicular cracks joining them. I approach the opening and peer down. It is deep. Fifty feet deep. I can discern a sandy bottom; no basalt is visible. The cracks do not appear to penetrate into the older volcanic rock, or if they do, then subsequent erosion and deposition have partially filled the fissures and obscured the evidence. I follow the lines of the cracks to their northern end, then make my way through the bushes to inspect them up close.

I stand at the entrance to a slot canyon that cuts a deep incision into the sedimentary cap of Black Point. As I enter into the narrow corridor, the light of day fades to a dim afterthought. The slot is narrow enough that I cannot extend my arms from my sides. I step slowly into the interior, caressing the cold walls with a delicate yet inquisitive touch. My fingertips meet hard, rounded convexities the size of ping-pong balls. They felt like bubbles, or blisters. I look to see that the walls are covered, encrusted, with a half-inch-thick armor of strangely textured evaporate minerals. Tufa. It forms when calcium-rich freshwater encounters carbonate-rich lake water. The two minerals combine and precipitate out of solution, forming calcium carbonate ($CaCO_3$), otherwise known as limestone. Any object that spends enough time beneath the surface of Mono Lake develops such a coating, and this includes rocks, boat hulls, and even people.

The crust gleams white in the otherwise gray, shady recess. I look ahead to see that tufa encrusts much of the surface area of the rock, but there are also areas with only a thin, soft veneer of gypsum. The presence of these crusts answers a question that has begun to develop in my mind: did these fissures form before or after the lake level receded? The mineral deposits I find insist the former. They would only have formed like this under water. But what caused Black Point to crack?

I venture further into the fissure. The air grows cold inside. I find myself walking on hard, old snow, sheltered from the warming rays of the May sun by slot walls that approach seventy feet in height. The sky is but a thin blue strip overhead. I walk across the frozen raised walkway, tilted this way and that. Then, to my astonishment, I discover the scattered, torn body parts of a California gull. Apparently the bird has been ripped apart and eaten. Not a string of meat remains on any part of it. I speculate on this but can come to no decisive conclusions. I doubt it is the work of a raptor, since California gulls are larger than most birds of prey—unless the raptor made the kill on site. Nearby I find the feathers of a magpie, then bones, then fluffy down, then the skull of a duck. Something is bringing its kill here to butcher and eat. Coyotes could be responsible, but why would they carry their dinner so far? What need would they have for the shelter of this slot? How could they catch so many birds? Gull beaks and other avian body parts litter the snow surface. No blood. I come back to my raptor theory. I've seen falcons take out green-winged teals before; why not gulls? A buteo could certainly take out a gull.

The slot grows increasingly shallow as I approach the southwestern end. Using hands and feet, I climb up and out of the fissure and into the warm late-morning sun. I climb back up on top of the sedimentary cap and look south, across the sweeping blue curves of Mono Lake.

Negit and Paoha Islands are inescapable features to even the most casual observer. While they appear to be benign islands, both are actually active volcanoes, mountains of a sort, like mini-Hawaiis rising up from the briny, shrimpy soup of Mono Lake. Negit, just off the north shore, is dark brown, black in some lights. It consists of a small andesitic cone and an associated flow. The name "Negit" means "gull" in the language of the Mono Basin Paiute. Receding lake waters from the 1940s into the 1990s resulted in a land bridge that connected the north shore of Mono to Negit, which had long been a premier nesting site for California gulls. Coyotes walked right out to the nests and greased their chins with fresh eggs and unsuspecting chicks.

When I first came to Mono Lake, I went in search of the island of Negit. It was well past sunset when I set out from my camp on the north shore, and by the time I neared the cries of gulls it was dark. After what seemed like hours I had still not reached the lakeshore, and I thought for sure something was wrong. Then I realized I was walking on andesitic pebbles. The silhouette of Negit's cone was a faint black smudge on the dark horizon. I stood there on gull island, after having followed in the footsteps of coyotes. Inadvertently, I had discovered the land bridge. Since the nineties the water diversions that resulted in decades of lake-level recession have largely ceased, and again the lake is full enough for Negit to be an island. But few gulls nest there these days, perhaps having lost their trust in their age-old grounds. Today the gulls prefer the smaller islets that surround Negit.

Further out across the water, the pale, gray-white form of Paoha contrasts starkly with dark Negit. Paiute tales describe the dancing mists and spirits out on the island which are its namesake. In the relatively short amount of time that has passed since Paoha poked its head above the lake, boat tours, a hotel, grazing sheep, and hot-spring fanatics have all left their mark on its muddy, steamy shores.

If the magma chamber beneath the Mono Basin is following the pattern of the Long Valley magma chamber, the eruptions of the Mono Basin should follow a similar pattern: basaltic, then andesitic, then rhyolitic. Black Point and the islands fit the model perfectly. Black Point, basaltic, extruded 13,300 years ago. Negit, andesitic, followed, erupting 1,600 years ago. Paoha, a mix of lake-bottom mud and some andesite, erupted only 310 years ago. Although there have been no eruptions in any living person's lifetime, documents from the nineteenth century report steam issuing forth from Paoha, earth-quakes, and huge waves rolling across the surface of the lake.

The fissures of Black Point are congruous with similar cracks and ridges in the Bodie Hills to the north, and in Negit, Paoha, and distant Cowtrack Mountain to the south. The existence of these fractures, as well as the abundance of volcanic landforms, suggests a fault system running through the basin. Through these cracks the immense Mono Basin magma chamber finds temporary relief. But the basin is des-tined to blow. Again and again and again.

As I descend Black Point, the winds of afternoon blow in my favor, dispersing the morning's no-see-ums outside my sphere of attention. Gnatcatchers flit about, calling noisily as they pick off the invisible insects on the wind. Near the base of Black Point, I watch with joy as an orange-crowned warbler flies across the sagebrush.

TWELVE

What Covers the Ground

Life is ever-changing, a veneer on landscapes that themselves are changing, on a planet that is changing, in a solar system that is changing, in a galaxy that is changing, in a universe that is changing. We tend to think that the picture we see of the world is somehow permanent, or at the very least a culmination of eons of effort. But the picture is but a frame in a film of greater length than we can yet tell. While each frame appears as an isolated snapshot of the world, it is but a small part of a great and dynamic theme in motion.

High on the stark, wind-blasted, Martian landscape of the White Mountains grow some of the oldest, gnarliest, most astounding life-forms on the surface of the planet. These beings go by the name *Pinus longaeva*: the Great Basin bristlecone pines. They can live to be over forty-six hundred years old. They can hold their needles for up to thirty years, fifteen times longer than most pines. They grow so slowly that it takes them a hundred years to put on one inch of wood. They are most successful in the worst possible growing conditions, showing a decided preference for highly alkaline and magnesium-rich dolomitic soils. Few other life-forms accompany the bristlecones onto their grim sites, where the pines' ice-sculpted, twisted trunks and disproportionately few bristly tufts of tenacious greenery contrast starkly with the bright, almost gleaming white-gray rock outcrops and coarse, chunky gravel into which the searching roots of the trees penetrate. In such sites, the trees themselves are mostly dead wood, so tough and resinous that a snag may stand in place for hundreds of years before the tree's roots decompose enough to cause it to topple. Once laid down, it may be thousands more years before the wood decomposes and goes back to the earth.

To cope with the triply fickle conditions of treeline, shoddy soils, and the high desert, where temperature, moisture, and nutrients are all limiting factors, Great Basin bristlecones have developed the ability to shut off vascular exchange to branches. In such an extreme environment, this means only one branch is kept alive at a time, and all the others are left naked, exposed to sun, wind, infestations, and the continuous blasting of windborne ice particles throughout the long subalpine winter. The oldest trees are the ones that most appear to be dead. These are the individuals who are able to strike a precarious balance with potentially disastrous natural forces by taking it slow and keeping their strand of life thin but strong. Staring in disbelief at a treeline stand of venerable bristlecones brings new meaning to the concept of going to extremes to avoid competition. The Great Basin bristlecone pines are fugitives, pushed to the far margins of livability in a fantastic evolutionary testimony to the great exclusion principle of ecology: one species, one niche. Thus far, no other species have challenged the ancient ones in their claim to some of the worst growing conditions on earth.

The dense, resinous nature of the wood of *Pinus longaeva* creates such a difficult environment for insects and bacteria that infestations are almost nil. As a trade-off, the trees are extremely flammable. In a mountain environment where summer thunderstorms are common, it is uncommon for tree species to explode under fire of lightning. After a fantastic August electric storm around White Mountain Peak, I retreated to the lowlands with my alpine ecology students and passed a burning bristlecone a few miles before the Methuselah Grove. We jumped out of our big white van and ran through the open spaces between the trees to get a firsthand look. A massive bristlecone, probably still a youngster at around a thousand years old, stood before us, burning furiously. The top of the tree had been blasted clean off, and its charred mass had rolled thirty feet downslope and come to rest against another tree, which had itself caught fire. Such a fire would not spread. The trees, so widely spaced out and with only bare, unlittered soil between them, would burn to their oblivion in isolation. Not even fire could live long in a bristlecone grove.

As a species, the bristlecones are infants. They only diverged from their close Sierran relative *Pinus balfouriana*, the foxtail pine, around twelve thousand years ago, as the last glacial advance came to an end. About this time, and continuing on through today, the Great Basin bristlecones of California and Nevada and their even closer relatives, the Rocky Mountain bristlecone pines of Utah, Arizona, New Mexico, and Colorado, began to diverge. Fossil evidence shows that prior to the last glacial retreat, at some point in time a common ancestor of all of these species and subspecies was geographically united as part of a vast system of coniferous forests that stretched across the American West. The warming trend that brought about glacial retreat changed the climate enough that the trees that made up these extensive coniferous forests could no longer regenerate. Some species went extinct. Some adapted to the new conditions and became new species. Others retreated to places where conditions were similar to what they were made for. They followed the cold and the wet. They sought refuge in the mountains.

The common ancestor of the foxtails and bristlecones diverged into the diverse species we know today for reasons similar to those that led Darwin's Galapagos finches to evolve into such a wide array of species in such a short time. Like the Galapagos, mountains are islands, but in seas of lowlands. As the climate warmed and the aridity of the West persisted, trees were pushed ever higher up into the mountains and became increasingly isolated from other stretches of forest as the dry, treeless valleys below them grew and spread upwards. The mountaintop habitats that the trees eventually took root in were clean slates, wiped free of soil and life by the mountain glaciers of the Pleistocene or abandoned by tundra species that themselves sought higher ground. Like the newly formed volcanic islands of the Galapagos, these habitats were wide open. It was a classic case of ecological release from competition. New kinds of life radiated into the vacuum. Isolated on geographically separate mountaintops, these Pleistocene refugees began to adapt to the specific conditions of their particular mountaintops. Over time, populations disjunct enough from one another became genetically dissimilar. What was once one species of *Pinus* diverged and expanded into three.

In the West, the foxtail pines persisted in arid subalpine areas where at least some precipitation fell the year round. Today they occur in the Sierra Nevada, between 10,000 feet—well below forest level—and 12,000 feet—at tree limit—in the vicinity of Sequoia–Kings Canyon National Parks and the adjacent Inyo National Forest. Here, summer thundershowers and an occasional storm system up from the Gulf of California bring slightly more water to the slopes than to the north, where foxtails are replaced by other species. A second, disjunct population of foxtail pines occurs hundreds of miles away, on the highest peaks of the Scott, Salmon, Yolla Bolly, and Klamath Mountains of Northern California—where granitic soils similar to those of the Sierra Nevada abound, and some moisture is available year-round. Both populations are remnants of the late Miocene and Pliocene Epochs, when ample summer rainfall allowed for extensive subalpine forests in upland regions along with the widespread mixed coniferous and hardwood forest of the lowlands. Subsequently, most species that were dependent on summer rainfall either died out or moved north.

Not surprisingly, considering their similar evolutionary background, foxtail pines share many adaptations with their evolutionary offspring, the bristlecones. Foxtails may grow to be up to three thousand years old. Needles may stay on the tree for up to seventeen years. And foxtails are extremely slow-growing; a tree thousands of years old may be less than six feet wide and fifty feet tall. The high amount of pitch in the wood makes the foxtails, like the bristlecones, susceptible to fire from lightning strikes, but like their eastern relatives, they are often spared because of the spacing between the trees and lack of understory. Another trait that foxtails bequeathed to bristlecones is their ability to shut off sections of their cambium layer (the inner bark, which transports nutrients and water to different parts of the plant) and maintain all of their functions through a strip of bark as narrow as a few inches. This is an extremely valuable adaptation for growing upright at the edge of the alpine zone, where winds and windborne ice blast their way across the land on a regular basis. The fact that bristlecones have retained, and even expanded upon, this adaptation indicates it has been successful. Growing upright under treeline conditions requires foxtail pines to be extremely strong structurally, as their tough, tight-grained, pitchy wood attests. This adaptation may have pre-adapted foxtails to be able to cope with the snow loads of the Sierran winters by making their branches strong enough to withstand breakage beneath the weight of snow.

East of the Great Basin, atop a few isolated mountainous areas of the Four Corners states, Rocky Mountain bristlecone pines grow as a recent divergence in the evolutionary tree of *Pinus*. These trees are toned-down versions of their western counterparts. They occupy less extreme sites than the Great Basin bristlecones, don't live as long, don't hold their needles as long, don't get as gnarly, and overall are less astounding. Nevertheless, the bristlecones of the Rockies boast ages and traits that push them to the extreme end of the spectrum relative to their associate species in the mountains of the continental interior.

Similar to the bristlecones and foxtails of the mountains of the American West, the giant sequoias of the western Sierra Nevada and the coast redwoods also have their origins in the climatic changes that began preceding the Pleistocene Ice Age and continue today. The paleontological record shows that three hundred million years ago, vast stands of primitive conifer forests covered much of the Northern Hemisphere. By one hundred and fifty million years ago, a common ancestor to all yews, redwoods, and sequoias emerged from this lineage, and the family Taxodiaceae was born. Closer relatives of the genus *Sequoia* (*S. Reichenbachii* and *S. couttsiae*) have been found fossilized among Cretaceous and Tertiary rocks, scattered widely over the Northern Hemisphere. These early sequoians eventually diverged into distinct genera: *Sequoia*, of which the coast redwoods (*S. sempervirens*) are representatives, and which are dependent on year-round moisture and mild temperatures, and *Sequoiadendron*, of which the giant sequoias (*Sequoiadendron giganteum*) are representatives, and which still require moisture but can tolerate periods of drought and a wider range of temperatures.

Ten to twenty million years ago, *Sequoiadendron* made its debut on the fossil record. At the time of their species origin, these ancestral giant sequoias ranged from present-day Idaho into western Nevada. As the interior of North America began cooling and drying, the sequoians began steady migration southwest, following the moist, mild conditions they grew up with. The *Sequoias* made it to the coast, where they eventually became restricted to river valleys between Big Sur and southernmost Oregon—areas watered by the drip of coastal fog throughout California's summer drought. The *Sequoiadendrons*, more tolerant of periods of drought, made it over several low passes of the still rising Sierra Nevada and rooted into the well-watered west slope. As the glaciers of the Pleistocene grew and scoured the bones of the Sierra Nevada, the narrow band of habitat in which the sequoias could survive was bulldozed off the west slope of the range and dumped as debris in the wide Central Valley below. The giant trees were never able to recover those sites lost to the gnawing of the ice. Only those montane places where the glaciers did not reach still host giant sequoias today.

The present-day range of the sequoias reflects this migrational trend. They are currently found only in seventy-five isolated groves along the west slope of the Sierra Nevada. All of these groves occur between five and seven thousand feet, forming a narrow, broken band running 260 miles north-south by only 15 miles east-west. This band runs from the northern part of Yosemite National Park southward and into Sequoia–Kings Canyon National Park. The range of the sequoias is kept at bay by winter conditions at its northern end and at higher elevations, and by aridity at its southern end and at lower elevations. The fact that the groves are isolated and do not form a continuous band reflects the scouring work of glaciers past, as well as possible separate migration routes through different passes.

The Tertiary climatic changes that preceded the Pleistocene resulted in the ecological conditions that gave rise to many of the natural communities we know today. As the Mesozoic Era rolled over to the Cenozoic in clouds of meteorite or volcanic dust and the wretched smell of reptilian corpses rotting on the wind, the embryo of a new world climate was beginning to take shape. The long, warm, wet period of the Cretaceous had been a remarkably stable time during which natural communities had climaxed and competition for space on earth was at a peak. With all of the continental landmasses gathered around the equatorial regions, the ocean waters warmed and cooled and circulated freely, and polar ice was a distant memory or a complicated foresight. In the warm, humid American West, much of the land was cloaked by a plant association of broad-leaved evergreens. Daniel Axelrod, a pioneer during the 1950s and 1960s in the field of paleoecology, studied the paleontological evidence for such a flora extensively. Based on morphological and taxonomical similarities with present-day tropical species, he suggested that this floristic group was of neotropical origin and migrated northward during that warm, wet period spanning the late Cretaceous to the middle Tertiary times (seventy to forty million years ago). As the continental landmasses drifted away from the equatorial regions and Antarctica approached the high latitudes of the south, Tertiary cooling commenced, and neotropical species were displaced in the north and at high elevations by newly evolving species of Holarctic origin. Collectively, Axelrod dubbed this floristic element the Arcto-Tertiary geoflora. From forty million years ago throughout the Pleistocene Ice Age, the Arcto-Tertiary geoflora diversified and expanded its range at the expense of the Neotropical-Tertiary geoflora. But as cooling continued and increasing aridity began to parch the American West, a new floristic element began to develop, centered around Mexico and the American Southwest. Beginning around twenty-five million years ago, a substantial number of species, mostly adapted to making a living in arid conditions, either evolved or migrated into the region, making inroads between and within the Neotropical-Tertiary and Arcto-Tertiary groups, as determined by local topography and climatic conditions. Axelrod named this most recent floristic element the Madro-Tertiary geoflora.

The coexistence of these three floras in the same region was dependent on the climatic and topographic conditions of the Tertiary Period. There were the warm-wet conditions that prevailed across much of California, changing to cool-wet in the mountainous regions and warm-dry in the interior, and there was the long lull in tectonic activity along the western North American Plate margin (mountain building had moved inland to the Rocky Mountain region, and Basin and Range extension had not yet begun). Thus there could be an extended period during which Tertiary floras would develop into distinct communities. Resumed uplift associated with Basin and Range extension, in concert with the onset of the Pleistocene Ice Age, brought an end to this period of development.

As the Ice Age became increasingly imminent, aridity increased, augmented by the rising of the Sierra Nevada and the resulting rain shadow to the east of the range. Pliocene climatic changes restricted the Neotropical-Tertiary species to the more moist regions of the coast. Some representatives from this retreating group include California bay-laurel (*Umbellularia californica*), and western sycamore (*Platanus racemosa*). Coniferous woodland and forest trees, including many Arcto-Tertiary species such as mountain hemlock (*Tsuga mertensiana*), Douglas-fir (*Pseudotsuga menziesii*), and red fir (*Abies magnifica*), became restricted to moist upland sites, moving with the rising lands to higher elevation. The Madro-Tertiary geoflora spread to become the live oak woodlands, chaparral, and deserts of today.

Migration pathways to and from the mountains of the coast, those of the Sierra-Cascade axis, and those of the desert were diverse. And it is important to always remember that the mountains themselves were changing, evolving, and growing as species changed, evolved, grew, and continuously moved around from place to place. The species of Arctic or boreal origins all came from regions, such as the Rockies and the far north, that predate the mountains of California. These taxa found their major inroads into California via the Sierra-Cascade axis, and during cooler times along the Coast Ranges axis, and became established in suitable habitats en route. Some species may have come to the Sierra region by alternative migration pathways, such as permafrost bogs that spanned the Great Basin during glacial times. Such bogs may have served as stepping-stones between the Rockies and the Sierra Nevada. However, there is a marked decrease in Rocky Mountain species as you move south along the Sierran axis, indicating their more probable migration pathway was via the

WHILE BIG CHANGES BRING big shifts in communities, smaller changes bring more subtle fluxes to systems. "Disturbances" such as fires, avalanches, storms, insects, bacteria, and fungal outbreaks, as well as human-induced activities such as logging, grazing, agriculture, mining, and development, all bring significant, quick changes to natural communities. As ecosystems respond to these changes, they follow predictable patterns, moving through a series of successional stages, trending ever closer towards stability and equilibrium when the longer ecological conditions are stable and unchanging. When a large-scale change, such as glaciation or volcanic activity, occurs that wipes the geologic slate clean of all preexisting vegetation and soil, or when new, previously uninhabited land is exposed (such as Hawaii, or Antarctica if it drifted away from the pole), a landscape undergoes *primary* succession. When less extreme changes occur, and the soil and its nutrients are left relatively intact, the landscape undergoes *secondary* succession. In both cases, the change is profound.

In the case of a postglacial landscape, the torn-up till and veneer of loess and other assorted debris that form the basis for soil development are alkaline in nature due to the exposed carbonate minerals from the bedrock. There are no organic compounds in the soil, and no nitrogen, and few other nutrients necessary for plant growth. The first and only plants that can get established in such circumstances are small annuals tolerant of low-nutrient conditions. As they root and go through their cycles of life and death, they slowly but surely add nutrients and organic material to the impoverished soil, thereby facilitating the establishment of other nitrogen-fixing plants, and eventually perennials, and even shrubs such as willows. These plants hold the soil together, and more and more soil accumulates. They also leach out the carbonate minerals from the soil, lowering the pH and facilitating the establishment of new and different species. In most postglacial landscapes this means alders, and the willow scrub is often replaced by alder thickets. The alders, with symbiotic nitrogen-fixing bacteria living on their root hairs, contribute still more nitrogen to the system via their leaf litter, which further acidifies the soil due to the tannic acid in the leaves. Once again the soil composition is changed. The alders facilitate the establishment of conifer forests.

Once the conifers become established (spruce in most places in the Northern Hemisphere; firs, hemlocks, and pines in the mountains of California), the successional cycle changes. When the new, previously uninhabited land was exposed for the first time, it was in a state of ecological release, much like those releases that follow mass extinctions. Innumerable niches were opened up and aggressive, opportunistic species rushed in to fill in the blanks. These species, usually annuals that put most of their life-energy into reproduction, typically produce thousands, sometimes millions of tiny seeds. Because these seeds are so small and numerous, they do not contain the nutrients necessary to send a root down through layers of organic material to reach fertile soil. Any divergence from ideal germination conditions means the seeds will perish by the tens of thousands. But if soil is scraped clean of overlying organic material, if it is somehow exposed as bare mineral soil, and if conditions are just right, the opportunistic species will propagate in astounding numbers. It comes down to who can get there first. Stunning arrays of opportunistic species often become established in the wake of change.

As the landscape undergoes its first stages of succession, diversity is high, and overall plant productivity is high. This trend continues as long as light is abundant and each successive community facilitates the growing conditions conducive to the next. But, as is the case in postglacial succession, once the conifers begin to get established everything changes. They block out the sun, and light that was once abundant becomes scarce, a limiting factor for many shade-intolerant species. When light becomes limited, both diversity and productivity plummet. The conifers also create and perpetuate growing conditions that favor themselves rather than facilitate further succession. Besides shading out other species, conifers, because the high lignin content of their needles slows down decomposition rates, acidify the soil to the point that species intolerant of acidic conditions cannot get established. As long as conditions do not change, the conifer forest will perpetuate itself indefinitely. Once this "climax" community gets established, the ecological release ends. All available niches are filled. Opportunistic species are displaced by specialized species as a more subtle competition for niches begins. The seeds of the specialists are large. They contain nutrient packages sufficient to support a root that may well have to penetrate several inches of organic material before it reaches the mineral soil it needs to grow. The cost of producing such seeds is greater, so trees produce fewer of them, but their survival rate is much higher. The dark, musty forest creaks in anticipation of change.

In the mountains, change comes regularly. Avalanches, landslides, and rockfall tear up slopes and make wreckage of the drainages. Fire and intense storms ravage the ridges. Needle miner moths and other infestations swarm through regions over the years. The mosaic of habitats that grace the diverse topography is further complicated by a constant flux of successional stages.

Lake succession, so commonly observed in postglacial environments such as the Sierra Nevada, Cascades, and Klamath Mountains, follows a different course. These glacial lakes have been slowly filling in with sediment ever since the glaciers pulled back. Generally, lakes at higher elevations are slower to fill in than those at lower elevations, due to the combined factors of smaller watersheds, shorter ice-free periods, shorter growing seasons, and slow soil development. Also, high elevation lakes were most recently exposed by retreating glaciers, some as recently as a few hundred years ago, during the Little Ice Age. Accordingly, the lower and older the lake, the more filled in it should be. These sediments may be dissolved in solution, suspended, or remain for the most part at the bottoms of lakes and streams. As sediments increase, nutrients are added to the lake water. Overall biological productivity increases as the lake fills in, a process called eutrophication, meaning "good nutrients," or "improved nutrients."

A somewhat predictable succession of ecological changes takes place as a Sierran lake undergoes eutrophication. Generally, as the lake becomes less deep the water is displaced outward, resulting in an increasingly wide and shallow body of water. As water levels fluctuate seasonally, well-adapted plants may eventually move in and inhabit the fringes. Soon the lake becomes shallow enough that rooted aquatic plants can move in from the periphery. All of these plants help stabilize the soil, and incoming sediment is less likely to wash out the outlet, and thus collects still more rapidly. As the cycle continues, the lake may evolve into a soggy wet meadow, inhabited for a few thousand years by those plants that can handle inundation by standing water throughout the growing season. At treeline and below, lodgepole pine seedlings may establish themselves where pocket gophers have churned up fresh mineral soil. Slowly but surely the trees move in, until an avalanche or insect infestation wipes them out. In the past and probable future, the ice comes back, wiping the slate clean and beginning the cycle anew.

Lake succession differs greatly from postglacial succession because facilitation is not performed solely by plants but is due in large part to the physical action of sediment input. Also, opportunists are not so clearly displaced by specialists, as the habitat, unlike in the case of dry land succession, changes from aquatic to terrestrial. Lake succession is similar to postglacial succession in that diversity and productivity are both high until the forest community becomes established, after which ecological release comes to an end and light becomes limiting, and both diversity and productivity decrease.

Postglacial succession and lake succession are but two successional models. There are many others that do not follow such an orderly cycle. In the case of bare rock surfaces, for example, lichen is both the pioneering and climax species, and our models of facilitation and successional stages prove inadequate and inconsiderate. Peat bog succession follows a similar course, where pioneering sphagnum moss creates such highly acidic conditions that nothing else can grow, and the bog may sustain itself in such a "climax" for thousands of years. Chaparral communities are defined by the regular presence of fire, and they would most often succeed into woodland if fire was not a constant presence. When fire moves through and burns the aboveground biomass, root systems are kept intact and they will resprout with vigor following the burn. Many chaparral species produce volatile oils that insure combustion and contribute to the spread of fire. Others have seeds that depend on fire to burn up organic material and expose bare mineral soil. With such examples at hand, words like "pioneer" and "climax" lose meaning. Even the word "succession" becomes questionable, almost teleological.

We tend to think that the world attained completion the day we were born into it. Trees like ancient bristlecones and giant sequoias, the oldest and the biggest, remind us that it is not so. They themselves are but torch carriers of the flame of change that has burned in countless species before them and will burn in countless species to come. The story is far from complete. The elevational range of the bristlecones rises and falls like the tide as temperature and aridity shift through the ages. The giant sequoias, often thought of as relicts of the past on their way out after a long, successful time on earth, may actually be expanding their range. An ecologist looking into the future might foresee many things over the horizon line of time, but there is only one certainty. Things tomorrow will be different than they are today.

Ecologists often call changes "disturbances," particularly changes that happen relatively fast, but this vocabulary is bound up in a bias for stability and equilibrium. Reflecting on the evolution of the universe, landscapes, and species, change is the rule, not the exception. The evolution of living communities, often as a result of physical landscape evolution and almost always involving species evolution, is no different. Big changes like the global climatic fluctuations associated with the Pleistocene Ice Age mean big shifts in communities of living things. Smaller, often cyclical changes, such as fires, avalanches, insect outbreaks, and a whole list of human-induced changes, effect smaller shifts in communities of living things. Regardless of its apparent magnitude, change affords the opportunity for entirely new versions of life to turn up, as the fossil record illustrates with glaring clarity. The Big Bang preceded the expansion of the universe. Mass extinctions precede greater diversification of life. Climate change preceded the realization of the spiraling roots of the bristlecone pine, the towering cinnamon trunk of a giant sequoia. An avalanche cleans the slate for an outburst of fluttering aspens.

No matter what timescale we are considering, whether hundreds of millions of years or the relative blink of an eye of a lifetime, we can see that the cloak of life that covers the ground is changing. From the dynamics of mass extinctions to recent climatic shifts to last summer's fires, the earth fluxes and life shifts, grows, and evolves. The change never stops, it just speeds up and slows down in a yet undeciphered set of rhythms within rhythms within rhythms.

THIRTEEN

At the Edge of the World

We live at the leading edge of a changing world, looking out into the unknown of what is to come, perhaps with a wind in our faces as the cosmic horizon expands into the void. Fifteen billion years ago the contraction of the universe birthed its expansion, involution birthed evolution, the Night of Brahm grew into the dawn of the Day of Brahm, and ever since, perhaps even before, the two forces of expansion and contraction have been at play, opposing yet co-creating, seemingly at odds but ever mutually dependent. In all cases, contraction, gathering, integration, union precede expansion, dispersal, disintegration, diversification, individuation. From the Big Bang to the muscle contractions that precede the birth of live young among mammals, contraction is the birthing force, and expansion is that which diversifies, moves outward, and turns what has never been into what is. From subatomic particles to the vast system of the universe, across the boundaries that delineate cosmology from quantum mechanics, expansion and contraction play out, regardless of the different physical mechanisms (gravity, nuclear forces, magnetic forces, etc.) behind them.

The first law of thermodynamics states that the energy in a system is constant. Energy cannot be added. It cannot be taken away. The energy just prior to the Big Bang, bound up in a universe so tightly packed that it was smaller than an orange, was the exact same amount as is in the universe today, fifteen billion years later, wider and more vast than any panorama of stars. And the cosmic horizon continues to expand with every passing moment. The law of the constancy of energy holds true regardless of whether the universe is expanding or contacting, or in some hypothetical state of suspended animation. But the second law of thermodynamics is contingent on an expanding universe. It informs us that entropy, the measure of energy unavailable for useful work in the system, is ever increasing. As energy is transferred from one thing to the next, more and more of it is "used up" in the business of doing. As the universe expands, its energy dissipates, disperses from a singularity to a multiplicity, from a unity to a diversity, from a simplicity to a complexity. If the universe were again to contract, one might speculate how the second law of thermodynamics would be turned inside out. But as long as the universe is expanding, matter, energy, and even mind take on ever-increasingly varied, ever-increasingly complex, and some would argue ever-increasingly beautiful and individualized forms. We get to take part in this. We get to watch it all happen.

From our human perspective, physical size puts us at a midpoint between the universe, which we perceive as immense, and subatomic particles, which we perceive as tiny. (It is worth noting here that there likely is no center, and orders of magnitude continue infinitely both smaller and larger than us.) As we look around, we first notice those things of the same order of magnitude as us: other beings on earth, like birds, mammals, and trees. As we look into the greatness of the small, the next order of magnitude down includes such wonders as fruits, flowers, and feathers, then the parts that make up those parts, and the parts that make up those, and so on. As we see further out and into the universe, the next order of magnitude up from us are things like ecosystems and mountains, then continents, then planets, with each successive context encompassing the previous one. There is even a multiverse that contains our universe, and a multi-multiverse beyond that!

Two aspects of the universal condition that we experience every day are the evolution of species, which is the biological expression of expansion, and the evolution of landscapes through the processes of plate tectonics—the geologic expression of contraction. Both of these symptoms take place near and dear to us, and they are not obscured by the high-powered microscopes, telescopes, and equations necessary to extend our perception to far-reaching orders of magnitude. Physics gives expansion and contraction context. Molecular biology and genetics analyze the microcosms. But the everyday experience of the common person, informed by a keen, inquisitive mind, can reveal much about the nature of the world.

We witness a world ever in the throes of creation. Earthquakes and volcanic activity tell us that the crust is still in the making, as radioactive decay deep within the earth generates heat and powers the convection cells that the lithospheric plates of the planet ride upon. Extinction and speciation inform us that life is ever on the rise, and despite the seemingly devastating effects of numerous mass extinctions, life is more diverse today than ever before in the history of the planet. We find seashells of long-extinct organisms embedded in layers of sedimentary rock that are five hundred feet thick and a thousand miles from the nearest sea. Fossilized skeletons of ancient massive reptiles lie scattered across the land, along with the imprints of primitive species of plants that have long since departed the spheres of the earth. Tropical seafloors once thousands of feet deep rest today almost at the top of the troposphere, thrust upward into mountains now gleaming with white mantles of snow and ice. Glaciers advance and retreat, quarrying rock and redistributing it, scouring bedrock clean of life and exposing it to entirely new possibilities. Hummingbirds, drunk on nectar, whir by in a mad rush in search of the color red. Lands are stretched, explosions happen, hot springs well up and then burst into boiling, sulfur-stinking geysers. The climate changes. Drought sets in. Treelines rise and fall. Insects destroy tens of thousands of acres of trees in a single summer. Fires burn life down to the ground. Then lupines spring forth profusely, their honey-butter scent thick on the wind. New life moves into open space and the universe invents a new part of itself day after week after month after year.

As we look forward we wonder where we are headed. Much can be deduced by looking at the patterns of the past and projecting their continuance into the future. But in a universe that is expanding, there is always an element of the unknown, the possibility of anything that none can foresee.

What of the mountains of California? They will change. We can assume with reasonable certainty (though never with total certainty!) that the Pacific Plate will continue its northwestward agenda, ripping and tearing away at western North America in the process. The Gulf of California will widen. New rifts will open in the Basin and Range Province, and seas will rush in to fill the widening gaps. As the last remnants of the Farallon Plate are subducted, the Mexican volcanoes in the south and the Cascades in the north will continue to erupt, spew forth ash and lava, and grow, until eventually those final pieces of the plate are devoured, and the slab gap that now underlies California and much of Mexico will widen, shutting off volcanic activity and introducing extensional faulting to Northern California, Oregon, and Washington, as well as southern Mexico. Then Shasta will sputter one last time, sigh, and submit to disintegration. The San Andreas fault system will grow and continue to deliver bits and pieces of Mexico and California towards Alaska. Baja will move up the coast like a patient beachcomber. It will likely rift as the action continues, and a true island of California will be born, bound for somewhere in the misty Aleutians. The Basin ranges, with no deep crustal roots to keep them rebounding isostatically, will erode, and their earth-toned sediments will continue to choke up their basins, eventually drowning the decrepit peaks in their own waste. The Sierra Nevada will continue to rise for a time and perhaps endure another glacial advance or two, becoming more and more dramatic in relief with each scouring, and eventually bow down to the uncompromising forces of water and gravity. The Santa Lucias, as well as the rest of the Coast Ranges, will likely become islands like Catalina, rising in steep, wrinkled curves above the dominating Pacific. The climate will change and change again. Conifers will migrate up the mountain slopes and be pushed back down. Alpine species will play musical chairs as the tundra expands and contracts. Glaciers will swell and wither in the shifting skies of time. New species will ever be diverging as conditions change and ecological releases allow for novelty. There may be an endemic Sierra Nevada hemlock, or a new species of pine particular to the conditions of the times. Sequoias may find their time on earth is up, or they may adapt to new changes and speciate yet again. It is likely that whatever relatively small changes occur, opportunistic species like Steller's jays, coyotes, and dandelions will always be there, though constantly reinventing themselves and adapting to new environments.

And what will be the fate of *Homo sapiens?* Many ecologists suggest that we are in the midst of the next mass extinction, and that human activity is responsible for this event. But a look to the past shows that life is more diverse now than it ever has been, and that mass extinctions are ever the heralds of still greater diversity to come. Will we make the cut? Will we be there to watch the Santa Lucias become emerald islands in the blue Pacific, the bright granite of the Sierra Nevada again be drowned in glacial ice, and countless unforeseen versions of life be born into the sunlit world? Will human eyes gaze upon the changes to come?

ALL OF THIS AND MORE will happen in less than ten million years. A blink of the eye of Brahm, a fleeting moment in the passing of the cosmic day.

BIBLIOGRAPHY

Ahrens, C. Donald. 1991. *Meteorology Today*. West: St. Paul.

Alt, David D., and Donald W. Hyndman. 1975. *Roadside Geology of California*. Mountain: Missoula.

Anderson, R. Scott. 1990. Holocene forest development and paleoclimates within the Central Sierra Nevada, California. *Journal of Ecology* 78: 470–489.

Arno, Stephen. 1973. *Discovering Sierra Trees*. Yosemite Association, Sequoia Natural History Association: National Park Service, US Department of the Interior.

————. 1984. *Timberline: Arctic and Alpine Forest Frontiers*. The Mountaineers: Seattle.

Axelrod, Daniel I. 1940. Late Tertiary floras of the Great Basin and border areas. *Bulletin of Torrey Botanical Club* 67: 477–487.

————. 1957. Late Tertiary floras and the Sierra Nevadan uplift. *Bulletin of the Geological Society of America* 68: 19–46.

————. 1958. Evolution of the Madro-Tertiary geofloras. *Botanical Review* 24: 433–509.

————. 1962. A Pliocene Sequoiadendron forest from western Nevada. *University of California Publications* 39: 195–268.

Barbour, Michael G., and William Dwight Billings (eds.). 1988. *North American Terrestrial Vegetation*. Cambridge University Press: Cambridge.

Barbour, Michael G., and Jack Major (eds.). 1990. *Terrestrial Vegetation of California*. California Native Plant Society: Sacramento.

Barry, Roger G., and Jack D. Ives. Introduction. In *Arctic and Alpine Environments*, ed. J. D. Ives and R. G. Barry, pp. 1–11. Methuen: London.

Beedy, Edward C., and Stephen Granholm. 1985. *Discovering Sierra Birds*. Yosemite Natural History Association, Sequoia Natural History Association: National Park Service, US Department of the Interior.

Bettinger, Robert L. 1991. Aboriginal occupation at high altitude: Alpine villages in the White Mountains of Eastern California. In *Natural History of Eastern California and High-Altitude Research,* vol. 3, ed. C. A. Hall Jr., V. Doyle-Jones, and B. Widawski. University of California: Los Angeles.

Billings, W. D., and H. A. Mooney. 1968. The ecology of Arctic and alpine plants. *Biological Reviews* 43: 481–529.

———. 1974. Arctic and alpine vegetation: plant adaptations to cold summer climates. In *Arctic and Alpine Environments,* ed. J. D. Ives and R. G. Barry, pp. 404–437. Methuen: London.

———. 1974. Adaptations and origins of alpine plants. *Arctic and Alpine Research* 6(2): 129–142.

———. 1978. Alpine phytogeography across the Great Basin. *Great Basin Naturalist Memoirs* 2: 105–117.

———. 1988. Alpine vegetation. In *North American Terrestrial Vegetation,* ed. M. G. Barbour and W. D. Billings. Cambridge University Press: Cambridge.

Bortoft, Henri. 1966. *The Wholeness of Nature: Goethe's Way toward a Science of Conscious Participation in Nature.* Lindisfarne: Hudson, NY.

Burt, William Henry, and Richard Phillip Grossenheider. 1952. *A Field Guide to the Mammals.* Houghton Mifflin: Boston.

Byron, Earl R., Richard P. Axler, and Charles R. Goldman. 1991. Increased precipitation activity in the Central Sierra Nevada. *Atmospheric Environment* 25: 271–275.

Chabot, Brian F., and W. D. Billings. 1972. Origins and ecology of the Sierran alpine flora and vegetation. *Ecological Monographs* 42: 163–199.

Chase, Clement G., and Terry C. Wallace. 1986. Uplift of the Sierra Nevada of California. *Geology* 14: 730–733.

Christianson, M. N. 1966. Late Cenozoic crustal movements in the Sierra Nevada of California. *Geological Society of America Bulletin* 77: 163–182.

Clark, Douglas H., and Malcolm M. Clark. 1995. New evidence of Late-Wisconsin deglaciation in the Sierra Nevada, California, refutes the Hilgard glaciation. *Geological Society of America Abstracts with Programs, Cordilleran Section* 27: 10.

Clark, Douglas H., Malcolm M. Clark, and Alan R. Gillespie. 1994. Debris-covered glaciers in the Sierra Nevada, California, and their implications for snowline reconstructions. *Quaternary Research* 42: 139–153.

Clark, Malcolm M. 1976. Evidence for rapid destruction of latest Pleistocene glaciers of the Sierra Nevada, California. *Geological Society of America Abstracts with Programs, Cordilleran Section,* pp. 361–362.

———. 1994. Reply to comment by M. Jakob on debris-covered glaciers in the Sierra Nevada, California, and their implications for snowline reconstructions. *Quaternary Research* 42: 359–362.

Clyde, Norman, and Wynne Benti, ed. 1997. *Close Ups of the High Sierra.* Spotted Dog: Bishop, CA.

Colinvaux, Paul. 1978. *Why Big Fierce Animals Are Rare.* Princeton University Press: Princeton.

———. 1993. *Ecology 2.* John Wiley and Sons: New York.

Collingwood, R. G. 1972. *The Idea of Nature.* Oxford University Press: Oxford.

Coonen, Lester P. 1977. Aristotle's biology. *Bioscience* 27: 733–738.

Crough, S. Thomas, and George A. Thompson. 1977. Upper mantle origin of Sierra Nevada uplift. *Geology* 5: 396–399.

Diamond, Jared. 1999. *Guns, Germs, and Steel: The Fates of Human Societies.* W. W. Norton: New York.

Dott, Robert H. Jr., and Donald H. Prothero. 1994. *Evolution of the Earth.* McGraw-Hill: New York.

Easterbrook, Don J. 1969. *Principles of Geomorphology*. McGraw-Hill: New York.

Edwards, Paul, ed. 1967. *The Encyclopedia of Philosophy*. MacMillan: New York.

Eicher, Don L., and A. Lee McAlester. 1980. *History of the Earth*. Prentice-Hall: Englewood Cliffs, NJ.

Eiseley, Loren. 1957. *The Immense Journey*. Time: New York.

Evans, Howard Ensign. 1993. *Pioneer Naturalists: The Discovery and Naming of North American Plants and Animals*. Henry Holt: New York.

Evans, Stephen G., and John J. Clague. 1994. Recent climatic change and catastrophic geomorphic processes in mountain environments. *Geomorphology* 10: 107–128.

Fagan, Brian M. 1990. *The Journey from Eden: The Peopling of Our World*. Thames and Hudson: London.

———. 2000. *The Little Ice Age: How Climate Made History, 1300–1850*. Basic Books: New York.

Farquhar, Francis P. 1965. *History of the Sierra Nevada*. University of California Press: Berkeley.

Fiero, Bill. 1986. *Geology of the Great Basin*. University of Nevada Press: Reno.

Fliedner, Moritz M., and Stanley Ruppert. 1996. Three-dimensional crustal structure of the Southern Sierra Nevada from seismic fan profiles and gravity modeling. *Geology* 24: 367–370.

Flint, Wendell D. 1987. *To Find the Biggest Tree*. Sequoia Natural History Association: Three Rivers, CA.

Gaines, David. 1988. *Birds of Yosemite and the East Slope*. Artemisia: Lee Vining, CA.

Gerrard, A. J. 1990. *Mountain Environments*. M.I.T. Press: Cambridge.

Gilbert, F. S. 1980. The equilibrium theory of island biogeography: Fact or fiction? *Journal of Biogeography* 7: 209–235.

Gillespie, Alan R. 1991. Quaternary subsidence of Owens Valley, California. In *Natural History of Eastern California and High Altitude*

Research vol. 3, ed. C. A. Hall Jr., V. Doyle-Jones, and B. Widawski. University of California: Los Angeles.

———. 1991. Testing a new climatic interpretation for the Tahoe glaciation. In *Natural History of Eastern California and High-Altitude Research* vol. 3, ed. C. A. Hall Jr., V. Doyle-Jones, and B. Widawski. University of California: Los Angeles.

Gilligan, David Scott. 2000. *The Secret Sierra: The Alpine World Above the Trees.* Spotted Dog: Bishop, CA.

Grater, Russel K. 1978. *Discovering Sierra Mammals.* Yosemite Association, Sequoia Natural History Association: National Park Service, US Department of the Interior.

Graumlich, Lisa J. 1993. A 1000-year record of temperature and precipitation in the Sierra Nevada. *Quaternary Research* 39: 249–255.

Graydon, Don, ed. 1992. *Mountaineering: The Freedom of the Hills.* The Mountaineers: Seattle.

Grayson, Donald K. 1993. *The Desert's Past.* Smithsonian Institution Press: Washington, DC, and London.

Hall, Clarence A. Jr., ed. 1991. *Natural History of the White-Inyo Range, Eastern California.* University of California Press: Berkeley.

Hamblin, W. Kenneth. 1989. *The Earth's Dynamic Systems.* MacMillan: New York.

Hambrey, Michael, and Jurg Alean. 1992. *Glaciers.* Cambridge University Press: Cambridge.

Hartman, William K., and Ron Miller. 1991. *The History of Earth: An Illustrated Chronicle of an Evolving Planet.* Workman Publishing: New York.

Harvey, H. T., H. S. Shellhammer, and R. E. Stecker. 1980. *Giant Sequoia Ecology.* United States Department of the Interior, National Park Service: Washington, DC.

Harvey, H. T., H. S. Shellhammer, R. E. Stecker, and R. J. Hertesveldt. 1981. *Giant Sequoias.* Sequoia Natural History Association: Three Rivers, CA.

Hawking, Stephen. 1988. *A Brief History of Time.* Bantam: London.

Heizer, Robert F. 1980. *The Natural World of the California Indians.* University of California Press: Berkeley.

Henson, Paul, and Donald J. Usner. 1993. *The Natural History of Big Sur.* University of California Press: Berkeley.

Hickman, James C., ed. 1993. *The Jepson Manual: Higher Plants of California.* University of California Press: Berkeley.

Hill, Mary. 1975. *Geology of the Sierra Nevada.* University of California Press: Berkeley.

Hughes, Donald J. 1975. *Ecology in Ancient Civilizations.* University of New Mexico Press: Albuquerque.

Jakob, M. 1994. Comments on debris-covered glaciers in the Sierra Nevada, California, and their implications for snowline reconstructions, by Douglas H. Clark, Malcolm M. Clark, and Alan R. Gillespie. *Quaternary Research* 42: 356–358.

Johnston, Verna R. 1994. *California Forests and Woodlands: A Natural History.* University of California Press: Berkeley.

Kennelly, Patrick J., and Clement G. Chase. 1989. Flexure and isostatic residual gravity of the Sierra Nevada. *Journal of Geophysical Research* 94: 1759–1764.

King, Clarence. 1997. *Mountaineering in the Sierra Nevada.* Yosemite Association: Yosemite National Park.

Klikoff, Lionel G. 1965. Microenvironmental influence on vegetational pattern near timberline in the central Sierra Nevada. *Ecological Monographs* 35: 187–211.

Leopold, Aldo. 1966. *A Sand County Almanac with Essays on Conservation from Round River.* Oxford University Press: Oxford.

Lopez, Barry. 1986. *Arctic Dreams.* Scribner: New York.

MacArthur, Robert H., and E. O. Wilson. 1963. An equilibrium theory of insular zoogeography. *Evolution* 17: 373–387.

———. 1967. *The Theory of Island Biogeography.* Princeton University Press: Princeton.

MacMahon, James A., and Douglas C. Andersen. 1982. Subalpine forests: a world perspective with emphasis on western North America. *Progress in Physical Geography* 6: 368–425.

Major, J., and S. A. Bramberg. 1967. Comparison of some North American and Eurasian alpine ecosystems. In *Arctic and Alpine Environments*, ed. H. E. Wright and W. H. Osburn, pp. 89–118. Indiana University Press: Bloomington.

———. 1967. Some cordilleran plants disjunct in the Sierra Nevada of California and their bearing on Pleistocene ecological conditions. In *Arctic and Alpine Environments,* ed. H. E. Wright and W. H. Osburn, pp. 171–188. Indiana University Press: Bloomington.

Major, J., and D. W. Taylor. 1977. Alpine. In *Terrestrial Vegetation of California,* ed. M. G. Barbour and J. Major, pp. 601–675. Wiley: New York.

Martel, Stephen J., T. Mark Harrison, and Alan R. Gillespie. 1987. Late Quaternary vertical displacement rate across the Fish Springs fault, Owens Valley fault zone, California. *Quaternary Research* 27: 113–129.

Matthes, Francois. 1950. *The Incomparable Valley.* University of California Press: Berkeley.

Mayr, Ernst. 1982. *The Growth of Biological Thought.* Harvard University Press: Cambridge.

McPhee, John. 1981. *Basin and Range.* Farrar, Straus and Giroux: New York.

Miller, D., ed. and transl. 1988. *Goethe: Scientific Studies.* Suhrkamp: New York.

Molnar, Peter, and Phillip England. 1990. Late Cenozoic uplift of mountain ranges and global climate change: Chicken or egg? *Nature* 346: 29–34.

Monasterski, R. 1993. Here comes the sun-climate connection. *Science News* 143: 148.

Moore, James G. 2000. *Exploring the Highest Sierra.* Stanford University Press: Stanford.

Muir, John. 1894. *The Mountains of California.* Century: New York.

Murie, Olaus. 1974. *Animal Tracks*. Houghton Mifflin: New York.

Munz, Philip A., and David D. Keck. 1949. California plant communities. *Aliso* 2: 87–105.

———. 1949. California plant communities supplement. *Aliso* 2: 199–202.

———. 1959. *A California Flora*. University of California Press: Berkeley.

Norris, R. 1985. Geology of the Landels-Hill Big Creek Reserve, Monterey County, California. *Environmental Field Program Publication* 16. University of California: Santa Cruz.

Page, B. M. 1970. Sur-Nacimiento fault zone of California: Continental margin tectonics. *Geological Society of America Bulletin*, 81: 667–690.

———. 1982. Migration of Salinian composite block, California, and disappearance of fragments. *American Journal of Science* 282: 1694–1734.

Peterson, Roger Tory. 1990. *Western Birds*. Houghton Mifflin: Boston.

Price, Larry. 1981. *Mountains and Man*. University of California Press: Berkeley.

Putnam, Jeff, and Genny Smith, eds. 1995. *Deepest Valley: A Guide to Owens Valley, Its Roadsides and Mountain Trails*. Genny Smith: Mammoth Lakes.

Radinski, Leonard B. 1987. *The Evolution of Vertebrate Design*. University of Chicago Press: Chicago.

Ransom, Jay Ellis. 1981. *Complete Field Guide to North American Wildlife*. Harper and Row: New York.

Reader, John. 1988. *Man on Earth*. University of Texas Press: Austin.

Roberts, J. M. 1993. *History of the World*. Oxford University Press: New York.

Schaffer, Jeffrey P. 1997. *The Geomorphic Evolution of the Yosemite Valley and Sierra Nevada Landscapes*. Wilderness: Berkeley.

Scuderi, Louis A. 1993. A 2000-year tree ring record of annual temperatures in the Sierra Nevada mountains. *Science* 259: 1433–1436.

Secor, R. J. 1992. *The High Sierra: Peaks, Passes and Trails*. The Mountaineers: Seattle.

Sharp, Robert P. 1972. Pleistocene glaciation, Bridgeport Basin, California. *Geological Society of America Bulletin* 83: 2233–2260.

Sharp, Robert, and Allen F. Glazner. 1997. *Geology Underfoot in Death Valley and Owens Valley*. Mountain: Missoula.

Sharsmith, C. W. 1940. "A Contribution to the History of the Alpine Flora of the Sierra Nevada." Ph.D. dissertation, University of California, Berkeley.

Shepard, Paul. 1998. *Coming Home to the Pleistocene*. Island: Washington, DC.

Shoenherr, Alan A. 1992. *A Natural History of California*. University of California Press: Berkeley.

Simberloff, D. S. 1983. When is an island community in equilibrium? *Science* 220: 1275–1277.

Skinner, Brian J., and Stephen C. Porter. 1987. *Physical Geology*. Wiley: New York.

Small, Eric E., and Robert S. Anderson. 1995. Geomorphically driven Late Cenozoic rock uplift in the Sierra Nevada, California. *Science* 270: 277–280.

Starr, Cecie. 1991. Biology: Concepts and Applications. Wadsworth: Belmont, CA.

Stebbins, G. Ledyard, and Jack Major. 1965. Endemism and speciation in the California flora. *Ecological Monographs* 1: 1–35.

Steiner, Rudolf. 1985. *Goethe's Worldview*. Mercury: New York.

———. 1988. *Goethean Science*. Mercury: New York.

Stevens, George C., and John F. Fox. 1991. The causes of treeline. *Annual Review of Ecology and Systematics* 22: 177–191.

Storer, Tracey I., and Robert L. Usinger. 1963. *Sierra Nevada Natural History*. University of California Press: Berkeley.

Swan, L. W. 1967. Alpine and aeolian regions of the world. In *Arctic and Alpine Environments*, ed. H. E. Wright and W. H. Osburn, pp. 29–54. Indiana University Press: Bloomington.

Swetnam, Thomas W. 1993. Fire history and climate change in giant sequoia groves. *Science* 262: 885–888.

Tierney, Tim. 1997. *Geology of the Mono Basin.* Kutsavi: Lee Vining, CA.

Troll, Carl. 1973. The upper timberline in different climatic zones. *Arctic and Alpine Research* 5: A3–A18.

Tudge, Colin. 1996. *The Time before History: 5 Million Years of Human Impact.* Touchstone: New York.

———. 1998. *Neanderthals, Bandits and Farmers: How Agriculture Really Began.* Yale University Press: New Haven.

———. 2000. *The Variety of Life: A Survey and Celebration of All the Creatures That Have Ever Lived.* Oxford University Press: Oxford.

Unruh, J. R. 1991. The uplift of the Sierra Nevada and implications for Late Cenozoic epeirogeny in the Western Cordillera. *Geological Society of America Bulletin* 103: 1395–1404.

Ward, J. V. 1994. Ecology of alpine streams. *Freshwater Biology* 32: 277–294.

Wardle, Peter. 1974. Alpine timberlines. In *Arctic and Alpine Environments.* ed. J. D. Ives and R. G. Barry, pp. 371–400. Methuen: London.

Weeden, Norman. 1996. *A Sierra Nevada Flora.* Wilderness: Berkeley.

Weinberg, Steven. 1977. *The First Three Minutes.* Bantam: London.

Went, F. W. 1948. Some parallels between desert and alpine flora in California. *Madroño* 9: 241–249.

Whitney, Stephen. 1979. *A Sierra Club Naturalist's Guide to the Sierra Nevada.* Sierra Club Books: San Francisco.

Worster, Donald. 1977. *Nature's Economy: A History of Ecological Ideas.* Cambridge University Press: Cambridge.

INDEX

LAURA BEEBE

ABOUT THE AUTHOR

David Scott Gilligan is a naturalist and a writer. He has taught natural history courses and led exploratory wilderness expeditions for Prescott College, Sierra Institute, and Sterling College, where he is currently a professor. His work and personal interests have taken him far afield to mountain and northern regions around the globe. His other books include *The Secret Sierra* (2000), *In the Years of the Mountains* (2006), and *I Believe I'll Go Canoeing* (2009).

HEYDAY

About Heyday

Heyday is an independent, nonprofit publisher and unique cultural institution. We promote widespread awareness and celebration of California's many cultures, landscapes, and boundary-breaking ideas. Through our well-crafted books, public events, and innovative outreach programs we are building a vibrant community of readers, writers, and thinkers.

Thank You

It takes the collective effort of many to create a thriving literary culture. We are thankful to all the thoughtful people we have the privilege to engage with. Cheers to our writers, artists, editors, storytellers, designers, printers, bookstores, critics, cultural organizations, readers, and book lovers everywhere!

We are especially grateful for the generous funding we've received for our publications and programs during the past year from foundations and hundreds of individual donors. Major supporters include:

Anonymous; Audubon California; Barona Band of Mission Indians; B.C.W. Trust III; S. D. Bechtel, Jr. Foundation; Barbara and Fred Berensmeier; Berkeley Civic Arts Program and Civic Arts Commission; Joan Berman; Peter and Mimi Buckley; Lewis and Sheana Butler; Butler Koshland Fund; California Council for the Humanities; California Indian Heritage Center Foundation; California State Coastal Conservancy; California State Library; California Wildlife Foundation / California Oak Foundation; Keith Campbell Foundation; John and Nancy Cassidy Family Foundation, through Silicon Valley Community Foundation; Christensen Fund; Compton Foundation; Creative Work Fund; Lawrence Crooks; Nik Dehejia; Donald and Janice Elliott, in honor of David Elliott, through Silicon Valley Community Foundation; Evergreen Foundation; Federated Indians of Graton Rancheria; Mark and Tracy Ferron; Furthur Foundation; George Gamble; The Fred Gellert Family Foundation; Wallace Alexander Gerbode Foundation; Richard & Rhoda Goldman Fund; Wanda Lee Graves and Stephen Duscha;

Evelyn & Walter Haas, Jr. Fund; Walter & Elise Haas Fund; James and Coke Hallowell; Sandra and Chuck Hobson; James Irvine Foundation; JiJi Foundation; Marty and Pamela Krasney; Robert and Karen Kustel, in honor of Bruce Kelley; Guy Lampard and Suzanne Badenhoop; LEF Foundation; Michael McCone; Moore Family Foundation; National Endowment for the Arts; National Park Service; David and Lucile Packard Foundation; Pease Family Fund, in honor of Bruce Kelley; PhotoWings; Resources Legacy Fund; Alan Rosenus; Rosie the Riveter/WWII Home Front NHP; The San Francisco Foundation; San Manuel Band of Mission Indians; Deborah Sanchez; Savory Thymes; Hans Schoepflin; Contee and Maggie Seely; James B. Swinerton; Swinerton Family Fund; Taproot Foundation; TomKat Charitable Trust; Lisa Van Cleef and Mark Gunson; Marion Weber; John Wiley & Sons; Peter Booth Wiley; and Yocha Dehe Wintun Nation.

Getting Involved

To learn more about our publications, events, membership club, and other ways you can participate, please visit www.heydaybooks.com.